THINKING WITHOUT DESIRE

Thinking Without Desire

A First Philosophy of Law

PANU MINKKINEN

·HART·
PUBLISHING
OXFORD – PORTLAND OREGON
1999

Hart Publishing
Oxford and Portland, Oregon

Published in North America (US and Canada) by
Hart Publishing c/o
International Specialized Book Services
5804 NE Hassalo Street
Portland, Oregon
97213-3644
USA

Distributed in the Netherlands, Belgium and Luxembourg by
Intersentia, Churchillaan 108
B2900 Schoten
Antwerpen
Belgium

Distributed in Australia and New Zealand by
Federation Press
John St
Leichhardt
NSW 2000

Hart Publishing Ltd is a specialist legal publisher based in Oxford, England.
To order further copies of this book or to request a list of other
publications please write to:

Hart Publishing Ltd, Salter's Boatyard, Oxford, OX1 4LB
Telephone: +44 (0)1865 245533 or Fax: +44 (0)1865 794882
e-mail: mail@hartpub.co.uk

British Library Cataloguing in Publication Data
Data Available
ISBN 1 84113–048–6 (cloth)

Typeset by Hope Services (Abingdon) Ltd.
Printed in Great Britain on acid-free paper
Biddles Ltd., Guildford and King's Lynn

διόπερ ἄνευ ὀρέξεως νοῦς νόμος ἐστίν.
Aristotle, *Pol.* 1287a 32

Jurisprudenz by Gustav Klimt

Contents

Acknowledgements

I am grateful to the private foundations and public institutions that have generously funded my work (in reverse chronological order): the British Council, the Emil Aaltonen Foundation, the University of Helsinki, the Research Institute of the Evangelical Lutheran Church of Finland, the Alfred Kordelin Foundation, the Finnish Cultural Foundation, and the Academy of Finland. In addition, I would like to thank my own department at the University of Helsinki, especially my supervisor professor Raimo Lahti, as well as everyone at the Department of Law at Birkbeck College.

I am indebted to my friends and colleagues at home and abroad who have encouraged and inspired me—you all know who you are! I can here specifically name but a few: my second supervisor associate professor Lars D. Eriksson, my preliminary examiner professor Martti Koskenniemi, my second preliminary examiner and my friend professor Kaarlo Tuori, my opponent and colleague at Birkbeck professor Peter Goodrich, all the members of the *Cercle Lacan* in Helsinki and especially its uncompromising president Hannu Sivenius, the active members of the Finnish National Section of the IVR, "my" students, everyone at Hart Publishing, and Ari Hirvonen, friend and colleague, who has, beyond the call of all duty, put up with me all these years.

Finally, I must mention my parents Ritva and Tapio Minkkinen, and my wife Johanna Jauho to whom I humbly dedicate this book.

Helsinki, January 1999
P.M.

Introduction

After occasional readings as a schoolboy and the odd courses at University, my first professional and more systematic encounter with philosophy was filtered through the writings of critical legal scholars of North American and British origin in the mid-1980s.[1] These texts seemed to be an answer to my profound doubts concerning the significance of my own discipline, namely, jurisprudence. Like most of my young peers at the time, I devoured the available literature with gusto. But living in the northern periphery of Europe made a difference that was to influence the development of my work. Driven to the outskirts of the Occidental world, Finns like myself are often by necessity knowledgable in the Continental languages with which this new thinking was originally both thought and written. In addition, the rather pedantic heritage of a fundamentally Germanic juridical culture required me to turn to the primary sources of this new "critique": first to contemporary French philosophy, and later to its German "sources", so to speak. This strategy was in full agreement with the academic policies that the University fostered then: Finnish jurisprudence was to be inter-disciplinary and international.

After spending a year in France, it became evident that everything was not as clear-cut and as simple as the critical legal scholars would have it. It often seemed to me that references to, for example, Derrida or Heidegger were made too light-heartedly, and that the philosophy that the primary sources were dealing with had little—if anything—to do with the social critique that was promoted in the name of "critical legal studies" or "postmodern jurisprudence". As sympathetic as I was to the political aims and goals of this critique, I felt that, *as a scholarly enterprise*, it could not be justified with the philosophical literature that was suddenly saturating the footnotes of legal journals.

As far as my own work was concerned, a professional choice had to be made. I could either devote my time to the political struggles that I found compelling—

[1] See, e.g., Kennedy and Klare, "A Bibliography of Critical Legal Studies," and Tushnet, "Critical Legal Studies: A Political History". It is, perhaps, symptomatic that, after Tushnet's "history", the amount of Critical Legal Studies (CLS)-inspired articles in the major American law journals has decreased radically. The British Critical Legal Conference first introduced itself in Fitzpatrick and Hunt (eds), *Critical Legal Studies*. The German journals like the *ARSP* or *Kritische Justiz* have never been too interested in the philosophical aspects of critical legal scholarship, and today "postmodernism" is often associated with the legal applications of system theory. See, e.g., Ladeur, *Postmoderne Rechtstheorie*, especially Pt. 2. In the francophonic countries of Europe, certain themes have come up in the work of some scholars based at the Catholic University of Brussels (Saint-Louis). See, however, Dethier, "Le droit par la bande".

at the time, I was seriously involved in, for example, the anti-prison movement—or I could concentrate on my theoretical work, redirecting it in accordance with the preliminary findings that I mentioned above. For reasons that I cannot explain here, I chose the latter option.

As I slowly started to work my way through the required primary literature, I became more and more aware of the fact that what I was doing could not be "critical theory", an honourable discipline supporting the work of the practising radical lawyer, but a "philosophy of law". Now, it is not lightly that a lawyer like myself uses the word "philosophy". It has a pompous ring to it, and from the moment the word is uttered, a myriad of suspect questions arises: Why "philosophy"? Of what use is it to the lawyer? What benefits does it involve? What answers does it promise? Such questions are, for the most part, rhetorical: the philosophy of law is regarded as an unnecessarily abstract and vain enterprise.

This evaluation of philosophy, shared by both the conservatives and the liberals of the juridical spectrum, and the questions that it implies, were to become the object of my work. What is a "philosophy of law"? Is there such a thing? Is it possible to begin with? The fundamental question concerning the possibility of a philosophy of law seemed to resonate well with much of the primary literature that I was now reading. Heidegger and Derrida, to stick with my two examples, did not radicalise law, *they radicalised philosophy*. So my initial question about the philosophy of law had to be somehow coupled with what "deconstruction" and the "destruction of Occidental metaphysics" were doing to philosophy in general. Derrida's *différance* and Heidegger's *Seinsfrage* were, then, not necessarily issues relating directly to the social institution of law as the jurisprudential discipline understood it, but to a particular way of *thinking* law, to a *philosophy* of law. For most of my colleagues at the faculty, this choice of perspective was hard to accept. A "philosophy of law" is not, I claim, a philosophy of *law*, it is a *philosophy* of law.

I was, of course, not the first lawyer to make philosophical claims about law. To my surprise, more reading revealed that the notion of philosophy that Heidegger had coined and the French had later adopted and made into their own particular brand of thinking—a contemporary *mos gallicus* of sorts—was not altogether new within my discipline after all. After the Second World War, a whole school of philosophers of law had developed readings of Heidegger that my original sources of inspiration, the critical legal scholars, seemed to be unaware of. I took it as my task to contribute to their venture by explicating this material. Ironically, digging yet deeper into the treasure chest of my own discipline, I soon realised that this movement within the philosophy of law was one attempt among others to reformulate and to overcome an essentially neo-Kantian understanding of philosophy.

Coming to terms with the neo-Kantians against whom my philosophers of law had turned, I had myself returned to the core of my discipline, to the jurisprudential heartland that I had tried to escape by turning to critical legal scholarship in the first place. A lesson learnt: before breaking the rules, it is good to know what they are.

From these more or less autobiographical remarks, I am able to schematise the structure of this book. My essential question concerns, then, the possibility of a philosophy of law. The discipline that usually designates itself with this name understands its objective in neo-Kantian terms: the aim of the philosophy of law—and of philosophy in general, as well—is to guarantee the "correctness" of knowledge. This "correctness", allegedly introduced into the language of metaphysics by the epistemological emphases of Kant, also marks the final victory of modern science and its preference for factual knowledge over truth. But the victory is possible only after a curious "juridisation" of metaphysics itself. Philosophy does not only assess the "correctness" of scientific knowledge, but it must also be brought to a test itself, it must be measured against the demands of reason. Such a measuring infers a law and a verdict. Philosophy is, then, articulated as "jurisdiction". Trying to justify its claims to the world, thinking itself takes on a juridical mode.

The *Gerichtshof der Vernunft* that Kant had set up was, of course, the "supreme court" that pronounced its verdict about the philosophy of law, as well. But a court of reason also implies a particular nostalgia for a lost age of metaphysical truth, a longing not unlike the resentment of romantics like Schelling for the epistemological considerations of critical philosophy. But what does this nostalgia suggest? Can such a lost truth be found by, for instance, turning back to the classical texts of Antiquity? My preliminary answer would be "no". I have attempted to portray the structure of metaphysical thinking—philosophy, as I will try to argue in the following chapters, is always "metaphysics"—through a fundamental desire that I claim to be at the root of all thinking. It is present in the Aristotelian *orexis tou eidenai*, the "desire to see" that precedes philosophical contemplation, as well as in the "objectless" desire that is at the bottom of Lacan's understanding of human Being. There is something towards which desire reaches out—an eternal truth, perhaps, or *la Chose*—and yet, this "thing" that is, by the same token, "no-thing" must necessarily remain non-appropriable. But neither is it in the array of human possibilities to resign from desire. Desire is fundamental, it is not a matter of choice; it is human Being, it is Dasein.

What does one, then, do? If this "thing" towards which desire reaches out is non-appropriable—even non-representable, as Lacan would probably say—, is there only lack? Is there only the ceaseless want of a truth that will, nevertheless, remain a mystery? This time my answer would be an ambivalent "yes". For even if the final truth remains out of reach, lack is complemented by a legal adjunct, and this is the point at which the juridical mode of philosophy is introduced. Face to face with a desire that it cannot appease, philosophy produces a verdict. Because its ultimate object is impossible, theoretical contemplation plummets into the decisions and the judgements of practical thinking: "correctness". If it can't be the "true" thing, it might as well be "correct". But even so, "correct" decisions are impossible without a truth that sustains desire; "correctness" is unthinkable without truth. Hence the irresolvable aporia, an "aporetic" structure.[2]

If this would be a crude compression of what I want to say in the first part of the book, the second part takes me back to my original point of departure: critical legal scholarship. Up to now, I have emphasised the difference between a *philosophy* of law and legal theory, and I may have even disregarded some of the social and political prospects and possibilities of my source material. The second part of the book is my attempt to reformulate the main idea of the first part in socio-political terms. If we understand "justice" as the truth towards which desire reaches out, we may also be able to envisage the corresponding "correct" decisions as "right". Even here human Being is understood in relation to an aporetic structure. A forever delayed "justice" that can be neither represented nor appropriated is essentially included in a fundamental desire, and the "rightness" of decisions and judgements is by necessity related to this "justice".

However, most of the chapters in the second part only address what justice is *not*. The textual excurses are my own attempts to come to terms with some of the claims of critical legal scholarship that I have found to be inaccurate. In the end, I am trying to deliver the philosophy of law from the theoretical elation of "postmodern" interpretations. Time and time again, this epochal label has been tagged on contemporary French thinking in order to either celebrate its alleged Dionysian flavour—a positive label that I find problematic, to say the least—or revive a new variant of francophobia in the grand tradition of, say, Edmund Burke. This is, then, not a "postmodern" theory. "Postmodernism", as it has been understood in the science of law, is a rather facile application of Continental philosophy, and I will try to demonstrate this in my reading of deconstruction and critical legal studies.

But even so, at least two things should be detectable from every individual excursus: first, my sincere wish to complicate things, to distance critical legal thinking from its unfounded poise that seems to merge the "uncertain" truth of justice with the self-assured composure of the master-rhetorician, and, secondly, the puzzling issue of desire, even my own desire, that is no less involved in political thinking than in metaphysics proper.

A book such as this one is, as I have already mentioned, the outcome of choices, of decisions and judgements the "correctness" of which will now be re-evaluated in other courts. However, the principal decision, that is, the choice of perspective, requires a short explanation. Many lawyers in particular may feel that I have deliberately concentrated on issues that are "irrelevant", that I have, in the end, defined myself outside the limits of even my own "inter-discipline". I disagree with such a narrow-minded view of law either as an entity or a science. Even in its "vanity", the philosophy of law is an accepted member of the jurisprudential family—in a truly profound sense, the philosophy of law must

[2] Cf. Finnis, *Natural Law and Natural Rights*, pp. 59–80.

be vain—but most expectations about its functions are rooted in a contestable understanding of philosophy itself. For the philosophy of law to be philosophy, it cannot serve the lawyer like the professional sophists of ancient Greece who were paid to, for example, teach public servants the devices of oratory. But neither can it assist either the practising lawyer or the jurisprudential scientist by furnishing them with the conceptual tools that they might require in their work. Indeed, any thinking that serves an end by producing a projected result is, by definition, not philosophy. This is not an unfounded opinion. In one way or another, the understanding of philosophy as metaphysics that I have adopted in this work extends from Plato and Aristotle through German classics such as Kant and Hegel all the way to my allegedly "postmodern" sources: Heidegger, Lacan, Derrida, and so on. I focus on these last mentioned thinkers for the very same reasons that I prefer Aristotle's *Metaphysics* over the *Nikomachean Ethics* or *Politics*.

But I feel that regardless of all my well-meaning efforts to explain myself and the following chapters, I must plead to my judges in advance about a certain feature that is characteristic of texts such as this one. My work is full of "obscurities", and most of them are, no doubt, of my own making, that is, impurities that are most likely due to the relative haste in which I have digested the issues at hand. But some of them are inherent in philosophy itself, even an indication that we are, indeed, dealing with "divine matters" as Aristotle might say. To take on a "first philosophy" that addresses "truth" and "human Being" cannot possibly be done with the same ease and simplicity with which, for example, the best textbooks on law are written.

Unfortunately philosophy offers no short-cuts for anyone concerned; the reader is obliged to take the same wearing route as the author, and every turn runs the risk of leading to an impasse. Anyone who has worked through the texts of, say, Aristotle, Heidegger, Lacan or Derrida must surely know this. I believe that one cannot "think" and "instruct" at the same time. I cannot do my own work while I insolently pretend to be "informing" my readers about literature that they have not had the chance to acquaint themselves with. For the thinker, every illustrative example or elucidating metaphor would ultimately require a diversion from the issue at hand. It would jeopardise any committed search for truth and, consequently, even compromise the possibility of "correct" or "right" decisions.

Much of the material presented in this book is revised and rewritten from articles and essays that I have published elsewhere during the past six years. A more colloquial and longer version of Chapter 1 has appeared as "Law, Science, and Truth", in Ari Hirvonen (ed.), *Polycentricity: The Multiple Scenes of Law* (London: Pluto Press, 1998), pp. 13–33. Parts of Chapters 3 and 4 have been published as "Right Things: On the Question of Being and Law", (1996) VII *Law and Critique* 65–84. Chapter 6 has previously been published as "The Juridical Matrix", (1997) 6 *Social & Legal Studies* 425–443; Chapter 7 as "The

Law-Giver's Place: On the Unethical Quality of Legal Wisdom," (1993) 2 *Social & Legal Studies*, 445–459; Chapter 8 as "Otherness and Difference: On the Cultural Logic of Racial Tolerance", (1992) III *Law and Critique* 147–167; Chapter 9 as "The Radiance of Justice: On the Minor Jurisprudence of Franz Kafka", (1994) 3 *Social & Legal Studies* 349–363, and, finally, the conclusion to Chapter 10 as "Pretexts," (1997) VIII *Law and Critique* 61–69. I thank all the publishers for permission to use these texts.

Part One

To Think Law

1

An Uncertain Science

"It is simply so that truth cannot be tolerant, it cannot concede to any compromises or limitations, and should another power wish to claim any part of it for itself, research must consider all elements of human activity as its own and be relentlessly critical."

Sigmund Freud

"All human knowledge is mediated by the desire of the other."

Jacques Lacan

I

The science of law, no doubt, considers itself an enterprise that pursues knowledge. And in this pursuit, law takes part in the tradition of modern science. But regardless of what specific form the science of law takes on—be it the philosophy of law, legal theory, or jurisprudence—the pursuit of knowledge about law is marked by an incertitude. For there seems to be a realm of human experience beyond the knowledge that is accessible to science, and this realm is usually depicted with the metaphorical arsenal of justice. But even if this realm beyond is inaccessible to science, it still directs and regulates the pursuit of scientific knowledge. Allegedly justice cannot serve as the object of the science of law, but neither can positive law be scientifically studied without taking into consideration the requirements of justice. This paradox accounts for the incertitude characteristic of the science of law.[1]

The lack of certitude is, for the most part, produced and reproduced within the discourse of this hesitant tradition that does not exactly know. In modern law, the incertitude has been restated by persistently attempting to respond to doubts brought into the juridical debate by juxtaposing the science of law to the scientific criteria of other disciplines and orientations.[2]

Within, for example, modern inter-disciplinary scholarship, a dialogue that initially involved state theory and later culminated into a more general "law and society" approach was predominantly a response to sociological doubts. The science of law was denied its claim to scientific knowledge because of its

[1] A classic formulation of the efforts of law to deal with this incertitude is Alf Ross's plea for what he understands as "realism". Incertitude is brought about by the legal scholar's persistent belief in law as a manifestation of some ideality in the real world. Ross claims that such duality can only lead to pseudo-objectivity, that is, non-science. Ross, *Towards a Realistic Jurisprudence*, pp. 19–20.

[2] Cf. Arnaud, *Critique de la raison juridique*, pp. 31–33.

reluctance to accept the fundamental determinants that constitute law as a social phenomenon. This is the way in which, for example, Jean Carbonnier differentiates jurisprudence from the sociology of law. According to Carbonnier, "the reality of law does not concur with jurisprudence, and it is even deformed by it. For jurisprudence is a matter of contentiousness, and contentiousness is pathological law, not normal law".[3] For Carbonnier, then, the deformation of the normal into the pathological is symptomatic of a delusional juridical tradition that cannot comply with the requirement of observation that the science of sociology represents.

In much a similar vein, contemporary critical legal scholarship has confronted the juridical tradition by referring to the explanatory potential of cultural theory. For instance, Peter Goodrich's radical variant of critical legal studies distances itself from the grand theories and the abstractness of modern jurisprudence. Goodrich's radicalism rejects the descriptive theories of "law as such" and the programmatic political theories that envelop them; the "patronising dogmas of truth" must now make way for theories of the particular. Radical critique abandons the "uninteresting" questions of what law is—an ontological question—or how one can know about law—an epistemological question—but, partly restating what has just been denounced, takes up "the historical and ontological question of how law is lived, what are its habitual forms, what is its deep structure that allows its repetition in ever different forms".[4] The initial arguments of the debate emphasise, then, the issue of scientific relevance and interest. Goodrich's dispute with the tradition is not merely about the essential characteristics of a particular entity, but also about how law should be studied. For my purposes here, it is only a matter of taste whether the object of the science of law is defined as "law as such" or as "deep structures".

But it would be more or less accurate to assert that both departures from the jurisprudential tradition of law make epistemological claims in so far as they *deny the ability of the science of law to know about its object of study*. Even though the political motivation behind the denial often concerns the abuse of scientific knowledge in the conservative maintenance of an unjustifiable social institution, the critical arguments are, nevertheless, formulated into what I propose to call the *epistemological question* of the philosophy of law, into what and how a particular science is able to know about its object of study. Law is, hence, deemed a social and/or a cultural entity the essential characteristics of which a misguided jurisprudential tradition cannot possibly recognise. During the past 150 years, such critique has resonated forcefully in law. The success this critique has enjoyed in the science of law presupposes that there is an opening in the very structure of juridical knowledge. The opening is, perhaps, best depicted by the incertitude that is so characteristic of the science of law, but it can also be accounted for by referring to the history of science and its relation to the philo-

[3] Carbonnier, *Flexible droit*, pp. 21–22.
[4] Goodrich, *Languages of Law*, p. 2.

sophy of the Enlightenment. In other words, if the modern science of law concerns rationally worked out knowledge—observable and verifiable juridical phenomena—the incertitude of law about its own scientific status is an indication of its uncomfortable relation to an "irrational" human experience beyond, that is, to justice.

Face to face with such irrationalisms, the science of law can either set these issues aside and banish them from the domain of knowledge, or, as law has done within the Continental tradition, attempt to account for this realm of human experience beyond observable phenomena within a specific epistemology. Before the formation of the institutional disciplines of modern academia, the science of law was placidly positioned amongst the other classical faculties, that is, theology, philosophy and medicine. But as the mathematical calculus heralded by the Anglo-French variant of the philosophy of the Enlightenment becomes the crowning pivot of scientific knowledge in the nineteenth century, the German *Aufklärung*, still inspired by the mores of Romanticism, takes on the idea of *Bildung*, of civilisation, in order to shelter the human spirit from the formal reductionism of numerical formulae. From this confrontation of philosophical orientations, a distinction between the natural sciences and the human sciences becomes apparent.

Within the German tradition, law is one orientation among others in an array of sciences that are commonly addressed as the *Geisteswissenschaften*, literally the "sciences of the spirit". This epithet implies the epistemological autonomy of the sciences that study the human world in relation to the experimental sciences studying the natural world. A similar distinction is apparent in the French term *les sciences de l'homme*, the "sciences of man". The term does not refer to the humanities in the narrow sense as it is applied in the disciplinary groupings of academic institutions today; the sciences of man include the human sciences, the historical sciences, the social sciences, the science of law, in short, all sciences that study the human world.

Both terms, however, entail a defensive reaction to an incertitude. They designate a division that establishes the sciences of man as distinct and dissimilar in relation to the mathematically assessable standards of the experimental sciences. Law is typically a science of man in that its scientific status has always been a matter of doubtful self-reflection; the primary position of the experimental sciences within the hierarchy of modern sciences seems to call for the justification of other orientations. The debate on the epistemological criteria of the science of law—How can one know about law?—is, then, built into the disciplinary orientation itself.

But despite all the reservations that are made about its scientific status, one can, nevertheless, claim that the science of law, regardless of its distinctive attributes and peculiar history, is epistemologically kin to the vast majority of the modern sciences in that it confers upon itself the *requirement of scientificity*.

This overtone is clearly audible in, for example, Hans Kelsen's foreword to the theory of pure law. The neo-Kantian theory is, among other things, an attempt to found the science of law on the epistemological standards of modern science by "purifying law of all political ideology and elements of natural science".[5] Kelsen's counterparts in this debate are, then, twofold: on the one hand, advocates of a speculative idealism that still defend notions such as voluntarism and, on the other hand, enlightened pantologists insisting on universal standards for all science. But even though the aim of the science of law is to present pure facts about its normative object of study, Kelsen, in the first edition of his theory, still identifies law with the *Geisteswissenschaften*.[6] From such a confrontation of pure facts and "spirit", only incertitude can arise.

Through this gap of incertitude, the social and cultural theories that advise the inter-disciplinary research of today have also entered into the science of law. The epistemological discourse that founds critical legal scholarship resembles a patricidal succession in which the claims of a previous scientific orientation in law have been rejected in favour of a new administration. The tradition that understands law as a "science of man" has made way for new insights. But if the criteria of scientific knowledge are formulated with the help of such a dialectic notion of critique, the response, that is, the epistemological status of a new orientation, will necessarily be formulated in an analogous way: law is either a science (*logos*, *ratio*), or it is merely a craft (*technē*, *ars*) embodying the artifice of the gifted individual. The confrontation of orientations is, then, articulated as an epistemology. Can a given mode of the science of law—including today's inter-disciplinary orientations—be understood as science to begin with, or is it, as the jurisprudential name indicates, merely a form of practical knowledge, the art of applying law that would be required of a good judge?[7] Does law merit the position of a science, or is it, even in its learned guises, only the technical skill of practical talent, the knowledge of how to use a normative instrument to reach a calculated resolution?

The two contemporary departures from the tradition of juridical thinking that I have alluded to—the sociology of law and critical legal scholarship—found themselves by penetrating the science of law through the epistemological incertitude that is established by the troubled position of the irrational human experience in a supposedly rational science of man. But in their scientific self-affirmation, these new orientations also run the risk of closing the opening through which they have entered and sealing their scientific enterprise into a system. In such an enclosure, something of the initial idea of the *Geisteswissenschaften* will, of course, necessarily be lost.

If the question of the scientific status of law is viewed from this angle, I believe that we can distinguish surprising affinities between law and the efforts of psychoanalysis to establish itself as a science. Not only are both orientations

[5] Kelsen, *Reine Rechtslehre. Zweite Auflage*, p. III.

[6] Kelsen, *Reine Rechtslehre. Erste Auflage*, p. 12. In the second edition, Kelsen speaks of law as a social science (*Gesellschaftswissenschaft*). I will deal with Kelsen in more detail in the following chapter.

[7] See, e.g., Aristotle, *EN* 1180b 23–1181a 12.

self-professed adherents of the *Geisteswissenschaften*, but they have also experienced similar external attacks undermining their respective claims to scientific knowledge. In addition, these sciences take such attacks seriously, for both entail lively epistemological controversies which, in contrast to the imperious silence of many other disciplines, is evidence of a vibrant tradition. If the problematic ingredient of law is justice and all the political implications that follow, psychoanalysis has had to answer for its foundational claim to truth: the unconscious. In this first chapter, my aim is to draw on these affinities in order to examine a possible avenue for the science of law to address its own epistemological question, that is, the strained relationship between scientific knowledge about law and an element of human experience that is allegedly incompatible with the demands of modern science.[8] In other words, what is justice? What is justice as the *truth* of law?

II

I will begin this account by sketching an aporetic structure from a less known psychoanalytic text. In the last section of his "new introductory lectures" from 1933, Sigmund Freud takes up the question of a *Weltanschauung* or a world-view.[9] The topic of the lecture is justified by referring to the constant inquiries presented about the status of psychoanalysis: can—or, indeed, should—psychoanalysis form a specific *Weltanschauung* of its own? The insistence of such inquiries and the corresponding eagerness of the lecturer to reply to them are an indication of Freud's dismay concerning prevailing notions about psychoanalysis. The ultimate issue at hand is, of course, the scientific status of psychoanalysis: is psychoanalysis a science?

Freud's answer, formulated in an easily accessible manner and, thus, possibly replying rather to popular misconceptions than to informed critique, is explicitly negative: psychoanalysis does not and cannot form a world-view of its own. As a scientific discipline, psychoanalysis can and must adhere to a more general "scientific world-view". For the most part, the lecture is dedicated to the discerning of such a scientific world-view or what Freud also calls the "scientific spirit [*wissenschaftliche Geist*]" from a religious world-view. There are good

[8] Formerly psychoanalytic theory was used in law as a form of social psychology that could contribute to the explanation of the communal experience of law. Kelsen, for instance, claims that even though Freud's theory of the libido can be used to describe the formation of various social groupings, it cannot account for the juridical specificity of the state, that is, its self-positing character (*Eigengesetzlichkeit*). Kelsen, *Der soziologische und der juristische Staatsbegriff*, p. 32. Cf. Legendre, *Histoire de l'administration de 1750 à nos jours*, pp. 43–44. In an attempt to surpass the dichotomy of positivism and natural law, Ehrenzweig refers to psychoanalysis in order to depict what he calls "the sense of justice". Ehrenzweig, "Psychoanalytical Jurisprudence: A Common Language for Babylon", 1356–1360. This attempt evolved into an eclectic *magnum opus*, Ehrenzweig, *Psychoanalytic Jurisprudence*. On psychoanalysis as a critique of legal positivism, see Goodrich, *Oedipus Lex*, pp. 223–247.

[9] Freud, *Neue Folge der Vorlesungen zur Einführung in die Psychoanalyse*, pp. 170–197.

reasons for understanding religion here in the broadest possible sense. For Freud, the shift from a religious world-view to a scientific one, as it is embodied in the science of psychoanalysis, also marks the threshold of modernity. As science, psychoanalysis represents the world-view of modernity.[10]

The lecturer is, however, well aware of an internal paradox within the employed term "scientific world-view". According to Freud, a *Weltanschauung* is a uniform, all-encompassing system of thought providing a closed and consistent explanation of the world, whereas science is necessarily incomplete, fragmentary and unable to construct self-contained systems. A world-view is, accordingly, unscientific in itself. How is, then, a "scientific world-view" possible? Freud claims that, as a *Weltanschauung*, science adopts:

> "the *uniformity* of the explanation of the world, but only as a programme the completion of which is relegated to the future. Apart from this, it is marked by negative characteristics, by its limitation to what is knowable for the time being and by its sharp rejection of certain elements alien to it. It asserts that there are no sources of knowledge of the world other than the intellectual working of carefully scrutinised observations or, in other words, what is called research, excluding knowledge from revelation, intuition or divination".[11]

The same paradox—perhaps displaying the influence of German Romanticism in Freud's thinking—haunts the use of the term "scientific spirit". During the course of his lecture, Freud extends the paradoxical tension between the closed and systematic characteristics of a world-view or the romantic *Geist* and the necessarily incomplete nature of science into an attempt to distinguish between, on the one hand, modern science—for Freud, science is always psychoanalysis—and, on the other hand, religion and modes of science-related thought such as philosophy, "political anarchism" and Marxism that still adhere to a religious world-view. Freud's account displays an apologetic tone, for he maintains that even modern science must be systematic. But in 1933, Freud's metapsychological ambitions have already been tempered; the lecturer emphasises that the systematic nature of science is merely programmatic and self-adjusting.[12]

In opposition to science, Freud specifies three human activities that include enough similarities to justify their treatment as a single unscientific world-view. Art is regarded as relatively innocent and innocuous because it explicitly declares itself illusory and seldom attempts to penetrate into the realm of reality. According to Freud, then, an unscientific world-view belongs to the order of

[10] It should be remembered here that, in his account on the omnipotence of thought in *Totem und Tabu*, Freud discerns three stages in the evolutionary history of world-views: magical, religious and scientific, representing respectively primitive, premodern and modern societies. Freud, *Totem und Tabu*, pp. 106–111.

[11] Freud, *Neue Folge*, p. 171.

[12] One of the best known critics of Freud's consistent belief in science was Oscar Pfister, a Swiss priest and psychoanalyst, who was especially critical about Freud's attempts to reduce religion to a neurotic illusion: Sigmund Freud, "Die Zukunft einer Illusion", pp. 323–378, in Freud, *Werke aus den Jahren 1925–1931*. Cf. Pfister, "Die Illusion einer Zukunft".

illusion whereas science belongs to the order of reality. The second activity designated by Freud, that is, philosophy, applies the scientific method of observation, but it displays its unscientific foundation in as much as it aspires to present a consistent and closed explanation of the world. Philosophy departs from the scientific spirit "by overstating the epistemological value [*Erkenntniswert*] of our logical operations and by accepting other sources of knowledge [than scientific observation] such as intuition". An unscientific world-view is, then, omniscient whereas science is restricted to the analytical description of made observations.[13]

The third human activity, religion, that Freud proceeds to discuss in detail serves as an archetypical example of an unscientific world-view. The exemplary character of religion is evident not only in its historical positioning in Freud's scheme of human evolution, but also in its alleged affinities and disparities in relation to modern science: Freud continuously juxtaposes the scientific spirit to religion. It would seem that we are not dealing with a sharp distinction between religion and science but, rather, with degrees of scientific thinking. Freud's concern is not religion as such, but modern science—psychoanalysis—and its relation to an unscientific world-view as it is exemplified in religion: how can the scientificity of psychoanalysis be accounted for?

Even for Jacques Lacan, the epistemological status of psychoanalytic practice lies "between science and religion".[14] Psychoanalysis pertains to the register of religion to the extent that it is a form of *re*search, an inquiry into something that precedes the investigation but has been forgotten. Such research implies that the investigation will eventually reach a terminal point by *re*appropriating a truth that has been forgotten. The object of science, however, is not stable or constant, but is subjected to the transformations of the search itself. Religion also includes the sacraments as inner operative elements that re-evoke its *au-delà*, its forgotten truth. But even if psychoanalysis also includes such an element of ceremony, it is not a religion. Its status is of an intermediate nature between the dialectics of the subject and the Other. Psychoanalysis has "nothing to forget, for it does not imply the recognition of a substance on which it tries to operate".[15]

From Freud's account of religion as the exemplary form of an unscientific world-view, we can distinguish three functions that a non-science adhering to the doctrinal burden of the past, be it religion, philosophy or art, fulfils. First,

[13] Freud, *Neue Folge*, pp. 172–175.

[14] Lacan, *Les quatre concepts fondamentaux de la psychanalyse*, pp. 11–17 and pp. 237–240. See also Lacan, *Écrits*, pp. 871–873. The indistinct character of this "between" must be emphasised. Lacan-interpreters such as Taureck allude to the intermediate character of psychoanalysis without contemplating its consequences in depth. Taureck, "Einleitung. Die Psychoanalyse zwischen Empirie und Philosophie", in Taureck (ed.), *Psychoanalyse und Philosophie*, pp. 7–31. Elsewhere Freud places psychoanalysis "between medicine and philosophy" referring to the psychosomatic character of its object of study. Freud, "Die Widerstände gegen die Psychoanalyse", pp. 97–110, in Freud, *Werke aus den Jahren 1925–1931*, p. 104.

[15] Lacan, *Les quatre concepts fondamentaux*, p. 239.

an unscientific world-view shares with science the concern to provide man with knowledge. Knowledge imbedded in an unscientific world-view is, however, rather specific. It is cosmogonic in that it attempts to give a closed explanation of the world by furnishing it with an origin, an ultimate foundation, or an *archē*. For Freud, scientific knowledge must necessarily be non-essentialist and anarchic. This can be called the *cosmogonic function* of an unscientific world-view.

Secondly, non-science is oriented towards the future in that it contains within itself a promise of redemption and deliverance. Freud maintains that even if scientific knowledge may occasionally succeed in assisting man in resolving his mundane problems, science itself does not entail the possibility—let alone a commitment—to relieve him of his everyday suffering. For Freud, scientific knowledge is contingent rather than determined by a redemptive ideal. An unscientific world-view fulfils, then, something that can be called its *messianic function*. Thirdly, an unscientific world-view applies its knowledge to impose normative constraints and ethical demands. Although rules and advice for the conduct of life are often derived from the application of scientific knowledge, science itself is "content to investigate and to establish facts".[16] According to Freud, then, scientific knowledge is descriptive rather than prescriptive. This third feature of an unscientific world-view can be called its *normative function*.

It is, therefore, in the realms of the cosmogonic, the messianic and the normative where the epistemological dividing-line between non-science and science must be drawn. Freud's account of religion—this account is itself rather unscientific—indicates, however, that such a dividing-line must necessarily be drawn into water. Science shares all the functions that non-science fulfils although the scientific tone is moderated: if religion gives "instructions", science provides "knowledge"; religion "consolidates", whereas science "teaches"; religion presents "requirements", science can only "advise". The conceptual tension of the paradox "scientific world-view" is, thus, operative to the end.

Freud understands philosophy as a borderline case, a human activity between science and non-science that commences from the scientific spirit—the scientific method—but displays its unscientific foundation in its consistent conclusions. A particular form of philosophical thought that Freud deals with is called intellectual nihilism or a reflection of political anarchism.[17] According to Freud, the starting point of nihilism is the scientific theory of relativity. Intellectual nihilism, however, forces the scientific spirit to annihilate itself by requiring science to denounce its own claims. Such an annihilation of science will, perhaps, provide a strategically motivated interim void into which a new world-view—a religion, an ethics, a politics—can later be installed.

In this struggle over hegemony, intellectual nihilism denies the existence of any criterion of truth which Freud understands as correspondence with the external world. According to the nihilist, truth is ultimately bound to the ever-

[16] Freud, *Neue Folge*, p. 174.
[17] *Ibid.*, pp. 190–191.

changing needs of man and, therefore, merely an illusion. Freud maintains that "a spirit of an epistemological orientation" will find the scientific incentive of such sophistries alluring, but their explicative power is restricted to mere abstractions. The nihilistic denouncement of truth leads science to an impasse in which it is hereafter futile to continue the scientific enterprise. Freud's examples are from the sphere of practical life—prescribing effective medicines, building solid bridges—but it is evident that even the nihilistic assertion still adheres to a certain degree of truth: the demise of truth is constituted as true.[18]

Freud finds the scientific enterprise necessary, but he does not explicate the "necessity" that demands its inception and continuance. Science, then, embodies a *desire for knowledge*, a desire the elaboration of which does not belong to the enterprise itself. This desire, perhaps too cosmogonic, messianic or normative for the rational scientist's liking, may also be one of the "alluring sophistries" that a philosophically worked out epistemology would require. But true to the dictates of modern science, Freud chooses fact and knowledge over truth.

III

In his lecture, Freud relates science primarily to man's practical concerns, but the intricate relationship between established facts and an irrational beyond is evident in the paradoxical tension between science and *Weltanschauung*. Critical legal scholarship has addressed this epistemic incertitude in a particular way. In today's scholarly environment, any reference to the requirement of scientificity would appear to be either more or less superfluous or as an indication of conservative political values. The overtones in contemporary debate have relativised the relevance of such a demand; the requirement of scientificity, so the argument runs, is founded on an outlived tradition and must, accordingly, make way for a more playful position, for a new *gaya scienza*. But much of the gaiety of today's critical thinking has only been possible by reducing the question of scientificity and the tradition that advocates such a demand to axioms. The occasional confrontations have all too often comprised of an indeterminate melange of confused nihilism and theoretical ruse that, blinded by its practical ambitions, has theoretically reduced itself to rhetorical persuasion.[19]

[18] On "historical" and "material" truth, see Freud, "Konstruktionen in der Analyse", in Freud, *Werke aus den Jahren 1932–1939*, pp. 41–56, and Freud, "Der Mann Moses und die monotheistische Religion," in Freud, *Werke aus den Jahren 1932–1939*, pp. 101–246 at pp. 236–240.

[19] On problems concerning such critical gaiety in law, see, e.g., Frankenberg, "Die Ernst im Recht". The same problems are confronted by psychoanalysis. Slavoj Žižek, an acute and sensitive reader of both Freud and Lacan, runs the risk of what Freud condemns as "wild psychoanalysis" by "simply" (*sic*) putting Lacan's theoretical apparatus to work. Such forced labour can only produce constrained interpretations. Žižek, *For They Know Not What They Do*, p. 3. Cf. Freud, "Über 'wilde' Psychoanalyse", in Freud, *Werke aus den Jahren 1909–1913*, pp. 117–125.

How should the science of law, then, respond to the battle calls of today's critical gaiety? Can it simply accept the challenge and partake in the contemporary critic's attempts to rhetorically transform the world? Such a position is often justified as an ethics of the "age of uncertainty", that is, as a playful stance after the demise of truth, as an apocalyptic philosophy after the fading away of the mirage of certitude.[20] But I would like to think that there is another route. The science of law can investigate the premises of its own incertitude, the tense relationship between what is accessible to science as knowledge and the truth beyond that seems to escape it. In Freud's account of psychoanalysis, the tension between scientific knowledge and a non-scientific world-view is more or less explicit. Even in his scientistic aspirations, Freud never eliminates the tension between psychoanalysis and the unobservable and "alluring" beyond that, nevertheless, seems to motivate his search.

Instead of reducing the science of law to mere "sophistries", I shall attempt to articulate the tension between science and the beyond through Lacanian psychoanalysis. In the second part of his seminar *Problèmes cruciaux pour la psychanalyse* from 1964–1965, Lacan analyses this tension as the relationship between knowledge and truth. The seminar dates back to the same period as Lacan's best known publication on epistemology, "La science et la vérité".[21] By analysing the relation between knowledge and truth, I hope to be able to formulate a feasible epistemological background for a philosophy of law that understands itself as a "science of man" in the most rigorous possible sense.[22]

In his earlier texts, Lacan's point of departure is the assessment that psychoanalysis belongs to the tradition of modern science.[23] In other words, if psychoanalysis is to either attain or maintain the status of a science, it must observe the same requirement of scientificity and exactitude as the other disciplines of modern science. At this stage, Lacan is still rather conventional: as the general requirements of science, epistemology precedes psychoanalysis, and scientific exactitude presupposes the ability to reduce a given phenomenon to formal lan-

[20] Cf. Derrida, *D'un ton apocalyptique adopté naguère en philosophie*, pp. 81–83. Such a self-affirmative playfulness would also constitute the traditional gesture of "paternal politics". On the necessary incertitude of the political space and the pacifying effect of the juridical subject, see Legendre, *Jouir du pouvoir*, pp. 87–109. On the production of axiomatic truths in law, see Legendre, *L'empire de la vérité*.

[21] Lacan, *Écrits*, pp. 855–877. On the significance and specific history of this *écrit*, see Roudinesco, *Jacques Lacan*, pp. 425–427. See also Lang, *Die Sprache und das Unbewußte*, pp. 266–304. Lacan seldom uses the term "epistemology" himself, but it has gained a certain status through Jacques-Alain Miller who has included it in the index he has compiled for *Écrits*. According to Miller, Lacanian epistemology marks "the position of psychoanalysis *in* the epistemological break in that, through the Freudian field, the foreclosed subject of science makes its return into the *impossibility* of its discourse. Therefore, Lacan theorises a single ideology: the 'modern ego' or, in other words, the paranoiac subject of scientific civilisation of which a misguided psychology theorises the imaginary at the service of free enterprise": Lacan, *Écrits*, p. 894. Cf. Miller, "La suture (Éléments de la logique du signifiant)".

[22] For an excellent overview of Lacanian psychoanalysis, see Dor, *Introduction à la lecture de Lacan 1* and *Introduction à lecture de Lacan 2*.

[23] Lacan, *Les écrits techniques de Freud*, pp. 7–19.

guage. In order to meet the requirement of scientificity, the ability to recede from the phenomenon observed to a formal abstraction must be respected within psychoanalytic theory, as well: "This is the problem of the foundations that must assure our discipline its place among the sciences: the problem of formalisation".[24] In the so-called "Rome discourse", the formalist ideal of science finds its summit in the structuralist anthropology of Claude Lévi-Strauss. In transforming the phenomenon observed into symbolic representations, certain principles must be taken into account if psychoanalysis is to fulfil the requirement of scientificity.[25]

But even if the necessity of formalisation is respected in psychoanalysis, the peculiar position of the subject in relation to the object studied seems to deny the possibility of any formal representation. For Lacan, only one subject as such can be recognised: the subject of science.[26] The possessive case of the notion reveals the double meaning from which Lacan draws his argument. The subject of science is the theory of the subject as it is elaborated by the science of psychoanalysis, but it is also the scientific subject that possesses knowledge about this structure. The constitution of the scientific subject—Lacan is here referring to the analyst as the possessor of knowledge—is, however, not the Cartesian *cogito* but what Lacan calls the *sujet supposé savoir*, a subject that is assumed to be knowledgable but whose inquiries into the world are tainted by the same fundamental desire that is innate in all subjectivity.[27] The *sujet supposé savoir* does not possess mere knowledge about the world, but also about the unconscious, that is, about truth.[28] The analyst posits himself in the place of the unconscious and allows it to speak, but:

> "the analyst is, of course, supposed to know, and yet all that is involved in the fundamental knowledge of psychoanalysis affirms us that he cannot be this *sujet supposé savoir* because the fundamental knowledge of psychoanalysis, Freud's discovery, denies it".[29]

[24] Lacan, *Écrits*, p. 284. On the ambiguous relationship between psychoanalysis and science, see Fink, *The Lacanian Subject*, pp. 145–146. On Lacan's different epistemological phases, see Milner, *L'œuvre claire*.

[25] A well-known interpretation of the scientific character of psychoanalysis is Althusser's claim that Lacan, in his reading of Freud, establishes psychoanalysis as a science by subjecting it to the general requirements of epistemology: "Lacan's initial point is to take [Freud's emphasis of theory] literally. And to draw the conclusion: to return to Freud in order to search, discern and define, from his texts, the theory that justifies everything else, both technique and practice": Althusser, "Freud et Lacan", in Althusser, *Écrits sur la psychanalyse*, pp. 22–53 at pp. 28–29. Lacan's reservation concerning Althusser's "scientism" is clearly audible in his laconic response depicting the manuscript as "profound and pertinent, complementing the subject with the dimensions of [Althusser's own] thought": letter of 6 July 1964, *ibid.*, p. 305. Cf. Roudinesco, *Jacques Lacan*, pp. 396–402.

[26] Lacan, *Écrits*, pp. 858–860.

[27] It should be noted that the Lacanian subject is *not* an inclusive rejection of the Cartesian *cogito* but a theoretical—albeit critical—development from it. Lacan's reading of Descartes has been elaborated in, e.g., le Gaufey, *L'incomplétude du symbolique*, pp. 174–186.

[28] Lacan, *Les quatre concepts fondamentaux*, pp. 209–220 and Lacan, *Le moi dans la théorie de Freud et dans la technique de la psychanalyse*, pp. 12–16.

[29] Lacan, *Problèmes cruciaux pour la psychanalyse*, p. 189.

The science of the psyche studies the possibility of a signifier that would permit the formalisation of the functioning of the object in analytic theory, to know the object that structures the human psyche. It is the phallic object with which the analyst deals in his relations between the subject and its psyche. But it is also the analyst's object, the object of analytic science.[30] The phallus as signifier is, however, marked by a radical absence. It is, therefore, only accessible to science as the lack that constitutes desire. Moreover, the object of science is causally determined by what Lacan calls the "Freudian thing" (*la chose*, *causa*), that is, the unconscious. As the fundamental lack that constitutes the subject's desire, the phallic signifier is compelled to function as the object of science merely as a swaying approximation without access to the exactitude of scientific formalisations:

> "the ambiguity of a subject's relation to knowledge, knowledge in so far as it still lacks the knowledge that, for us, is the activity of the existence of a subject, precisely this makes it inconceivable to presume that a subject founds itself on a harmonious ensemble of systemic signifiers . . . there is a lack somewhere that I articulate for you as being the lack of a signifier".[31]

This structure is intimately bound to the unique position of the affect of anxiety in philosophy. According to Bernard Baas, anxiety is:

> "the dynamic element that animates a certain movement towards truth, and it characterises or signifies this movement as the movement towards truth".[32]

In order to fulfil the requirement of scientificity, the structure accounting for the subject and the object of science would also have to be fully transmissible or, in other words, it would have to be elaborated into a formal representation that can be conveyed forward without reference to a nominal authority such as a name. To realise this requirement, the formal representation would have to be eradicated of all intersubjectivity.[33] For Lacan, such formal purity is, however, inconceivable because psychoanalysis, as a "human science", requires that the world must be represented with the true man taking into account his position as subject. The subject is a place without which there would be no representation because otherwise representation would not be "in the world":

> "Our aim, our ideal, is mathematical formalisation. Why?—because only formalisation is *mathēme* or, in other words, capable of transmitting in full. Mathematical formalisation is writing, but it only subsists if I, in presenting it, employ the language that I use. Here is the objection: no formalisation of language is transmissible without the use of language itself. With my saying, I make this formalisation, the ideal metalanguage, exist".[34]

[30] Lacan, *L'identification*, p. 534.
[31] Lacan, *Problèmes cruciaux*, p. 192. Cf. Lacan, *La relation d'objet*, pp. 36–39.
[32] Baas, *Le désir pur*, s. 98.
[33] Lacan, *Les psychoses*, p. 76.
[34] Lacan, *Encore*, p. 108. Cf. Lacan, *Problèmes cruciaux*, p. 204.

As science, psychoanalysis must, accordingly, take into consideration a problem peculiar to its specific nature. There is something that cannot be formalised: the truth of the unconscious. There is meaning in the unconscious, but no signifier can represent it.[35] According to Lacan's starting point, the requirement of scientificity would be fulfilled only if everything can be formalised, including that which is not conscious. But for Lacan, the unconscious must necessarily remain unconscious; the truth of the unconscious remains out of reach. In other words, the science of psychoanalysis does not deal merely with facts, but it also contrives postulates or, using Lacan's own terminology from the period of the "Rome discourse", conjectures. As a conjectural science, psychoanalysis studies phenomena the cause of which—the unconscious—is not in its jurisdiction. But this does not mean that a science that presents its arguments as approximations would be futile or impossible:

> "The introduction of the unconscious changes the status of knowledge totally . . . we do not know where the subject that is presumed to know settles down in relation to the signifier but, on the other hand, this knowledge, even if it is unconscious, refers in a fundamentally interdicting way to the pole that determines itself in its function as knowledge; there is something that this subject, this knowledge, must not know".[36]

The interplay between fact and conjecture also designates the relationship between knowledge and truth:

> "The reference of psychoanalysis as science to that with which one can, in effect, realise the particular relation in connection to a particular place where truth reappears in the modern dialectic of knowledge, . . . this reference, in effect, determines what there is in [knowledge] that we can speak of in the name of psychoanalysis".[37]

The unconscious is introduced into science through language. Even if science could be understood as a formalised and systematic enterprise, one would be obliged to use conventional and non-formal language. A mundane phenomenon can, perhaps, be structurally accounted for by using formal, mathematical symbols, but one is, nevertheless, obliged to conceive the symbols themselves and define their application with conventional language. We can, perhaps, deduct any given phenomenon into a logical formulation, but even the use of logical formulae in science requires the explication of how one has come about the employed symbols.[38]

[35] According to Lacoue-Labarthe and Nancy, "[t]he subject cannot *know* this truth the theory of which requires, in turn, the theory of the subject. Truth is anterior or exterior in relation to all knowledge because it must be understood . . . as the identification of truth to speech itself without any other reference and, in particular, to the exclusion of all metalanguage or, in other words, of the sense of sense": Lacoue-Labarthe and Nancy, *Le titre de la lettre*, p. 92.

[36] Lacan, *Problèmes cruciaux*, p. 203.

[37] *Ibid.*, p. 217.

[38] Lacan, *Encore*, p. 108.

IV

This means that we must confront several consequential difficulties. Within the conjectural sciences—the "sciences of man" including the science of law—the ideal of the formal model does not seem to pertain to unconscious meaning; the requirement of scientificity is in contradiction with the intersubjective relations of the human world. We can, perhaps, display the systemic characteristics of a given phenomenon with the help of a formalised model, but the truth of the unconscious remains beyond scientific models. This is the paradox: on the one hand, we can, for example, speak of exact, formalised knowledge that is transmissible but, on the other hand, science is also tainted with unconscious meaning. If the science of law is understood as a conjectural science, its domain of study would necessarily include a peculiar truth that cannot be formalised or transmitted but of which mere approximations can be presented: the truth of the unconscious. Does this, then, mean that, for example, scientific knowledge about law and truth are incompatible, that, as a science, law can only inquire into observable phenomena the truth of which has been introduced into the world through a language mastered by the unconscious? Does the science of law have access to its object of study merely as it is posited into the world, but never as the truth of law?[39]

Such an exclusion of truth, typified by the pathos of modern science, would merely restate the original opposition: the science of law is either knowledge or a craft, either *logos* or *technē*, *ratio* or *ars*. And in this presentation of oppositional positions, the conjectural science of law that must also approximate to the unscientific notion of "justice" would, indeed, remain a skilled way of applying the law, the *prudens* of the talented *iudex*. More generally speaking, as a conjectural science, law would be reduced to an hermeneutic art of interpretation. But this need not be the case. In order to fulfil the requirement of scientificity, the relationship between scientific knowledge and the truth of the unconscious must be inscribed into the very epistemological basis of the conjectural sciences.

Are, then, knowledge and truth incompatible as modern science seems to claim? Playing on etymology, Lacan contends that science and truth are, indeed, compatible to the extent that they "compathise". They "suffer together" from a similar lack.[40] They are unable to clarify one another and are flawed by the same defect: the inability to reach a totalising perfection. Even the epistemological basis of the so-called exact sciences consists partly of unverifiable postulates. It is, for example, impossible to verify the principle of observation itself by way of observation, and it must, consequently, remain an axiom. Face to face with their

[39] On the inability of science to recognise truth, see Lacan, *Écrits*, pp. 73–80. For an influential but unfortunately polemical criticism of Lacan's "scientific" project, see Roustang, *Lacan, de l'équivoque à l'impasse*, in particular pp. 23–63.

[40] Lacan, "Radiophonie," p. 92.

own imperfections, the traditional "sciences of man" have usually either set such irresolvable aporias aside as, for instance, Kelsen's legal positivism does by positing, due to epistemological necessity, the *Grundnorm* into the "transcendental-logical" domain that the science of law itself does not address,[41] or they have served as the justification for external scientific support as, for example, the sociology of law does by submitting the science of law to the epistemological dictates of the social sciences and, simultaneously, restating doubts about the scientific credibility of the science of law itself. In this sense, the critical legal scholarship of today resembles its predecessors; cultural theory is called upon to appease the desire for knowledge that cannot be satisfied.

What I understand by scientific imperfection is that the relationship between the object of science and the subject that studies it can never be mended fast; an opening will remain in the scientific *suture* that prevents the totalising rationalisation of the human world. In Lacan's notion of the conjectural sciences, this aperture is filled with the unconscious. Therefore, the impossibility of a scientific *suture* is related to the imperfection of truth. But even conjectures can be presented with rigour and, accordingly, the antinomic opposition of knowledge and truth is unnecessary:

> "The opposition between the exact sciences and the conjectural sciences is unsustainable from the moment when conjecture is susceptible to an exact calculus (probability) and when exactitude founds itself only on a formalism classifying the axioms and laws of grouping symbols".[42]

As a conjectural science, the science of law cannot simply refuse to deal with the requirement of exactitude and freely venture a truth that it claims to account for. But even if the phenomenon of law could be presented in a formal model, the unconscious truth of the conjectural sciences punctures a hole into the ideal of scientific exactitude. Respectively, even if the truth of law must remain a conjecture, the science of law must comply with the requirements of scientificity: the knowledge of science and the truth of the unconscious are not incompatible.

Lacan maintains that no epistemological metalanguage is possible and, accordingly, the distinction between knowledge and truth, between fact and conjecture, must be incorporated and inbuilt into the very epistemological structure of science itself. Lacan uses one of his topological representations, the Möbius strip, to demonstrate this.[43] In other words, the relationship between

[41] Kelsen, *Reine Rechtslehre. Zweite Auflage*, pp. 224–225 and 443–444. On Kelsen's relationship to neo-Kantianism, see Kelsen, "Rechtswissenschaft und Recht. Erledigung eines Versuchs zur Überwindung der 'Rechtsdogmatik'," in Sander and Kelsen, *Die Rolle des Neukantianismus in der Reinen Rechtlehre*, pp. 279–411. It is, perhaps, worth noting that Heidegger regards Freud's notion of the unconscious as a neo-Kantian attempt to guarantee the closed nature of causal relations within the science of psychoanalysis: Heidegger, *Zollikoner Seminare*, p. 260.

[42] Lacan, *Écrits*, p. 863.

[43] Joël Dor maintains that Lacan's topological representations such as the Möbius strip do not indicate the mathematisation or the formalisation of psychoanalysis as science. The representations are, rather, metaphorical illustrations the dynamics of which are revealed in that the illustration actualises the representation at the same time as it makes use of it. Dor describes this *mise en acte*

the science of law and its object of study is an intersubjective structure in which the incompleteness of a structural representation must be set against the indeterminate suspension of truth.

The rapport between knowledge and truth remains irresolvable, paradoxical and strained. The language of the science of law can be read as a symptom that arises as the subject of science attempts to find access from the imaginary order of its enterprise, afflicted with intersubjective relations and identifications with which man understands his position in the world, into the symbolic order of a formal and closed system where the meanings of language are formed. But without the phallic master signifier that would fix the system conclusively, man is imprisoned by his unconscious hopes and nightmares and obliged to use a metaphorical and figurative language.[44] In the science of law, the subject attempts to capture law in an altogether rational, formal and scientific structure, but such a task will necessarily lead to juridical rhetoric.

Kelsen's attempt to "purify" law is also an effort to found law as a modern science. His delusional gesture is in eradicating the subject of science from the world to which the science of law and its object of study belong; in Kelsen's world of pure knowledge, there is nothing called "human". An acute reading would, perhaps, indicate the passages in which the neo-Kantian jurisprudent was obliged to repress truth, but the repression itself already introduces the fragments from which the truth of law can be addressed. In a very similar fashion, the critical variant of contemporary legal scholarship represses its own incertitude with the rhetoric of crisis that accompanies its criticism.[45] Confusing object and objective, critical legal scholarship is preceded by an axiology of social values, and in this sense we are, indeed, dealing with a "legal" science in which the directives of social criticism fill the void of the unconscious truth. As critical theory, the science of law is unable to either criticise or to analyse the modern Cartesian subject that it seemingly denounces, but can merely *reaffirm* it in its self-assuring tonality.

The strong opposition against Lacan's antihumanistic epistemology robbing man of the sovereign position he has possessed ever since the beginnings of the Enlightenment—this is why Lacan was so uncomfortable with the notion of a "science of man" and preferred to use the term "conjectural science"—can be interpreted as the symptom of a failing Cartesian humanism. Human being in the world is not, in the last instance, affirmed by God in the sense that Descartes understands it but remains in a disturbing incertitude.[46] This cannot, however, be indifferently acknowledged. The incertitude concerning the ultimate scien-

of the representations as "epistemological acting out" that does not take place within the common prescriptions of science: Dor, "Approche épistémologique des paradigmes mathématiques lacaniens", 95. On the Möbius strip in particular, see Dor, *Introduction 2*, pp. 129–138.

[44] See, e.g., Lacan, *Les psychoses*, pp. 221–231. On the phallic "symbol Φ", see Lacan, *Le transfert*, pp. 277–291.

[45] See de Man, "Criticism and Crisis", in de Man, *Blindness and Insight*, pp. 3–19.

[46] On God as the non-deceiving foundation of science, see Lacan, *Les psychoses*, pp. 77–78.

tific clarification of law is also at the core of a desire for the science of law understood as a conjectural science. It is the root for the original desire to know, for the question that is worth asking even if no conclusive answer is to be expected:

> "science is animated by a mysterious desire, but it does not know, any more than anything in the unconscious, what this desire means".[47]

An epistemology that founds itself on the certitude of the subject concerning itself and its world can never acknowledge the unconscious, a repressed truth that is present only because it is absent, a truth that is recognised only because it is next to impossible to unveil. In the last instance, the epistemological basis of the science of law would necessarily have to be the question concerning man's inaptitude to master the surrounding world he has created. For if the truth of law was already at hand, scientific knowledge would also be undesirable.

A science, then, called "law", an object of knowledge that bears the same name, and, finally, a truth that we clumsily approach with the grandiloquence of "justice": as truth, justice can never be conclusively appropriated, and, yet, it is the desire of the subject of science for this very same truth that makes any scientific enterprise possible to begin with. But even if justice as the truth of law must necessarily remain out of reach, what the subject of science does catch a glimpse of is altogether different than the mundane facts of positive law.

If one cannot realise justice but need not settle for positive statutes, we are, perhaps, dealing with something called "correctness".

[47] Lacan, *L'éthique de la psychanalyse*, p. 374. See also Lacan, *L'envers de la psychanalyse*, pp. 9–24.

2

A First Philosophy of Law

"By nature all men desire to see [*tou eidenai oregontai*]."

Aristotle

"For metaphysics as a science to be able to demand recognition not only for its deceiving oratory but also for its insight and authority, the critique of reason itself must present the whole array of *a priori* concepts, their division according to the various sources—perception, understanding, and reason—and, further, categorise them fully and analyse them including anything that can be inferred from them."

Immanuel Kant

I

It is, however, no coincidence that a treatise on the philosophy of law should begin with an account of epistemology. One could well claim that the philosophy of law only commences with Immanuel Kant. Such a claim would not necessarily be referring to the Kant of the *Second Critique* or to his *Rechtslehre*, for the tradition that understands law as a mode of practical thinking can be traced back to the beginnings of Occidental philosophy. It would be equally acceptable to assert that it is, indeed, the epistemologist of the *First Critique* who is the true initiator of the philosophy of law as a modern science. Within this explicitly modern tradition of juridical thinking, the impact of Kant reaches its culmination point some two centuries after the philosopher's death. The modern "paradigm" of the philosophy of law is unquestionably neo-Kantian, and as such, the paradigm articulates the *metaphysical question* of the philosophy of law into an epistemology: how can one know about law? What are the *a priori* conditions of such knowledge? How is correct knowledge about law possible?

As I have tried to indicate in the previous chapter, the epistemological question usually involves a denial: the scientific status of former orientations—in Kant's case we would be dealing with the dogmatic doctrines that precede the age of rational science—is contested. But there is another side to the question that I would now like to take up in more detail. To enunciate on the "correctness" of knowledge in such a way necessarily requires that philosophy must also establish its own "right" to address the world. The metaphysical question takes on, then, a juridical form: how can philosophy justify its claim to correct knowledge? And the philosophy of law will, consequently, involve a peculiar multiple reference to law: the metaphysical question of the philosophy of law concerns the *right* to present *correct* knowledge about *law*.

Contemporary articulations of the metaphysical question in philosophy are often presented by mentioning the name of Martin Heidegger. One could hardly overestimate Heidegger's impact for philosophy in general, but surprisingly little has been done to assess the significance of the German thinker's *œuvre* for the philosophy of law. Heidegger has virtually nothing to say about law as such, but in the following chapters, I will try to illustrate possible avenues for a Heideggerian account of law. For now, it suffices to briefly review what Heidegger had to say about philosophy and what the reaction of the philosophy of law was. It has been argued that Heidegger's "fundamental ontology" radicalises the metaphysical question to such an extent that no philosophy of law is thereafter possible. As the philosophy of law does not and cannot address the fundamental question of philosophy, that is, the question of Being or the *Seinsfrage*, the philosophy of law can but reduce itself to the theoretical elaboration of juridically significant entities, to a science of law:

> "If the philosophy of law turns out to be impossible, if it cannot make law into juridical reality or justify philosophy, then juridical thinking has no other alternative but to take, in the Kantian spirit, the 'safe path of science': to reduce itself to a science of law".[1]

Furthermore, if we take in earnest Jacques Derrida's claim that Heidegger is still reluctant to take the destruction of Occidental metaphysics to its conclusion,[2] Heidegger's position *vis-à-vis* the philosophy of law—and Derrida's, for that matter—becomes even more problematic. The philosophy of law, then, remains a possibility that requires a justification. Can philosophy deal with law? Can the science of law be philosophical? Is there a philosophy of law that is distinct from the science of law?

The philosophy of law must justify its claim to its theoretical enterprise. *Quid iuris*? What is law? What right does the philosophy of law have to address law? And the answer that modern science requires is: the philosophy of law has earned its right to exist only if it can *guarantee the scientific nature of knowledge about law*. Jean-Luc Nancy has called this self-legitimation of philosophy "jurisdiction".[3] Especially after Kant, Nancy maintains, philosophy, no longer able to unveil the world in the sense of classical metaphysics, becomes the scientific discourse of reason that pronounces what is "correct" (*richtig*) and what is "right" (*recht*). Philosophical jurisdiction is an epistemological fiction the initial model of which is a geometrical figure, that is, Kant's "tribunal of reason"

[1] Girardot, "Ist Rechtsphilosophie überhaupt möglich?", p. 160.

[2] Derrida, *Marges—de la philosophie*, pp. 73–78.

[3] Nancy, "Lapsus judicii," in Nancy, *L'impératif catégorique*, pp. 33–60, especially pp. 38–44. An analogous theme is presented in Rose, *Dialectic of Nihilism*, in relation to neo-Kantian philosophy of law, especially pp. 25–49.

in which reason operates as the ruling *tertius*.[4] Jurisdiction assigns meaning by pronouncing the rightful limits within which a concept can make sense.

An entity—a rainbow, for instance—does not exist before philosophy has given its verdict. From the bench, philosophy must judge whether the perception of a rainbow is correct or merely a deceptive image. But at the same time, philosophy must also institute its own right to pronounce judgement. As jurisdiction, philosophy fuses correctness and right (*ius*) with enunciation (*dictio*). By enunciating (*dicere*), philosophy, however, does not constitute. It merely refers (*indicere*) to the causal principle (*causam dicere*) that establishes the correctness of the entity in question. In Nancy's account, this initially "Latin" discourse can no longer bring the first causes and principles of metaphysics to light as the *logos* of the Greeks did. It can only furnish evidence on the relationship between cause and effect.

The cause of Aristotle's rainbow, for example, is reflection (*anaklasis*). For the Greeks, the reflected beam radiates from the eye of the observer reaching out towards the sun. In a profound sense, then, it is the light in the beholder's eye that creates the colours of the rainbow.[5] In jurisdiction, however, the rainbow must precede the observer and exist independently of his observations. The observer can only participate, as a sensory recipient, in an optical phenomenon in which the light of the sun reflects through droplets of water.

When philosophical jurisdiction enunciates on the correct nature of such an optical phenomenon, it does not create correctness. It gives it a form (*formula*). To verify the correctness of the causal relationship between reflection and rainbow, philosophy must figurate an analogy between an individual entity and a universal regularity. If it can do so, it will also legitimise its right to pronounce judgement. Because this right to philosophise is subjective, philosophy must, at the same time, constitute itself as a juridical subject; it must formulate its right to address the world. The holder of such a privilege is a judge (*iudex*) who corrects erroneous knowledge by giving it the correct form. Philosophical jurisdiction subsumes an individual case like a rainbow under the universality of the law of reflection. A case is, by nature, an event that takes place by chance. Because the probability of a rainbow under specified meteorological conditions has already been established into scientific knowledge, it would hardly constitute a case. For philosophy is only called upon to evaluate the correctness of cases that have taken place by chance. But when philosophy enunciates the correctness of such a case, it also annuls chance by subsuming the case under the universality of a law. A universal law involves no chance, and yet all laws must be established by evaluating the correctness of singular cases.

Philosophical jurisdiction has, then, a peculiar double structure. It must enunciate what is *hic et nunc* correct and, at the same time, annul the chance that brings about individual cases. The correct evaluation of the rainbow has veri-

[4] See the preface of the first edition of Kant, *Kritik der reinen Vernunft*, p. 15. Kant's own term for the tribunal (*Gerichtshof*) also connotes the "court" (*Hof*) where the king presents his rulings.

[5] My example of the rainbow is taken from Aristotle, *Mete*. 372a 16–21.

fied a universal law: the causal relationship between light and water that produces the rainbow is accounted for with the law of reflection. Strictly speaking, the rainbow has never been a case because there is no chance involved. But on the other hand, the universal law of reflection that accounts for the rainbow is established by chance because philosophy can only evaluate individual cases: correctness cannot be evaluated before we know what particular case we are talking about. But a rainbow cannot be equated with the law of reflection. The case of the rainbow can only be subsumed under the law of reflection if the former is formulated correctly. Correctness, then, is a fictive analogy between law and case. When the philosophical *iudex* establishes what is correct in a particular case, the facts are pronounced correctly and the "essence" of the case formulated (*fictio*). This is what Nancy calls the juridical fiction (*fictio iuris*) of philosophy.[6]

But the *iudex* does not constitute itself as an autonomous subject; only a judgement (*iudicium*) is presented. A judgement is not a conception (*conseptio*) with which the subject of metaphysics "conceives" both itself and the world. Trying to recognise the world, a judgement forces the world to disconnect from its representations while the signs that ensure correct knowledge are distinguished. The tribunal is, of course, also summoned with a judgement. But the *a priori* law that legitimises the summoning judgement is not a metaphysical one. It is posited at the same time as the court is summoned, and it auto-institutes the tribunal's right to assert what is correct. Philosophy must, then, endlessly justify its own claim to the world.[7]

In this chapter, I will investigate the metaphysical question of the philosophy of law from a rather traditional perspective. I will mainly focus my analysis on three neo-Kantian authors and attempt to demonstrate the auto-institutive structure of their philosophies. This involves an assumption that will govern the arguments arising from my readings, namely, that the "philosophical jurisdiction" of the philosophy of law is epistemological to the extent that, as an individual entity, *law is meaningful only in as much as it makes correct knowledge about the human world possible.* Law serves as the epistemic justification of philosophy, as the "juridisation" of knowledge concerning the human world. This involves a peculiar conspiracy between philosophy and juridical thinking: for philosophy to be a science, the knowledge that it provides must be "correct" (*richtig*) or "right" (*recht*).

The conspiracy will prepare the way for my second argument. Nancy's reading of the "Latin" discourse of philosophy seems to imply a nostalgia, a longing for an "original" Greek metaphysics that has been lost in the "juridisation" of philosophy into a science. My reading of Aristotle will hopefully show that the conspiracy between philosophy and juridical thinking may have already been inscribed into the opening words of *Metaphysics*. But even if we maintain with

[6] On juridical fictions, see Vaihinger, *Die Philosophie des Als Ob*, pp. 46–49.

[7] On the auto-institutive discourses of philosophy, see Derrida, *Du droit à la philosophie*, pp. 95–102.

Heidegger that the question of Being is the axis around which philosophical thinking revolves, we can, in a preparatory manner, characterise the premises of a "metaphysical" account of law. I will argue that a being that is "what it was to be"—this is the *to ti en einai* of Aristotle's "first philosophy"—must necessarily remain inaccessible to man. Animated by a desire for truth, a desire the structure of which I have tried to elaborate in the previous chapter, philosophy can merely pronounce what is "correct" or "right". In the chapters to follow, my eventual aim will be to demonstrate that law or, more accurately, "right" (*Recht*) is not only the entity of a regional science, but also a constitutive factor in the very structure of human Being. And only such a perspective entitles us to speak of a *philosophy* of law.

II

I have argued that, as a *modern* science, the traditional paradigm of the philosophy of law is neo-Kantian. Rudolf Stammler is usually mentioned as the founding representative of this lineage of epistemologically bent lawyer-philosophers. Inspired by the so-called Marburg school of neo-Kantian philosophers, Stammler claims that law can be regarded as a science only if the specificity of juridical consciousness is consistently and logically imbedded in the general scheme of the human order of consciousness.[8] The point of departure of a scientifically legitimate philosophy of law is Kant's distinction between transcendental-logical form and content. Form is universal, while content is human consciousness that is ordered in accordance with form.[9] The object of the philosophy of law is, accordingly, the logical form (*Form*) of law. The form of juridical thinking is the specific way in which juridical representations (*Vorstellung*) are ordered in human consciousness.[10] Form represents universality in relation to the ever-changing nature of content:

> "The form of a thought content is the unity of the permanent elements in contradistinction to those that are subject to change".[11]

On the other hand, the "correctness" (*Richtigkeit*) of law is "the form of the material evaluation of a content of law". For Stammler, correctness is not the equivalent of justice (*Gerechtigkeit*) as the English translations often seem to imply, but *the formal guarantee of knowledge*.[12] Forms such as correctness are basic concepts that establish a "founding experience" ordering the contents of human consciousness. Within the neo-Kantian scheme, philosophy offers the rigour of a scientific method to understand these universal forms of human con-

[8] Stammler, *Theorie der Rechtswissenschaft*, pp. 34–35. On philosophy and science in general, see *ibid.*, pp. 62–68.

[9] *Ibid.*, pp. 6–10.

[10] *Ibid.*, pp. 10–11.

[11] Stammler, *Die Lehre von dem richtigen Rechte*, p. 217.

[12] I will return later to the "ethical" implications of correctness.

sciousness. The transcendental-critical method of the *First Critique* was, however, developed for the scientific observation of nature and cannot, accordingly, be used as such in the analysis of the human world. Stammler's neo-Kantian position, that is, his preference for Kant the epistemologist, is clearly audible in his reservations about Kant the jurist whose account of law Stammler finds technical and unscientific.[13] The method developed in the *First Critique* must, then, be revised in order to make it valid for the analysis of law and other human phenomena.

For Kant, only one ordered form of human experience was accessible as knowledge, namely nature. Therefore, a critical philosophy of law requires the elaboration of a second dimension.[14] Nature is the bulk of all temporal and spatial observations. In these observations (*Wahrnehmen*), human beings establish causal relationships as knowledge. In nature, human beings perceive "becomings" (*Werden*), that is, necessary temporal sequences from something anterior to something posterior. One can, for instance, observe how seeds germinate into plants under particular meteorological circumstances. Knowledge about the human world is not, however, structured as the causal relationships of nature. The individual entities of the human world can only be recognised as acts of volition (*Wollen*), that is, as purposive means determined from the ends towards which they are directed. Volition involves realisations or effectuations (*Bewirken*) in which logically necessary and purposive acts are determined from posterior circumstances. Farming, for instance, is human volition where a purpose—vegetation understood as a harvest—has determined the means—the germination of seeds understood as cultivation.[15] The sciences that deal with the social world could, then, also be called the "purposive sciences" (*Zweckwissenschaften*).

Law is a "formal characteristic of human volition"[16] or, in other words, juridical volition. Juridical volition depicts the way in which the substantial needs of human beings are ordered into a particular form, that is, into positive law. Juridical volition is, then, the *a priori* foundation of all positive law. This foundation must, accordingly, be the object of the scientific study of law. A technical jurisprudence—*all* jurisprudence, in fact—deals merely with temporary legal norms, while the philosophy of law applying the critical method must account for the transcendental-logical foundation of the juridical experience, for what is universal in law, or, in other words, for law as a concept (*Rechtsbegriff*).[17]

Three specific characteristics distinguish juridical volition from volition in general. First, juridical volition is not an isolated and individual expression of will but, rather, the articulation of the binding character of social unity

[13] Stammler, *Die Lehre von dem richtigen Rechte*, pp. 65–68.
[14] *Ibid.*, pp. 177–187; Stammler, *Theorie der Rechtswissenschaft*, p. 55.
[15] *Ibid.*, pp. 49–55.
[16] *Ibid.*, p. 69.
[17] *Ibid.*, pp. 340–344.

(*Verbindung*). Juridical volition unites reciprocally the purpose of one individual to the means of another. If, for instance, the farmer's harvest is, at the same time, the means for another's sustenance, the relationship between the two is by nature binding. The binding character of juridical volition is also external regulation (*äußere Regelung*) or, in other words, an order of intentional representations in relation to the inner nature of, for example, ethical volition.[18]

Secondly, juridical volition is marked by autocracy or sovereignty (*Selbstherrschaft*) in that it overrules other expressions of volition. The validity of social customs is governed by conventional rules, and such customs are adhered to merely at will and *in casu*. Law does not grant the individual will such significance. If, for instance, the farmer cultivates his land on the basis of a hereditary right of possession and usufruct (*dominium utile*), his claim to the land remains contestable until it has been established as a juridical institution, that is, as an expression of juridical volition. The power of juridical volition over individual wills and desires indicates its sovereign nature.[19]

Lastly, juridical volition is both factually and normatively inviolable (*Unverletzbarkeit*) in that it is formally consistent even if its substance alters historically. Juridical volition is not capricious, or if a social will proves to be *de facto* arbitrary, it is not law. If the farmer has established his claim to his land as the juridical institution of property, it cannot be evoked at whim. The expression of juridical volition cannot, then, be arbitrary (*willkürlich*).[20]

Thus we arrive at the concept of law. For Stammler, law as a transcendental concept is an inviolable, autocratic and unifying volition.[21]

The concept of law cannot, however, regulate the ever-altering substance of individual norms; it is merely a method of thought for the verification of the transcendental-logical conditions of law. Neither does it evaluate the morality of law. The ethical quality of law is derived from the idea of law (*Rechtsidee*). It should, however, be noted that the idea of law is also a *method of thought*, but unlike the concept of law that evaluates the *a priori* conditions of law, the aim of the idea of law is to assess the morality of juridical volition. Or, to rephrase this in Stammlerian terms, the idea of law evaluates the correctness of law.[22]

But being a method of thought, the idea of law has no normative authority in itself. It merely couples juridical volition with the teleological nature of human volition in general. Even if juridical volition is a particular expression of human will, it must also participate in the general scheme of volition. Volition is teleological to the extent that it comprises within itself a particular social ideal: the community of free-willing men.[23] When the idea of law directs positive law

[18] Stammler, *Theorie der Rechtswissenschaft*, pp. 90–95.

[19] *Ibid.*, pp. 101–105.

[20] *Ibid.*, pp. 109–113.

[21] *Ibid.*, p. 113.

[22] Stammler, *Die Lehre von dem richtigen Rechte*, pp. 158. On the relationship between natural law doctrine and Stammler's idea of law, see Coing, *Grundzüge der Rechtsphilosophie*, pp. 147–150.

[23] Stammler, *Die Lehre von dem richtigen Rechte*, pp. 196–200; Stammler, *Theorie der Rechtswissenschaft*, pp. 470–475. Cf. Schmitt, *Der Begriff des Politischen*, pp. 33–34, n. 9.

towards the realisation of the ultimate social ideal of volition, law is correct. This is, however, not an ethical judgement. As volition, law must necessarily contain within itself the teleological constitution of human will *lest law would be incorrect* or, to put it in another way, it would not be law at all.

Correctness is assessed with the use of principles. Stammler classifies the four basic principles of correct law (*richtiges Recht*) into two main categories. The principles of consideration (*Achten*) maintain the will of individual members in a juridical community within the limits of a correct autonomy. The first principle establishes the juridical nature of social relationships: the substantial will of an individual may not be arbitrarily subjected to the will of another. In a juridically bound community, law establishes the specific conditions under which the will of one must make way for the will of another. The second principle governs the execution of the first: the will of another, presented as a juridical claim, is valid only in as much as the individual under obligation remains a neighbour in relation to himself.[24] The obligated remains a neighbour to himself as long as he is able to fulfil his proper will, that is, regard himself as a purpose in itself.[25]

The second set of principles deals with participation (*Teilnehmen*), and they evaluate the correctness of the juridical demands presented by the community at large to its individual members. The first principle establishes the juridical nature of the social union: the member of a juridically bound community may not be arbitrarily excluded. Law defines the particular circumstances under which the juridical bonds between an individual and the community can be broken. The second principle, once again, regulates the execution of the first: a juridically determined right to exclude a member from the community is valid only in as much as the individual excluded remains a neighbour in relation to himself.[26]

Because the philosophy of law only deals with what is universally valid and unchanging in law, its essential question is: is law what it should *a priori* be?[27] *This evaluation does not indicate to the normative authority of ethics or justice but to the epistemological correctness of juridical knowledge.* Does knowledge concerning law as the object of a scientific enterprise measure up to the requirements of correctness? The philosophy of law must elaborate "a theory of what can be regarded as universally valid in the things [*Dinge*] of law".[28] With its concepts, such a philosophy, first, establishes the scientific nature of juridical thinking and, secondly, provides the measure with which the ultimate correctness of law can be evaluated. The philosophy of law is, then, a scientific account of the taking place of correctness, of *Richtigkeit*.

[24] Stammler, *Die Lehre von dem richtigen Rechte*, pp. 208–210.

[25] *Ibid.*, pp. 285–291.

[26] *Ibid.*, pp. 211–213.

[27] Stammler, "Über die Methode der geschichtlichen Rechtstheorie," in Stammler, *Rechtsphilosophische Abhandlungen und Vorträge. Erster Band*, pp. 1–40 at pp. 10–18.

[28] Stammler, "Begriff und Bedeutung der Rechtsphilosophie", in Stammler, *Rechtsphilosophische Abhandlungen und Vorträge. Zweiter Band*, pp. 1–26 at p. 25.

Stammler's influential attempts to conceptualise a scientifically independent foundation for the philosophy of law—and for the "purposive sciences" in general, as well—were also severely criticised. The most stern objections were provided by a new orientation in the social sciences that attempted to establish its own scientific rationality in relation to the claims to universality of the neo-Kantian philosophers. Max Weber, for example, reviews Stammler's position on the "regularities [*Gesetzmäßigkeit*] of all human knowledge concerning social entities" in an unusually scornful tone. Weber's lengthy close-reading of Stammler and his parodic account of the rules of skat—indeed, Weber's "scat-ology"—is developed into a general condemnation of philosophical approaches to law as "scholastic mystification". For Weber, law is:

> "circumstances that can be determined as a fact and, as such, also be recognised by a multitude of human beings . . . These circumstances effect, both directly and indirectly, the formation of empirical regularities in the factual relationships of human beings with each other and with material goods".[29]

If Weber's confrontation with Stammler illustrates the intricate dividing-line between the philosophy of law and the empirical sciences—or between "juridical dogmatics" and the social sciences, as Weber would have it—Stammler's neo-Kantian epistemology is also vulnerable in its spiritual overtones. Trying to remain faithful to the demands of Kant's theoretical reason, the philosophy of law cannot indicate what one "ought" to do. And yet, the spectre of practical reason underlies in the very idea of being human, in the perfection of juridical volition as a "community of free-willing men". For Kant, the teleology of the human world only had an heuristic and regulative function, whereas in Stammler's philosophy of law, teleological perfection has acquired a foundational significance.[30]

But for my purposes here, there are two interrelated issues that I would like to emphasise. First, Stammler does not understand law merely as an entity among others. *Law is, first and foremost, a gateway to knowledge concerning the human world.* After Kant, knowledge was allegedly possible only in relation to the causal regularities of nature, but Stammler proposes to develop a philosophy that can adequately depict man and the environment in which he dwells. Secondly, the objective of philosophy is not to unveil the mysteries of this human environment as classical metaphysics would suggest, but, rather, in the name of reason and modern science, to *affirm conclusively the correctness of this knowledge.* There is a double relation to law, then: a normative entity serving as the founding constituent of the human world, and an evaluation or a judgement concerning the scientific status of philosophical knowledge.

[29] Weber, "R. Stammlers 'Ueberwindung' der materialistischen Geschichtsauffassung," in Weber, *Gesammelte Aufsätze zur Wissenschaftslehre*, pp. 291–359, p. 355.
[30] Kaufmann, *Kritik der neukantischen Rechtsphilosophie*, p. 20.

III

Whatever the inconsistencies of Stammler's theory may be, it had a profound influence on what was to be understood as the philosophy of law during the following decades. The most prominent of the neo-Kantians was, of course, Hans Kelsen. Although Kelsen seldom mentions philosophy, the aim of the "pure theory" is defined in philosophical terms: "to answer the question, what and how law is, and not the question, what it ought to be or what it should be made into".[31] In order to understand fully the relevance of Kelsen's theory, one must bear in mind its manifestly epistemological character. Its aim is not to, for instance, supply a theoretical foundation for the practice of adjudication as jurisprudential readings of Kelsen suggest, but only to know its object and to describe it. Law, then, is meaningful only as the object of scientific knowledge. And this accounts for the constitutive character of the theory; for Kelsen, *law must be conceptualised in a particular way in order to enable correct knowledge about the human world.*[32]

Kelsen, as all juridical thinkers of the modern era, is well aware of the doubts that taunt the scientific status of his discipline. He claims that the confusions of juridical thinking are due to the lack of methodological rigour. The adversaries of the theory are designated in an explicitly neo-Kantian manner: adherents of "methodological syncretism". The pure theory will "free" the science of law from elements that are alien to it. This promise of liberation is peculiar. It refers retrospectively to a golden age before the causal explanations of the natural sciences and the "ideological" disposition of the social sciences have damaged juridical thinking.[33] No such foregoing age of purity, of course, exists. And without the foundational authority of such a past, the theory must necessarily constitute its own methodological purity.

For my concerns, the specificity of law is less important than the epistemological postulates on which the theory is founded. One cannot repeat too often that, for Kelsen, law is meaningful only to the extent that it enables the presentation of scientific knowledge concerning human phenomena. Instead of answering the ontological question the theory originally presented—What and how is law?—the theory reformulates its response in epistemological terms: law must be conceptualised as normativity in order to guarantee the scientific nature of knowledge concerning the human world. In distinguishing such knowledge from the knowledge of the natural sciences, Kelsen originally claimed that the science of law is a human science in the traditional German sense:

[31] Kelsen, *Reine Rechtslehre. Zweite Auflage*, p. 1.

[32] Cf. Bobbio, "Hans Kelsen".

[33] Kelsen, *Reine Rechtslehre. Zwerte Auflage*, pp. 60–61. On the sociology of law in particular, see *ibid.*, pp. 107–113.

> "In as much as the pure theory of law distinguishes law from nature, it seeks the limit that distinguishes nature from spirit [*Geist*]. The science of law is a human science [*Geisteswissenschaft*], not a natural science".[34]

Defining the limit does not, however, establish the science of law as a human science. The theory investigates a limit that must logically precede it. The specificity of a particular human science in relation to the natural sciences can, then, only be established in a constitutive act in which the theory lays down the foundations of its own existence. This self-constitutive element is, as I will try to indicate, the key element in understanding Kelsen's neo-Kantian affinities.

The identity of law in relation to other phenomena is dependent on the parallel Kantian distinction between the factual and the normative, between *Sein* and *Sollen*. The distinction also constitutes the specificity of the science of law in relation to the natural sciences. For Kant, knowledge is possible only as causality in the realm of nature, but Kelsen, like all neo-Kantian philosophers of law, insists that the world that man inhabits can be scientifically analysed by extending the critical method to observations about the human world. The constitutive element of man's social life is normativity.[35] Normativity, then, is a particular form of human knowledge.

The theory distinguishes further between the norm of law (*Rechtsnorm*) and the statute of law (*Rechtssatz*). The former is an imperative and the object of the science of law, while the latter is a hypothetical evaluation in which a possible sanction has been coupled with a possible activity. As the object of Kelsen's theory, the norm of law cannot, however, be identified with the science that studies it. For "[l]aw commands, permits or authorises, but it does not 'teach' ",[36] whereas the science of law "can only *de*scribe law, it cannot *pre*scribe a certain behaviour".[37]

As knowledge (*Erkenntnis*) about the human world, normativity is the theoretical object of the science of law that it must itself constitute. The function of this constitutive creation (*Erzeugnung*) is, then, epistemological. The pure theory of law can describe a norm of law only after it has first been "created" in an act of legislation.[38] But the statute of law that the legislator has prescribed is, from an epistemological perspective, only of secondary importance. The theory must, in an act of constitutive creation, posit its own object, that is, the norm of law.

Because the pure theory of law constitutes a specific form of knowledge other than nature, it must establish its scientific identity in relation to the natural sciences. The science of law is a social science—in the revised and expanded sec-

[34] Kelsen, *Reine Rechtslehre. Erste Auflage*, p. 12. The first edition, published originally in 1934 some 25 years before the better known second edition, is usually regarded merely as an historical document.

[35] Kelsen, *Reine Rechtslehre. Zweite Auflage*, pp. 78–79.

[36] *Ibid.*, p. 73.

[37] *Ibid.*, p. 75.

[38] *Ibid.*, pp. 74–75.

ond edition, Kelsen speaks of law as a *Gesellschaftswissenschaft*—and its specificity in relation to the natural sciences is defined by way of the regularities that establish the relationship between cause and effect in nature. If any social science exists, society must, accordingly, be understood as a non-causal and normative order of reciprocal human activity. Causal relations are regulated by the laws of nature, while the normative character of human action is "imputated" (*Zurechnung*) with juridical laws (*Rechtsgesetz*). A juridical law does not account for the factual or probable consequences of particular modes of behaviour, but stipulates that an illegality "ought" to be followed by a sanction. The structure of the principle of imputation—"if an action takes place, a sanction ought to follow"—indicates the normativity that is allegedly distinctive to knowledge concerning the human world, the characteristic that Stammler identified as purposiveness.[39]

In the statute prescribed by the legislator, "the word 'ought' only has a descriptive character".[40] It connects two facts—an act and a sanction—causally together just as the law of nature. A norm of law, on the other hand, does not depict the relationship between an act and a sanction in causal terms. It emphasises that a specified act must literally be "accounted for" (*zurechnen*) with a specified sanction.[41]

The idea of causal laws dominates the natural sciences as well as the social sciences that adhere to the scientific ideal of causality. On the other hand, the normative sciences, that is, the sciences of law and ethics, analyse norms that man has posited for himself. But the science of law is not a social authority that either prescribes these norms or affirms their ethical value. It is a scientific enterprise that merely describes them.[42] But the object of the theory, that is, the norm of law, does not exist as such. Its status as the expression of normativity is entirely dependent on the constitutive character of the theory itself.

As normative expressions of legislated statutes, the norms of law are created in volition (*Wollen*). Because volition belongs to the world of nature, the norm of law cannot be identified with the will that posits it.[43] But who or what is this "will"? As science, the pure theory of law must account for the outcome of a "subjective" act of volition as "objective" normativity, that is, without reference to intention. The normativity of the norm is, consequently, derived from the objective authority of a higher norm, and with the notion of authority, the system of norms can then be presented as the pyramid of positive law.

But in order to guarantee the scientific status of the theory, the pinnacle of the pyramid must be presumed as a non-positive basic norm that cannot logically be posited by an anterior or higher authority.[44] The normativity of all norms of

[39] *Ibid.*, pp. 93–95. According to Stammler, "the measure of the correctness of a particular law [is] its purposive character [*Zweckmäßigkeit*]": Stammler, *Theorie der Rechtswissenschaft*, p. 469.
[40] Kelsen, *Reine Rechtslehre. Zweite Anflage*, p. 83.
[41] *Ibid.*, pp. 78–80.
[42] *Ibid.*, pp. 89–93.
[43] *Ibid.*, pp. 4–9.
[44] *Ibid.*, pp. 196–197.

law is, then, ultimately founded on the basic norm. The basic norm is a transcendental-logical postulate that must be presumed (*voraussetzen*) so that the science of posited (*gesetzen*) law would be possible.[45] The basic norm is the epistemological precondition of the pure theory of law, and it interests Kelsen only to the extent that it ensures the possibility of scientifically correct knowledge about law.

This is where the self-constitutive character of Kelsen's theory becomes most evident. In 1963, only three years after the influential second edition of *Reine Rechtslehre* was published, Kelsen was forced to revise his understanding about the basic norm. Kelsen himself emphasises the radicality of the revision, but his interpreters have more or less neglected it. The pure theory of law is entirely founded on the possibility of a basic norm that cannot be the outcome of an act of volition. Now Kelsen refers to a "double fiction" of sorts:

> "The basic norm is a *fictive* norm that requires a *fictive* act of volition that posits the norm. It is a fiction according to which an authority wills for the norm to exist".[46]

The early Kelsen was rather categorically opposed to epistemological fictions, but he later moderated his view considerably.[47] If we read the pure theory of law as an exercise in epistemology, the fictive character of the basic norm will come as no surprise; the basic norm seems to be an "analogical fiction".[48] But what is significant about Kelsen's later admission is the fiction's two-foldedness: both norm *and* volition are now fictive. The fictive volition, that is, the precondition of the basic norm and, consequently, also the precondition of normativity in general and all correct knowledge about the human world, accounts for the self-constitutive gesture of legislation with which Kelsen's theory posits its own object: the authority that "wills for the norm to exist" is the theory itself. Normativity does not exist outside the pure theory of law.

Kelsen, then, shares with Stammler an understanding of law or normativity as the key to knowledge about the human world. His main considerations involve the status of knowledge as the notion "pure theory" already suggests. I believe that traditional readings of Kelsen—even critical estimates—are misled to believe that the aim of the pure theory of law is to furnish a solid foundation for adjudication and juridical practice. *Kelsen's principal concern is the correctness of philosophical knowledge*, and in the end, such correctness can only be ensured with the evaluative gesture of a fictive volition that posits the basic norm.

[45] Kelsen, *Reine Rechtslehre. Zweite Anflage*, pp. 204–209.

[46] Kelsen in a discussion in Schmöltz (ed.), *Das Naturrecht in der politischen Theorie*, p. 120.

[47] See, e.g., Kelsen, *Hauptprobleme der Staatrechtslehre entwickelt aus der Lehre von Rechtssatze*, p. VIII. Cf. Kelsen, *Reine Rechtslehre. Zweite Auflage*, pp. 301–304, and especially Kelsen, *Allgemeine Theorie der Normen*, pp. 206–207.

[48] See Vaihinger, *Die Philosophie des Als Ob*, pp. 39–46. A fiction is a psychic image (*Gebilde*) or a conceptual fabrication (*Kunstgriff*) operating as a tool of thinking. Vaihinger's question is: "How is it possible that we come up with correct judgements using intentionally false representations?": *ibid*., p. XXIV. On Kelsen and Vaihinger, see Jöckel, *Hans Kelsens rechttheoretische Methode*, pp. 74–83.

IV

The debate concerning Kelsen's basic norm has often focused on its transcendental quality. Despite Kelsen's stern objections, the basic norm has commonly been seen as the necessary ethical ingredient in the theory and not as the epistemological precondition it was meant to be. But the emphasis on the "correctness" of juridical knowledge at the expense of justice in the philosophy of law has also generated peculiar hybrids of neo-Kantian thinking and natural law. The influence of natural law doctrine is, perhaps, most evident in Latin thinkers such as the Italian Giorgio del Vecchio. In addition to a substantially "indifferent" logical dimension and a phenomenological dimension comprising a universal history of juridical thinking, law necessarily involves a deontological dimension, as well, that is, the idea of law as the measure of justice. Natural law operates as the ideal that the logical concept of law "ought" to be. The history of law is the teleological completion of the ideal of natural law.[49]

These tensions are best portrayed in the singular work of Gustav Radbruch. Radbruch belongs to the South-Western or Badener school of neo-Kantian philosophers of law and assimilates most of his philosophical influences from the Heidelbergian jurist-turned-philosopher Emil Lask. Radbruch's point of departure is, to no surprise, the notion of methodological dualism (*Methodendualismus*). Knowledge about nature and knowledge about the human world also constitute the difference between fact and norm, for "it is impossible from what *is* to derive what is *valuable*, what is *correct* [*richtig*], what *ought* to be".[50] Radbruch clearly gives correctness an ethical tone. But the true essence of law is to bridge the gap between fact and norm. Essence is here understood as the "nature of things" (*Natur der Sache*) that determines the substantial specificity (*Stoffbestimmtheit*) of the idea of law. The nature of things comprises the natural, cultural and juridical circumstances that the legislator subjects to its legislation.[51]

Law is a fact that aspires to become normative, a projective movement of sorts from the "is" towards the "ought". Law, then, is a scientifically accessible fact the necessary fate of which is to become a value. Law is the realisation of the idea of law, a reality (*Wirklichkeit*) the sense of which is to "serve justice"[52]:

> "Law may be unjust (*summum ius—summa iniuria*), but it is law only because its sense is to be just".[53]

The idea of law or, in other words, the value that law aspires to, is justice. Justice, however, has a double meaning for Radbruch. In a more restricted

[49] Del Vecchio, *Lezioni di filosofia del diritto*, pp. 358–361.

[50] Radbruch, *Rechtsphilosophie*, p. 97.

[51] *Ibid.*, p. 98. Cf. Radbruch, "Die Natur der Sache als juristische Denkform", in Hernmarck (ed.), *Festschrift zu Ehren von Rudolf Laun*, pp. 157–176.

[52] Radbruch, *Rechtsphilosophie*, p. 127.

[53] *Ibid.*, p. 95.

sense, justice serves as the measure of positive law. But it is also the *a priori* foundation of all positive law. In other words, only law that is to become just is correct, or, to rephrase this in yet another way, *correctness is becoming just.* The idea of law pertains to the foundational meaning of justice. Foundational justice involves three distinct dimensions: first, justice in the narrower sense or, in other words, the formal equality of the *Rechtsstaat*; secondly, the purposiveness of law or the substantial standards of the welfare state; and, lastly, legal certainty or the fundamental nature of positive law. Radbruch clearly departs from his neo-Kantian predecessors in that the positivity of law is understood in relation to the idea of law rather than as the epistemological precondition of the science of law.

As to the first dimension, it is enough for my purposes to indicate to the affinity between formal equality (*Gleichheit*) and an Aristotelian doctrine of justice.[54]

The purposiveness (*Zweckmäßigkeit*) of law, on the other hand, takes on the ethical virtue of morality in three different forms: personal values, social values, and, lastly, cultural values—aesthetics, for instance—that Radbruch calls *Werkwerte*. Depending on which values are given priority, we can distinguish between individualistic, supraindividualistic and transpersonal perspectives. From an individualistic perspective, cultural and social considerations must make way for individual values. The arts and the humanities, for example, serve primarily to civilise and to cultivate individuals, just as the existence of the state is justified with the demands of its citizens. From a supraindividualistic perspective, individual virtues and talents serve to enrich society at large, and cultural, transpersonal values such as the environment require allocating responsibilities to both individuals and communities. These three perspectives have been condensed into three key notions of modern law: liberty, nation, and culture.[55]

Legal certainty (*Rechtssicherheit*), the third dimension of justice as the idea of law, is by necessity related to the positivity of law:

> "Legal certainty requires the positivity of law: if one cannot *firmly determine* [*feststellen*] what is just, one must *firmly posit* [*festsetzen*] what ought to be right, and, in addition, from a position where one can *thoroughly* realise [*durchsetzen*] what has been *firmly* prescribed".[56]

However, the requirement of certainty creates tensions that cannot be resolved theoretically. Such tensions are the antinomies of law. For instance, the substantial demands of purposive welfare values can only be enhanced by reducing the import of legal certainty, that is, the positivity of law. On the other hand, the promotion of cultural values such as tolerance and solidarity may require

[54] Radbruch, *Rechtsphilosophie*, pp. 125–127.
[55] *Ibid.*, pp. 146–155.
[56] *Ibid.*, p. 169.

that a particular statute is deliberately left unapplied. Antinomies, Radbruch emphasises, can only be resolved in the practice of law.[57]

The philosophy of law, however, leaves the adjudicator confronted by the antinomies of law in a state of epistemic ignorance; it is impossible to "know" what one "ought" to do. In line with its fundamentally neo-Kantian nature, Radbruch's philosophy of law can only inquire into the possibility of a designated judgement, into the *a priori* conditions of juridical evaluations. This has given both Radbruch and his interpreters reason to call the theory relativistic. But it is "theoretical relativism"; it does not and cannot exempt the juridical thinker from decisions as such.[58] Quite the contrary, it seems that antinomies themselves commit the juridical thinker to action and decisions. Because of the antinomic nature of law, the jurist is obliged to confront the world and to decide. The philosophy of law can—and must—address this obligation, but it cannot—and must not—tell him what he should do.

After the horrors of the Second World War and the theoretical inability of the neo-Kantian philosophers of law to address them, the "agnostic" relativism of Radbruch's earlier position was reformulated into a more affirmative ethics of justice. Regardless of possible epistemological inconsistencies, the philosophy of law is now committed to develop the idea of law into a rough scheme of priorities that would facilitate the resolving of possible antinomies. Radbruch claims that, in a conflict of interests, the purposiveness of law—the legal policies of the welfare state—must make way for the demands of both equality and legal certainty. This claim is in line with what is today understood as the minimum content of the modern *Rechtsstaat*. But in certain cases, the antinomy between equality and legal certainty may require the use of non-positive elements. Legal certainty is also an expression of equality because it requires that even an unjust law—a law that does not treat individuals as equals—must, all the same, be applied in a uniform way. The antinomy between equality and uniformity is, then, an internal antinomy of justice:

> "Where the injustice of positive law reaches such measures [*Maß*] that the legal certainty guaranteed by positive law no longer functions as the counter-balance of this injustice, unjust positive law must make way for justice".[59]

Another formulation of this "question of measure" states that legal certainty intervenes between purposiveness and justice as equality. Purposiveness requires uniformity in adjudication, but uniformity is also an expression of equality and, hence, of justice, as well. Most antinomies are, then, merely apparent, internal within justice.

A true antinomy is a situation in which the application of positive law would undeniably result in an unjust outcome. In such cases, the conflict must be resolved in accordance with a "suprapositive right" (*übergesetzliches Recht*).

[57] *Ibid.*, pp. 168–173.
[58] *Ibid.*, pp. 100–105.
[59] Radbruch, *Vorschule der Rechtsphilosophie*, p. 33.

Positive law that does not aspire to the idea of law, that is, that does not "serve justice", is incorrect, it is a "positive wrong" (*gesetzliches Unrecht*). A system of norms that serves legal injustice is not correct law, and in such a case, one must decide in accordance with a suprapositive right. Justice in the wider sense is now also the ethical measure of positive law.[60]

Once again, the philosophy of law has been put to the test: it must be able to justify its right to address the world. But unlike the epistemological emphases of his predecessors—philosophy provides correct knowledge about law—for Radbruch, correctness as *Richtigkeit* has also acquired an ethical overtone: correct law is a factual entity that "serves justice" in that *it aspires to become an ethical norm*. Correctness can, then, be understood as the inclination to become just. And it is the nature of this correctness that has made philosophy "Latin" and juridical long before Kant summoned the tribunal of reason. What is the metaphysics of such a correctness, the becoming just of a factual entity like law? What is the "first philosophy" of law? I propose to address these questions with the help of Aristotle's understanding of philosophy in *Metaphysics*.

V

When a jurist thinks about Aristotle and the philosophy of law, he usually reflects on justice as a virtue or the political talents of a good judge or law-giver. The perspective adopted in the *Nikomachean Ethics* or in *Politics* is, however, of a practical, almost non-philosophical nature. The science of ethics deals with the individual and social requirements of a good life. But such happiness falls short of what true philosophical contemplation can offer. For a science serving the practical requirements of a good life cannot possibly provide the exaltation of philosophical wisdom. This tension in Aristotle's thinking is referred to often enough, but its consequences for the philosophy of law have not been evaluated.

Aristotle's *Metaphysics*, representing the theoretical counterpart of the practicality of ethics, does not advise us how to live a good life. It elaborates on what is called the "first philosophy" (*prōtē filosofia*), on a science that deals with "beings as beings" (*on hē on*). The tradition of Occidental metaphysics has understood this initial question of philosophy to concern the timeless "essence" (*ousia*) of divine, human and non-human beings. But if we rephrase and radicalise the question in Heideggerian terms, the question of philosophy addresses the occurrence of Being (*to einai*) itself. Literally, the question of Being addresses the way in which a being—any being—comes into Being, a being that is "what it was to be" (*to ti en einai*). But it is not only a question about things thought, it is also about the being that thinks, about its "noetic" ability to conceive the Being of beings.

[60] Radbruch, "Gesetzliches Unrecht und übergesetzliches Recht," in Radbruch, *Rechtsphilosophie*, pp. 347–357 at pp. 352–355.

If philosophy is understood as the "first philosophy", what possible place could law or justice occupy in the questioning of the Being of beings? Is, indeed, any philosophy of law possible? The question is, of course, rhetorical: such a "first philosophy" of law is not only possible but also necessary. For the Greeks, all things relate to justice (*dikaiosunē*) by necessity, they are necessarily in accordance with *dikē*. What is, then, a "just" thing (*to dikaion*)? It is complete; it lacks nothing of its ownmost "essence". The relationship between things and *dikē* indicates that when a thing is "what it was to be", it must by necessity also entail a future as its original possibility of Being. A thing that is "what it was to be" has come into Being because Being itself was a possible future to begin with. This possible future "to be" is justice, and a thing that manifests its original possibility to be what it is, is just.

For the most part, the Greeks articulated justice as the possible future "to be" in terms of deserts and merits. For Plato, for instance, justice requires that every thing must receive what essentially appertains to it. It is, therefore, in the nature of all things to expect something that is rightfully regarded as their own. Justice demands, for instance, that a man is to expect his due as the qualification of being human.[61] Justice, then, is the initial possibility of a thing to come to be as what it is. Even Aristotle's notion of justice requires that everything should receive their due. Law (*nomos*) establishes a relationship between a thing and a merit that is rightfully to be expected. It is just that a thing should be given its due, that is, that it should come to be as what it is. Justice, then, is the foreclosing of a proper future, the actualisation of a thing as what it essentially is. Law adjoins a thing with its proper future to be,[62] and everything that accords with such a law is also just.[63] As adjoinment, the accord is the perfection of a thing in relation to an other.[64] When a thing is just, it contains within itself its due—its proper future—as "what it was to be". Lacking nothing, such perfection is justice: a just thing is a being that is absolutely singular in relation to any other. It is self-sufficient and cannot be otherwise.

But the use of the word "justice" in this context does not really capture what is at stake. In most Continental languages of today, one would rather say that such things are "real" (*richtig*) as, for example, in the German expression *eine richtige Angst*, an anxiety that is the "real" thing and not a fabrication of the imagination. As such, a real anxiety is also "correct" to the extent that it is not a "false" sensation. "Correct", on the other hand, is both semantically and etymologically akin to "right" (*recht*) as in the rightness of an evaluation. If we use these juridical idioms to address people, we would, for example, be able to indicate that someone is a "true human being" (*ein richtiger/rechter Mensch*). In the Romance languages, however, "correctness" (*correction*, *correttezza*, *corrección*) refers to courteous and considerate behaviour, while "rightness"

[61] Plato, *R*. 332b.
[62] Aristotle, *Rhet*. 1366b 7.
[63] Aristotle, *EN* 1129b 11–12.
[64] Aristotle, *EN* 1129b 25–27.

(*droiture*, *dirittura*, *derechura*) connotes the moral uprightness and rectitude of a righteous man, resonances that are not altogether absent in German but are detectable only in the more subtle dimensions of tone. So if things are "correct", perhaps human beings would rather be "upright".

The Latin root *rectus*—literally "that which is set straight", from *regere*—can also depict the qualities of correctness and beauty. For instance, the early Roman poet Propertius uses the word to praise the colour of the maiden's blushed cheeks that are not blemished by artificial rouge: *ut natura dedit, sic omnis recta figura*.[65] The perfection of such natural beauty is of an almost divine quality that is reminiscent of the philosophical and poetic attempts of the Greeks to capture the just nature of all things.

However, all etymologies of correctness and right—*richtig*, *recht*, *correctus*, *directus*—can be traced back to the Greek verb *oregein*, "to reach out", "to yearn for". Perhaps, then, the perfection of things, their just nature, is something that true human beings as upright men strive for. The desire to know or to see (*orexis tou eidenai*) that, according to the opening sentence of *Metaphysics*,[66] characterises all men, is a relationship between an upright desire and the justice towards which it reaches. This profoundly human desire, or even appetence, to reach out for the justice of things is curiously related to *orthos*, something "straight", but also "true", "right", and even "correct". Aeschylus uses a juridically significant compound to depict the "right and just way" (*orthodikaion*) in which land and city should be governed,[67] while Sophocles claims that the "true law" (*orthos nomos*) of loyalty prescribes friendship.[68]

The "first philosophy" of law does not address the practical questions of an ethics as it is formulated in what is usually understood as an Aristotelian account of law. But neither can it conclusively determine the divine quality that makes up for the justice of a thing making it "what it was to be". It is an account of man's desire to see, to know the world and to appropriate it, and about the knowledge that reveals itself to his "orectic" appetite. In order to examine the possibility of this "first philosophy" of law, two questions must be asked: what is philosophy? and how and what does philosophy know? If we can formulate plausible answers to these preliminary questions, we can continue our questioning into the wisdom (*sofia*) that relates to law.

For Aristotle, thinking is ordered into a three-fold hierarchy where the theoretical science of philosophy represents the crowning pivot of the human endeavour. A productive science like architecture involves the creation (*poiesis*) of useful entities, and the product can be clearly distinguished from the act of production. A temple may be the result of the architect's creative activities, but it could have just as well been a residence. On the other hand, a good life, that is, the aim of the practical science of ethics, is inseparable from the activity

[65] Propertius, *Elegiarum*, II XVIII 25.
[66] Aristotle, *Met.* 980a 22.
[67] Aeschylus, *Eum.* 993–994.
[68] Sophocles, *Aj.* 350.

(*praxis*) that such a science entails. But architecture and ethics are not theoretical sciences or, in other words, philosophy. Philosophical contemplation (*theoria*) involves no benefits or profits as such. To contemplate on, for instance, the essence of the elements will neither facilitate the building of temples nor improve the ethical quality of one's life. It is contemplation for the sake of contemplation, philosophy for its own sake.[69] But it does involve the promise of exaltation resulting from the philosopher's proximity with the gods.

Within the unproductive and useless science of philosophy, we encounter yet another three-fold distinction that establishes a second hierarchy. The three theoretical sciences—the three philosophies—are physics, mathematics, and, lastly, theology or metaphysics. This last mentioned "first philosophy" precedes all others in significance, and while it is of no use in itself, in grants its pursuer wisdom about what is most general, about the divine origin of things. Such origins are the primary causes and principles that govern all beings.[70] The "first philosophy" that deals with things as "what they were to be"[71] contemplates on (*theōreion*) beings as beings (*on hē on*) in their ownmost essence (*kath' auto*).[72] To know of such matters is to refine what is godly in man, to partake in divinity, and it is this affiliation with the gods that accounts for the exaltation of philosophical wisdom.

But even Aristotle must recognise that such wisdom does not come easily. The nature of philosophical wisdom can only be determined by examining the problems that philosophy encounters. Philosophical problems are aporias.[73] Face to face with aporias, theoretical contemplation seems to be tied into a knot, and one can open the knot only by looking at it.[74] Although philosophical contemplation does not involve sensual pleasure, the metaphor of "theorising" suggests that looking at a knot resembles the way in which celestial divinities amuse themselves by observing the entangled intricacies of the human world. While the onlooking gods are left to entertain themselves, the aporetic encounter seems to leave the philosopher with "no way out" (*a poros*). But it also leaves the philosopher in want, desiring for something (*aporeō*) as Sophocles seems to indicate.[75] And perhaps this something that man desires is the leisurely way (*rheia*) in which the gods go about their business, a carefree existence that, however, remains forbidden to man (*aporrētos*). For Plato, an aporia is a state of ignorance that causes pain and suffering, and theorising can but regard such anxiety.[76] But if the ancients understood the aporia as a perpetual mystery to which no clear explanation could be given, Aristotle clearly presumes that every

69 Aristotle, *Met.* 1025b 19–25.
70 Aristotle, *Met.* 1026a 6–13.
71 Aristotle, *Met.* 1004a 3.
72 Aristotle, *Met.* 1003a 22–32.
73 Aristotle, *Met.* 995a 25.
74 Aristotle, *Met.* 995a 31–32.
75 Sophocles, *Ph.* 898.
76 Plato, *Tht.* 151a.

problem has its solution. So how can one come about a solution? How can one see the knot and undo it?

The theoretical gaze of philosophy that resembles the way in which the gods amuse themselves by looking on to the world is executed by man as wonder (*thaumazein*). Metaphysical wonder does not bring pleasure because it neither produces anything to enjoy nor serves the practical necessities of a good and happy life. And further, the wonder that enables theorising can only take place by letting time while away (*diagōgeus*). Philosophy is born only from and at leisure; only unproductive wonder enables true philosophical theorising.[77] But although wondrous theorising does not bring pleasure, it involves the promise of a bliss that is related to the unfolding of philosophical aporias as time whiles away. In this heavenly idleness, the philosopher who wonders at leisure may catch a glimpse of a thing that is "what it was to be", a just thing, a perfect being that entails its proper future. As the virtue (*aretē*) of ethics, justice always requires the other, whereas both theory and what it contemplates are self-sufficient and perfect in themselves (*autarkēs*).[78] By letting time while away in wonder, man can partake in this singular perfection.[79]

So what does the philosopher wonder about? That a thing is as it is,[80] that it is perfect, that it lacks nothing and entails nothing in excess, that it is "just". But is the perfection of a just thing a divine matter that only the gods are permitted to see? Is the justice of a thing, that it is "what it was to be", an aporia in the sense of the ancients, an irresolvable mystery? The alleged privilege of the gods to know about such matters would seem to be based on a law that denies man access to godly concerns, that is, to matters concerning the primary causes and principles that govern all things, to the aporias of metaphysics. Aristotle claims that the gods have no reason to withhold such knowledge.[81] But philosophical wisdom can only be acquired in a certain way. By letting time while away in idle contemplations, the philosopher imitates the gods,[82] he is their "likeness" (*homoiōma*). A *homoiōma* is an image or a correspondent that is always in a derogatory relationship with an original. For example, Aristotle's rhetorics is but "like" dialectics,[83] just as for Plato worldly entities are always "resemblances" of divine things.[84]

As a semblance of the gods, man attempts to appease his desire to see by letting time while away and pass. In this idle wonder—this *désœuvrement*—he is allegedly initiated into godly concerns with a glance of the divine origin of things, of the primary causes and principles that govern all things. But what does the philosopher see? Is it a resolution to the aporia of metaphysics, or could the

77 Aristotle, *Met.* 982b 11–25.
78 Aristotle, *EN* 1177a 27–1177b 1.
79 Aristotle, *EN* 1097b 7–8.
80 Aristotle, *Met.* 983a 13–14.
81 Aristotle, *Met.* 983a 3–5.
82 Aristotle, *EN* 1178b 21–22.
83 Aristotle, *Rhet.* 1356a 31.
84 Plato, *Phdr.* 250b.

philosopher perhaps be deceived by some knowledge other than true wisdom? Even Aristotle seems to say so, for:

> "Thinking [*nous*] is always correct [*pas orthos*], but desire [*orexis*] and fantasy are either correct or not. Therefore the thing desired is the common source. But it may be the perfect good [*agathon*] or its appearance [*phainomenon*]. It is, then, not any perfect good but only that which is produced in action [*prakton agathon*]. The perfect good produced in action can also be otherwise".[85]

Human beings desire to see, to know and to appropriate the aporias of metaphysics and, in the last instance, to resolve the mystery of the perfect good. But unlike the theoretical insight imitating the gaze of the gods, the desire to see of metaphysics always runs the risk of erring about its object, of taking sophisms for wisdom or an appearance for the "real" thing. Because all philosophy is conditioned by man's desire to see, the divine truths that metaphysics seems to confer to its practitioner must necessarily remain out of reach. For man, the world unfolds merely as possibly correct, and it remains for philosophy—even for a "first philosophy"—to pronounce judgement on the correctness of the world. This is the juridical moment of metaphysics, the "first philosophy" of law.

As a desiring being, man is but an image of the deities. The philosopher is merely a semblance of the gods because only the latter have an infinity to pass. The philosopher is "all too human" because even the time that whiles away in idle wonder is productive to the extent that it exhausts itself and eventually desists: philosophy is a mortal enterprise. Lost in wonder, the philosopher is perhaps closest to the gods, but as a mere likeness, he will never attain the bliss of true wisdom. This unsurmountable difference between the divine and the human accounts for the aporetic and agonising nature of the object of philosophical wonder.

In his human desire, the upright philosopher can but reach out and marvel at the eventual justice of a thing, at a thing that will ultimately occur as "what it was to be" and complement itself in a perfection that lacks nothing and entails nothing in excess. Justice constitutes the desired object (*to orekton*) of a "first philosophy" of law, but in the judgements of correctness that a mortal man is capable of, such justice is forever delayed.

For the ownmost essence of things, that is, justice in itself, or the future that will come to be, is a matter fit only for infinite gods.

[85] Aristotle, *De an.* 433a 27–31.

3

In an Orderly World

"Shortly after World War I, I asserted: 'Sovereign is he who decides on the exception'. After World War II, at the dusk of my life, I claim: 'Sovereign is he who enjoins the waves of space [*wer über die Wellen des Raumens verfügt*].' "

Carl Schmitt

I

In the previous chapter, I attempted to indicate how, even in its Greek origins, the "first philosophy" of law involves a certain juridisation of metaphysics. From my arguments, it should have become more or less clear that I am not trying to elaborate on a philosophy that studies law but, rather, on a metaphysical discourse that attempts to justify its claims to the world as correct. There are, of course, particular approaches to law that can well be considered philosophical; hence, there are philosophies of law that deal with law as an individual entity. But taking into account the core of my argument, their purport is not in what they say about this thing called "law", but, rather, in the way in which they understand their philosophical enterprise.

Even though the juridical tradition is more or less inclined to accept the argument that the question of Being that Heidegger has phrased makes any "truly" philosophical approach to law impossible, there have, nevertheless, been at least three law-related assimilations of the German philosopher's thinking. The first orientation in which Heidegger's name is often mentioned, a discipline with a continuing history from the beginning of this century to this day, is the *phenomenology of law* that acquires its philosophical import from the phenomenologies of Edmund Husserl[1] and Maurice Merleau-Ponty.[2] The phenomenology of law attempts to define the specificity of the phenomenon of law with the help of the reductive method. The second orientation, originating in the 1950s, involves an existential reading of Heidegger and, in its juridical interpretations, is strongly influenced by, for example, the social philosophy of Karl Jaspers,[3] the existential theology of Max Müller,[4] and the existentialism of Jean-Paul Sartre.[5] The *existential philosophy of law* addresses primarily the

[1] e.g. E. Husserl, *Ideen III*, pp. 76–92.
[2] e.g. Merleau-Ponty, *Phénoménologie de la perception*, pp. 469–495.
[3] e.g. Jaspers, *Existenzphilosophie*, pp. 26–54.
[4] e.g. Müller, *Existenzphilosophie im geistigen Leben der Gegenwart*, pp. 160–183.
[5] e.g. Sartre, *L'être et le néant*, pp. 275–364.

issue of human existence and its rapport to the social dimension of law.[6] The third assimilation that takes place during the following decade is the elaboration of an *hermeneutics of law* which finds its Heideggerian undertow mainly from the philosophies of Hans-Georg Gadamer[7] and Paul Ricœur.[8] The principal concern of this approach concerns the interpretation of texts, and it has since developed into an established field of both mainstream legal theory and its critical counterpart.

But even if the existence of these three assimilations can be historically accounted for, the problematic question remains unanswered: what does Heidegger have to offer the philosophy of law? Can we simply avoid the question by declaring that the claim concerning the impossibility of a philosophy of law after Heidegger is merely a strategically motivated cathedratic appeal for tradition? Or is there a philosophically relevant relationship between the question of Being and law? Although the existing approaches mentioned above are all insufficient in themselves to cover the full radicality of Heidegger's philosophy, they do indicate three distinct themes through which the relevant issues can be addressed and elaborated. The first theme would be an inquiry into law as a being. In 1913, Husserl writes:

> "Every concrete empirical objectivity, together with its material essence, finds its proper place within a highest material genus, a 'region' of empirical objects. To the pure regional essence belongs, then, a *regional eidetic science* or, as we can also say, a *regional ontology*".[9]

The *regional question* of the philosophy of law addresses law as an individual entity: what is law? How is law? The regional question covers what is traditionally understood as the ontology of law, and, following Heidegger, one may well claim that phenomenology represents the culmination of a Platonic tradition that attempts to discern the true essence of an entity in its *eidos*; the idea of law would, then, be its true essence. For Heidegger, a phenomenological explication is, however, inadequate. Phenomenology as the science of "essence" can only be ontology or, in other words, the science of the Being of beings. Phenomenology and ontology together characterise what is known as philosophy or the "universal phenomenological ontology that arises from the hermeneutics of Dasein".[10] The analysis of an entity such as law must be preceded by a more fundamental inquiry into the way in which man encounters individual beings in general.

The second theme that I will deal with can be called the *ontological question* of the philosophy of law. Instead of addressing law as an individual phenomenon,

[6] On Heidegger and existential philosophy, see, e.g., Gadamer, "Existentialismus und Existenzphilosophie", in Gadamer, *Neuere Philosophie I. Hegel—Husserl—Heidegger*, pp. 175–185.

[7] e.g. Gadamer, *Hermeneutik I. Wahrheit und Methode*, pp. 258–269.

[8] e.g. Ricœur, *Le conflit des interprétations*, pp. 222–232.

[9] E. Husserl, *Ideen I*, p. 23.

[10] Heidegger, *Sein und Zeit*, p. 38 (§ 7).

entity or being, a fundamental ontology of law understands law—or, to be more precise, "right" (*Recht*, *droit*)—as part of the *Seinsfrage*, as an essential ingredient of the question of Being: how does law relate to the Being of beings? How is law involved in the way in which individual beings come to be? Needless to say, such an approach will lead my inquiries far from the questions and perspectives that are cherished by the juridical tradition. Nevertheless, I hope to have demonstrated the relevance of such a question already in my account of "just things" and correctness in the previous chapter.

Finally, the issue of interpretation will be addressed in a working-out of the hermeneutical starting points of understanding: how can and how does man understand law? Can understanding lead to a committed involvement with the world that is demanded by critical legal scholarship? Is critical interpretation possible within the "hermeneutics of Dasein"? This marks a return to the original "critical" starting points of my argument. The *critical question* of the philosophy of law, today frequently elaborated with the help of a theory of "deconstruction", addresses the issue of interpretation as a tool that would enable the decision-maker to distinguish between various meanings of a given juridical text. All too often this issue is approached from a finalistic perspective: the theory is formulated to meet the demands of a politically "correct" outcome. The perspective adopted here, however, requires me to elaborate the initial preconditions of understanding and to inquire whether any interpretative departure from the tradition is possible.

In working out the possibility of a philosophy of law, all three themes sketched above overlap and demand each other. It is not only a question of complementarity: any regional ontology necessarily implies a fundamental ontology, a cornerstone of which is a theory of understanding. In addition, the order in which these themes follow one another here is not necessarily the best. It mimics a traditional jurisprudential mode of inquiry that would first deal with law as an individual entity and only then proceed to the more "abstract" issues of the *Seinsfrage*. On the other hand, the issue of understanding and interpretation is dealt with last because it furnishes a background for the general theme of the second section of this book, namely, the relationship between law and the social usually addressed in critical legal scholarship.

In this chapter, then, my first aim is to analyse the way in which two very different phenomenological accounts of law have attempted to capture the ideality of the phenomenon in question. I hope to be able to indicate the reason why today's phenomenologists of law have often seen Kelsen and the pure theory of law as their forerunner and ally. I will next clarify the way in which Heidegger understands individual entities as equipment. Heidegger's critique of the philosophical tradition that phenomenology represents is overwhelming to the extent that it indicates why an original experience of existents such as law is not accessible through theoretical reflection and a reductive method. But even as equipment, I will argue that law constitutes an order of sorts in which the world that man inhabits appears as meaningful. Any such order requires a grounding, and

I will finally try to depict the constitutive elements of this grounding with the help of Carl Schmitt's notion of law as the unity of localisation and order.

II

The origin of the phenomenology of law is usually attributed to Adolf Reinach, a philosopher and Husserl's pupil who wished to demonstrate the appropriateness of the phenomenological method in the analysis of normative phenomena.[11] Jurists, however, only discovered phenomenology much later after the Second World War. This delay partly explains why Heidegger's name comes up—for better or worse—in the phenomenology of law of the post-war period. Alois Troller, for instance, follows Heidegger's path concerning the question of science but, rather inconsistently, also feels inclined to rely on a Husserlian methodology. The science of law is not merely logical; it must found itself on human being understood as Dasein that, in turn, can only be revealed through the method of phenomenological reduction.[12] Such a complicity between the philosophies of Husserl and Heidegger should lead to difficulties that Troller seems to be rather naive about. I will, however, concentrate my analysis here on two distinct authors: an unlikely "phenomenologist" better known for his pioneering work on Hegel, and a phenomenologist proper well appreciated in the francophonic world of law. My aim is to indicate how both authors—as different as they are in their approaches—can embrace the eidetic purity of law as a phenomenon only by explicitly rejecting the fundamental questions that Heidegger's critique of the philosophical tradition raises.

In 1943, the Hegelian philosopher Alexandre Kojève completed a manuscript on the phenomenology of law that remained unpublished until 1981. Kojève's point of departure is what he calls a "behaviouristic" method that depicts the external form of a particular human phenomenon, that is, that studies the observable actions that characterise a juridical situation as such and that distinguish it from all other human situations.[13] The essence of law reveals itself in the phenomenon "to have a right to . . ." involving two distinct beings and the possibility of an intervention by a disinterested third party. Without an intervention, it would be impossible to confirm that one or the other "has the right to . . .". Therefore, the constitutive element of law is an intervention without which a behaviouristic definition would be impossible.[14]

A juridical phenomenon requires an interactive relationship between the two beings involving an action and a reaction that both consist of three elements: volition, action, and intentionality. For an action to be juridical, it must provoke

[11] Cf. Reinach, *Zur Phänomenologie des Rechts*, pp. 11–20. Husserl on Reinach, see E. Husserl, "Adolf Reinach", in E. Husserl, *Aufsätze und Vorträge (1911–1921)*, pp. 300–303.

[12] Troller, *Überall gültige Prinzipien der Rechtswissenschaft*, pp. 213–214, n. 2.

[13] Kojève, *Esquisse d'une phénoménologie du droit*, p. 19.

[14] *Ibid.*, pp. 22–24.

a reaction that, in turn, aims to suppress the original action.[15] The disinterested third party must be distinct in relation to the two beings of the original interactive relationship. The existence of the third party indicates that law is essentially a social phenomenon.[16] So far, Kojève's theory could well be taken for a phenomenology of law in the usual sense of the word. The key to Kojève's Hegelian thinking lies in his notion of the idea of justice. Justice is an unsubstantial or theoretical interest that motivates the otherwise impartial intervention. Justice can be law only if a third party exists in the original confrontation of the two parties that Kojève understands as the original battle for recognition between master and slave:

> "The source of the *idea of Justice* is the anthropogenic desire of desire that is realised in and through the Battle for recognition. And this idea is created in and through the consciousnesses of the two adversaries that confront each other in this Battle. But the ultimate source of *Law* [*Droit*] is the penetration of this idea into the consciousness of a third party, that is, a human being other than the two adversaries in question".[17]

The third party intervening in the battle cannot recognise the winner in its particularity but only the universal aspect of its human existence. This means that the individual participants are interchangeable and that the third party will remain disinterested because the only motivation to intervene and to arbitrate is to recognise the universal humanity of the winner—the master—by denying its particularity. Kojève calls this the aristocratic law of the master. But even the defeated participant of the battle—the slave in its potential humanity—represents a law, namely bourgeois law. The autonomy of the phenomenon of law lies in the antithetic relationship between two "rights": an existing law of the master and a law of the slave that is inclined to materialise. The actuality of the one and the potentiality of the other synthesise into what Kojève understands as the law of the citizen.[18]

In a more Husserlian tone, Paul Amselek defines the phenomenology of law as the systematic application of a philosophical and eidetic reduction to the study of law. Because of the reductive nature of the phenomenological method, Amselek explicitly recognises Kelsen as a notable forerunner of his own theory. The phenomenology of law is, accordingly, a particular development of the pure theory of law.[19]

Three perspectives must be taken into account. In its essence, law is a collection of norms and, therefore, its eidetic genus is normative. In addition, the

[15] Kojève, *Esquisse d'une phénoménologie du droit*, pp. 62–68.

[16] *Ibid.*, pp. 73–75.

[17] *Ibid.*, p. 260.

[18] *Ibid.*, pp. 257–266. This should make it more than clear that Kojève's "phenomenology" is Hegelian rather than Husserlian. The "reductive" logic inherent in Kojève's theory is limited to the ruling out of neighbouring phenomenons such as religion (*ibid.*, pp. 207–214) and morality (*ibid.*, pp. 214–225). On the dialectics of history in general, see Kojève, *Introduction à la lecture de Hegel*, pp. 161–195.

[19] Amselek, "La phénoménologie et le droit", pp. 197–199. On a melange of Kelsen and phenomenology, see also Schreier, *Grundbegriffe und Grundformen des Rechts*, pp. 6–12.

norms that law consists of are specifically ethical in that they are equipment that function as commands. Lastly, in their functioning, the commands that law consists of belong to the domain of the public direction of human behaviour. These three perspectives, that is, the generic, the specific, and the particular eidetic elements of law, account for the eidetic singularity of law as a unique phenomenon in the world.[20] It is, however, worth noting that the normative character of law in Amselek's theory is intimately bound to efficacy. The normative character of legal commands is merely an indication of the obligation to conform to the dictates of an effective positive law. For Amselek, the phenomenology of law is, then, a science in the Kelsenian tradition rid of all moral considerations.[21]

As a norm, the phenomenon "law" has a measuring function. The norm is an object of reference or a model, a ground for the evaluation of things in relation to a preceding set of qualities. To measure is to juxtapose a model and an object in order to indicate their differences. The value of the object is established in its relationship to the standard represented by the norm. Amselek distinguishes two different standards. In some cases, it is possible to give an infinitely divisible and multipliable standard unit with which the object is then compared. Such comparison is quantitative measurement and is confined to objects that are measurable on a numeric scale. Rules and norms, however, are not divisible or quantifiable. The qualitative value of the object in relation to the standard is, then, either uniformity or the lack thereof. The mental process is, however, the same regardless of whether the relationship is announced in quantitative terms or not: measurement is the verification of the consistency between the object and the standard.[22]

Legal norms are commands which, according to Amselek, refer to a specific instrumental function: they furnish yardsticks that are to be heeded due to coercion. They are, then, a specific technique of directing human behaviour clearly distinguishable from recommendations that do not involve constraint. The coercive nature of law allegedly gives cause to numerous misunderstandings about the relationship between law and power. Amselek emphasises that even though commands require the existence of some element of force, coercion is a factual or an existential feature of law that does not belong to the *eidos* of a command.[23]

But if all commands are not law, what, then, is the crucial element that would enable us to see the eidetic core of law? Several answers can be given: law is coupled with sanction, law governs the exterior behaviour of human beings, law is a dual structure of rights and obligations, and so on. Amselek emphasises two specific traits that seem to differentiate law from all other commands. First, law consists of commands that are made public and, secondly, these commands have a specific instrumental function, namely, the regulation of human behaviour.

[20] Amselek, "La phénoménologie et le droit", p. 200.
[21] Cf. Amselek, *Méthode phénoménologique et théorie du droit*, pp. 312–355.
[22] Amselek, "La phénoménologie et le droit", pp. 205–208.
[23] *Ibid.*, pp. 240–246.

The existence of law implies, then, two fundamental postulates: man lives in social communities, and the communal existence of man is regulated by authoritative commands. These commands do not regulate inter-human relations but individual human beings.[24]

Regardless of what can be said about the merits of the two distinct approaches briefly characterised above, Kojève's and Amselek's phenomenologies of law are akin as far as they include a self-professed deficiency. Kojève elucidates the shortcomings of his "superficiality" by affirming that a comprehensive analysis of law would require not only his specific brand of phenomenological research, but also a *metaphysics of law* accounting for the existence of law in relation to other beings, as well as an *ontology of law*, that is, an elaboration of the Being of law in particular and law's relationship to Being in general.[25] Kojève's "phenomenology" is, of course, essentially Hegelian, but it clearly relies on a reductive method that attempts to distinguish a stipulated phenomenon by eliminating unnecessary attributes. But in order to insure the scientific nature of this venture, Kojève must also set aside the philosophical questions that concern man's original experience of law.

On the other hand, Amselek, commenting on the theoretical prospects of phenomenology, distinguishes the three different phases of the reductive method as they are elaborated by Husserl: the philosophical, the eidetic, and the transcendental reductions. He, however, rejects a broad definition of the third and ultimate phase of phenomenology judging it as a "debatable and more or less metaphysical [doctrinal theme], developed by diverse phenomenologists (and by Husserl himself)".[26] If Kojève can be commended for his openness concerning the limited nature of his "phenomenology", Amselek emphasises the epistemic advantages of an impaired phenomenology that evades the philosophical difficulties that even Husserl felt obliged to confront. It is this forceful consideration given to the "scientific" nature of a phenomenology of law that characterises the affinity between thinkers like Amselek, Kojève and Kelsen. But it is also the dividing-line that separates the phenomenology of law from what Heidegger would consider the thinking of "true" philosophy.

III

The philosophical "difficulties" that beset such a scientific phenomenology are articulated in Heidegger's *Sein und Zeit*, a book dedicated to Husserl, but also an overwhelming critique of the philosophical tradition of which phenomenology is regarded as the culmination. Heidegger rejects Husserl's conviction that the essence of a being—including the human being or Dasein—could be revealed with the help of a reductive method executed by the reflective thinker.

[24] Amselek, "La phénoménologie et le droit", pp. 251–254.
[25] Kojève, *Esquisse d'une phénoménologie du droit*, pp. 11 and 17–18.
[26] Amselek, "La phénoménologie et le droit", p. 188.

How can one, then, account for man's original encounter with individual entities such as law?

The starting point of what the early Heidegger calls an "hermeneutic phenomenology" is the way in which Dasein encounters individual beings while being simultaneously absorbed in its everyday practical activities. When Dasein confronts the world concernfully, it does not come across senseless existents. For Dasein, beings appear in a meaningful way as purposive tools, as equipment (*Zeug*) that it manipulates in accordance with a specific in-order-to (*Um-zu*) that designates the tool. The in-order-to of an equipmental being is not its function but, rather, a referential totality interconnecting one being to another without which any one being would remain senseless for Dasein.[27] As equipment, a being is, then, defined by its in-order-to, its purposiveness within a structural totality. For a being to make sense to Dasein, it must function within a context of meaningful activity that Heidegger calls involvement (*Bewandtnis*). In its purposive involvement with beings, Dasein encompasses a for-the-sake-of-which (*Um-willen*), a conclusive albeit non-intentional motivation for Dasein to use equipment. By using equipment, Dasein displays a particular knowledge about how they function within a totality, within a wherein (*Worin*) of available beings.

As Dasein is concernfully involved in its everyday activities, it does not reflect on the equipmental being used or the totalities that define it as a particular being but, nevertheless, displays a pre-theoretical familiarity with these merely by knowing how to use the tool. Using a shovel, a farmer digs a ditch into his field demonstrating, at the same time, a necessary understanding of agriculture and, yet, does not reflect on the shovel or farming in any theoretical way. But without such an understanding, the individual being "shovel" would remain senseless: "ditch", "soil", "irrigation", "cultivation", and so on. Heidegger calls the general phenomenon of Dasein being "always already" socialised into a world of meaningful beings Being-in-the-world (*in-der-Welt-Sein*). The fundamental characteristics of any given being are determined by its in-order-to, its use as equipment in relation to a particular for-the-sake-of-which. As Dasein uses an equipmental being in its everyday practical activities, the tool has a specific way of Being that Heidegger calls availableness (*Zuhandenheit*).[28]

The particularities of the juridical tradition present obstacles in trying to conceptualise an example that would be relevant to law. Juridical thinking seldom regards law as operative except when it is violated and, for reasons that should become clear later, this is a plausible solution only to a certain extent. But law exists in the world of Dasein even when things are running smoothly: it secures safe passage within urban traffic, it sets standards for commerce and trade, it directs social comportment within certain parameters, and so on.

[27] Heidegger, *Sein und Zeit*, pp. 67–69 (§ 15).

[28] *Ibid.*, pp. 52–54 and 69 (§§ 12 and 15). For phenomenological accounts of world and law, see, e.g., G. Husserl, "Recht und Welt", in G. Husserl, *Recht und Welt*, pp. 67–114 and G. Husserl, "Erfahrung des Rechts", in G. Husserl, *Recht und Zeit*, pp. 67–86.

In such situations, Dasein encounters law as an equipmental being with a specific in-order-to and for-the-sake-of-which. An obvious parallel to the farmer and the shovel would, of course, be the professional lawyer using law as equipment in his work. The lawyer displays a pre-theoretical familiarity with law by, for example, recognising a document as a contract laden with legal significance without having to reflect on the matter theoretically. At the same time, he must necessarily possess some understanding of a referential totality without which law would remain senseless to him: "volition", "intention", "obligation", "process", "settlement", and so on. Law is not, however, equipment restricted to the use of legal professionals. Regardless of the merits of the professional approach, it can hardly touch the surface of a being as complex as law. I shall, then, attempt to depict the way in which law is encountered by the non-professional Dasein.

In its everyday activities, Dasein is involved with available law continuously without being reflectively aware of it. For Dasein, law functions as equipment with which Dasein directs its social comportment within the world; we do not pick pockets or threaten others with violence because, regardless of the contents of individual statutes protecting the property and personal integrity of others, *we abide by the law*. The fundamental characteristics of law are not, then, revealed exclusively in its professional use as a yardstick for measuring the legality of social relations as the bulk of legal theory contends but, rather, in the way in which Dasein encounters law in relation to its own comportment within the world. The referential totality of law, its in-order-to, is, in a sense, self-referential: if a shovel "is" in order to dig ditches, law "is" only to be abided by. Dasein abides by the law encompassing a specific for-the-sake-of-which: law orders the world in a way that enables Dasein to maintain sense and meaning. Law standardises Dasein's comportment.

A literal translation of the German expression for abiding by the law (*das Gesetz einhalten*) would read: to keep law as one, to keep it intact. The connotation is similar as in the English expression "to keep a promise" and other such idioms. We do not keep a promise because we are persuaded by its force or because we direct our behaviour in accordance with the contents of its normative efficacy but, rather, because we wish to secure the unity of the promise. Should we "break" the promise by refraining from an obligation, its unity would be in jeopardy. In a similar way, law seems to manifest a two-fold tension between the order of unity and the disorder of decay. On the one hand, law has become one and, by abiding by the law, we uphold its integrity. Its original structure is not one of unity but, rather, of conflict and chaos. On the other hand, law has an inclination to disintegrate back into chaos, to lose the unity that only our law-abiding comportment can maintain. Because of this inclination, we act, not to maintain ourselves in accordance with the law, but to keep law itself as one. In this sense, law represents the order of the world that enables it to "make sense".

In its normal—and primordial—mode of Being, that is, availableness, law appears to Dasein in a way that does not involve any form of reflective awareness. What Dasein encounters is, quite simply, availableness. As an equipmental being, law is transparent and dissolves in such a way that Dasein is not aware of its characteristics. In order to be available, law must paradoxically withdraw from Dasein that is concernfully engaged in its practical activities. As law-abiding citizens, we are normally unaware of law that we keep intact by acting in a certain way; we pay for a paper at the newsstand without being reflectively aware that law requires us to do so. In a corresponding way, Dasein's own grasp of its law-abiding comportment is not inspection in the sense of a methodological stance in relation to a set purpose, but circumspection, that is, purposive involvement "in the world" to which both Dasein and law belong; by paying for the paper, we are merely engaged within a world encompassing both us and law.[29]

Dasein articulates its understanding of law by comporting within three consecutive totalities. First, there is an equipmental totality (*Zeugganze*) of law including such interrelated equipment as, for example, "law", "norm", "rule", "principle", and so on. Secondly, there is a referential totality (*Verweisungsganzheit*) of law which comprises the structural relations between the individual beings. Thirdly, there is an involvement totality (*Bewandtnisganzheit*) of law which adds Dasein's purposiveness, its concern to keep law intact, to the two others.[30] Structurally the involvement totality makes up what is known as the world or, in other words, significance (*Bedeutsamkeit*), the background against which law "always already" makes sense in the disclosure of Dasein and world.

Should Dasein always be involved in its everyday activities in such a transparent way, it would never be able to account for the world in which it and its equipment dwell. The primordial mode of Being of Dasein and of law lies, however, in the way in which available law is used in absorbed coping, in the way in which Dasein is involved in keeping law intact. An awareness of the fundamental characteristics of law is only possible when it fails to perform in the way it usually does and becomes unavailable (*Unzuhandenheit*) unravelling all that it normally performs with. In such a case, the world, that is, the specific way in which individual beings such as law and referential totalities are accessible to Dasein in a meaningful way, is discovered. Heidegger, however, denies that the fundamental characteristics of beings could be explained by referring to a subject/object-relationship in which, for example, the subject intentionally theorises about law.[31]

From the modes of disturbance defined by Heidegger,[32] we can distinguish the three different ways in which law is unravelled to Dasein. Conspicuousness

[29] Heidegger, *Sein und Zeit*, pp. 69–70 (§ 15).

[30] *Ibid.*, pp. 83–87 (§ 18).

[31] *Ibid.*, p. 73 (§ 16). According to Heidegger, the theoretical reflection of science requires the decontextualisation of aspects into occurrent properties that do not belong to the equipmental whole. For example, the efficacious aspect of law is decontextualised into "efficacy", an isolable property that can then be attached to any other entity, as well. In Heideggerian terms, this would mean overlooking the equipmental character of law: *ibid.*, pp. 356–364 (§ 69).

[32] *Ibid.*, pp. 73–75 (§ 16).

(*Auffälligkeit*) is the brief acknowledgment that law has somehow not performed in the way it should. We pick up a paper at the newsstand and start to walk away suddenly remembering that we have not paid for it. The law that we are to keep intact by directing our comportment in a specific way suddenly becomes unavailable but, as we pay the attendant, quickly withdraws back into availableness. Obstinacy (*Aufsässigkeit*) occurs when the function of law, that is, that it is kept intact, becomes impossible. As we are looking for the attendant of the newsstand who has mysteriously vanished, we become more fully aware of law, of the requirement to keep it intact, and of the referential totality that encloses the requirement: "law", "payment", "price", "merchandise", "business", and so on. Only after a few reflective thoughts can we secure the unity of law by, for example, leaving the coins at the counter and be on our way.

In the third variant of disturbance, obtrusiveness (*Aufdringlichkeit*), a transition occurs from involved practical activity to a theoretical reflection on the impossibility of fulfilling the task, that is, to keep law intact. Sitting in the underground with an unpaid paper under our arm and with no possibility to rectify our infraction, we reflect on the matter with ambiguous sensations of unaccomplishment. We are fully aware that we have broken the law and are withheld from resuming our practical activity, that is, keeping law intact, and helplessly gaze at the paper we have unlawfully taken into our possession. Only now does a theoretical position enabling the explanation of the causal relations between law, commerce and our own behaviour become possible but, at the same time, law has become occurrent (*Vorhandenheit*) and is deprived of its worldly character and, accordingly, its fundamental characteristics.

As an hermeneutics of the everyday, the first division of *Sein und Zeit* attempts to define this "method" for the interpretation of Dasein's involvement with meaningful beings in its everyday practices. Heidegger claims that the tradition has overlooked Dasein's primordial relationship with the world and has, thus, evaded the question of Being: How "is", for example, law for Dasein?[33]

The hermeneutic interpretation (*Auslegung*) of law is already implicit in Dasein's everyday understanding of law. Interpretation is always the articulation of a latent capacity that Dasein usually exercises in its everyday purposive involvement: by keeping law intact, Dasein interprets law that it must necessarily already possess an understanding of. For Heidegger, interpretation is grounded on a three-fold fore-structure of understanding. First, Dasein must necessarily possess a fore-having (*Vorhabe*), understand the functional totality to which law belongs: "norm", "rule", "position", "social world", and so on. In other words, in interpretation, Dasein manifests its understanding of using law and other related equipment for a variety of purposes. Secondly, Dasein must possess a fore-seeing (*Vorsicht*), understand that, as serviceable equipment, law can be used to achieve a specific end. In other words, in interpretation, Dasein displays its understanding of law as a being that can be kept intact. Thirdly,

[33] Heidegger, *Sein und Zeit*, pp. 17–18 (§ 5).

Dasein must possess a fore-conception (*Vorgriff*), an understanding of how law must be manipulated in order to achieve this end. In other words, in interpretation, Dasein anticipates that by comporting in a specific way it can keep law intact.[34]

As law designates a particular order for the world—by, for example, uncovering a particular meaning of the world for the paying customer at the newsstand—it directs our comportment in a specific way. Dasein conducts itself in relation to law due to a certain pressure present in its Being-with (*Mit-sein*) in the world with other Dasein. Dasein occupies positions in relation to other Dasein in a way that is, so to speak, proper. Dasein directs itself towards a "normality" in the sense that, for example, paying for the paper is "what one does". This involves no normative pressure in the legal or moral senses; "one keeps law intact [*man hält das Gesetz ein*]" because that is what is expected of Dasein. For Heidegger, the "one" or the "they" (*das Man*) of the passive tense is a non-ethical, formal description of Dasein's tendency to conform.[35] By conforming to the normalising impact of law, that is, by keeping law intact because that is what one usually does, Dasein avoids differentiation from others and aims at an averageness. It upholds a shared background necessary to sustain the world and, at the same time, an order without which any understanding of individual beings would be impossible; law-abiding Dasein is merely conforming to the normality of the "one". Conforming, however, prevents Dasein access to its true Being. Therefore, Dasein's relation to the normalising impetus of law is supported by common normality. In other words, Dasein's mode of Being in relation to law can only be unauthentic (*uneigentlich*).[36]

If Dasein keeps *law* intact, it is not merely conforming to a norm; Dasein does not relate to, for example, social norms and law in the same way. Even if social norms constitute the bulk of positive law, we do not write out an official document according to a prescribed formula in the same way as we pay for a paper at the newsstand. Unlike norms, law indicates to a norm that can be kept intact and, at the same time, specifies such comportment as "correct" and "right" (*recht*). We pay for a paper and, simultaneously, contend that it is "correct" to do so. If abiding by the law and keeping law intact accounts for the order without which the world of Dasein would appear as senseless, how can Dasein attest the "correctness" or the "rightness" of this order? Dasein must somehow ground itself into its world, establish for itself a fast location that would secure the stability of the order of law. I will attempt to clarify this aspect with the help of Carl Schmitt's philosophy of *nomos*, the understanding of law as the unity of localisation and order.

[34] *Ibid.*, p. 150 (§ 32).

[35] *Ibid.*, pp. 126–129 (§ 27).

[36] In some interpretations of Heidegger, there is a disposition to understand "unauthenticity" as a pejorative mode of existence. This is, however, not the case. For the most part, Dasein's relationship with the world is unauthentic as in, for instance, coping with the everyday and, indeed, should remain so.

IV

Schmitt's final working phase, lasting from the mid 1930s until his death in 1985, can well be called the philosophy of *nomos* in that it embodies a more metaphysical approach to law than his previous writings on, for example, public and international law.[37] However, Schmitt's philosophical ambitions involve a paradox. On the one hand, he still subjects his philosophy to the dictates of the science of law and the epistemological requirements inferred thereof. But in clear contrast to this scientific tone,[38] Schmitt dedicates much of his later work to the working out of what he calls "fundamental words" (*Urwort*). The philosophy of *nomos* is not:

> "a vocabulary of a given philosophical system applied to juridical questions but the development of concrete concepts from the immanence of a concrete legal and social order".[39]

The "violence" of such conceptual poesy and its relationship to a "concrete order" have called for much speculation on the relationship between Schmitt's philosophy and the politics of the Third Reich. According to, for instance, Karl Löwith, this last phase in Schmitt's decisionism can be called "occasional" because it substitutes the conceptual decisionism of the exception or the distinction of friend and enemy with a *decision* concerning the "concrete order" of the state and the stability engendered by such an order.[40]

But even if the concrete and successive epochal orders that Schmitt designates are established in decisions, the decisionism of the philosophy of *nomos* stands or falls on an original appropriation that must necessarily precede any given order. Nor is *nomos* stable in the conventional sense of the word. It is a synergetic order in which the elementary forces of the world—for Schmitt these are primarily land and sea, but in its epochal extensions also air and fire—are in constant and tense play. It is the tension (*Spannung*), not stability, that characterises the elements of the order. *Nomos* is:

> "the immediate form in which the political and the social order of a nation [*Volk*] becomes visible as having space, the first measure and distribution of the pasture, that is, the appropriation of land [*Landnahme*] and the concrete order that lies in it as well as follows from it".[41]

[37] For an historical account of Schmitt's last intellectual period from 1937 onwards, see Hofmann, *Legitimität gegen Legalität*, pp. 198–205.

[38] e.g. Schmitt, *Der Nomos der Erde*, p. 5.

[39] Schmitt, "Die Lage der europäischen Rechtswissenschaft", in Schmitt, *Verfassungsrechtliche Aufsätze aus den Jahren 1924–1954*, pp. 386–429 at p. 427. On *nomos* as a concept, see, e.g., Meier, "Zu Carl Schmitts Begriffsbildung—Das Politische und der Nomos", in Quaritsch (ed.), *Complexio Oppositorum*, pp. 537–556 at pp. 552–553.

[40] Löwith, "Der okkasionelle Dezisionismus von C. Schmitt", in Löwith, *Heidegger—Denker in dürftiger Zeit*, pp. 32–71 at pp. 59–60. Later Löwith attempts to see a similar mode of decisionism in Heidegger: *ibid.*, pp. 61–68.

[41] Schmitt, *Der Nomos der Erde*, pp. 39–40.

Space (*Raum*) is, then, concurrent in relation to *nomos*. It represents the orderly aspect of *nomos* that is apparent only as the tension between disparate elements. In working out the notion of space, Schmitt takes on a clearly metaphysical tone:

> "Only today is a certain thought possible for us, a thought that would have been impossible in all other epochs and that a German philosopher of the present has articulated: the world is not in space but space is in the world".[42]

What does Heidegger, Schmitt's "philosopher of the present", say about space and world? As Dasein's essential constitution is Being-in-the-world, its formal existential expression is Being-in. Being-in is the ontological relationship between beings that, each within their respective localities (*Ort*), approach one another "in" space.[43] Dasein expresses a spatial concern with equipment that Heidegger calls the existentiale of dis-stancing (*Ent-fernung*): Dasein has a tendency to bring equipment near in order to gain access to them. The degree of availableness is the nearness of Dasein's concern in relation to equipment or, to put it in another way, available equipment has the character of nearness (*Nähe*).[44]

What Schmitt adopts from Heidegger is an understanding of space and spatiality as an order that contains within itself the elementary tensions of human existence. *Man inscribes himself into an orderly world by occupying a locality in an original appropriation of land*. Schmitt emphasises the terrain character of man's locality, its relationship to land. Dis-stancing or, to paraphrase Schmitt, man's inclination to appropriate the world, is the orderly tension between a terrain locality and an outside, between "land and sea". In a spatial order, man localised in land approaches the element of sea.

Space is, however, not a closed order. *Raum* is a fundamental German word, an *Urwort*. A phonetic analysis reveals that the diphthong "*au*" represents the first and the last vowels of the German alphabet, the alpha and the omega, the beginning and the end. But beginning does not enfold in end:

> "The *R* forms . . . the active adjunct, and *M* is an end coming together at the horizon, surpassing the horizon. *Raum* is, then, not a closed circle nor a domain but a *world*, and this world is not an empty space, nor is it *in* an empty space, but our *Raum* is a world filled with the tension of different elements".[45]

[42] Schmitt, *Land und Meer*, p. 106. The same reference can also be found in, e.g., Schmitt, "Völkerrechtliche Großraumordnung mit Interventionsverbot für raumfremde Mächte—Ein Beitrag zum Reichsbegriff im Völkerrecht", in Schmitt, *Staat, Großraum, Nomos*, pp. 269–371 at p. 319.

[43] Heidegger, *Sein und Zeit*, p. 56 (§ 12). On locality and space, see also Heidegger, "Bauen Wohnen Denken", in Heidegger, *Vorträge und Aufsätze*, pp. 139–156 at pp. 148–152.

[44] Heidegger, *Sein und Zeit*, pp. 104–110 (§ 23). For a political comparison of Heidegger's and Schmitt's concepts of space and spaciality, see Hofmann, *Legitimität gegen Legalität*, pp. 236–247. See also Pöschl, *Raum und Raumordnung*, pp. 18–22.

[45] Schmitt, "Raum und Rom—Zur Phonetik des Wortes Raum", in Schmitt, *Staat, Großraum, Nomos*, pp. 491–495 at pp. 492–493.

From the elements of land and sea Schmitt develops his notion of *nomos* as the unity of localisation and order.[46] Man is a terrain creature bound to the earth in three ways. In its crop, the earth bears the measure of how human toil and work are transformed into the fruit of the land, while the tillage marks firm boundaries for the distribution and the division of the land. Finally, in its harvest, the earth supplies a solid foundation for the unity of localisation (*Ortung*) and order (*Ordnung*), that is, for *nomos*:

> "*Nomos* is the *measure* [*Maß*] that distributes and localises the ground and the soil of the earth into a specific order as well as the figure [*Gestalt*] of the political, social and religious order that follows. Thus measure, order and figure form a concrete, spatial unity".[47]

By way of contrast, the sea represents a point beyond the order of the land, a free zone open for trade and commerce. Because human existence is by nature terrain, the origin of all *nomoi* is the appropriation of land.[48] Yet all epochs have their own *nomos*, and the thalassic expansion (*Seenahme*) of the great maritime powers represents the extension of the order of the land to the sea. The relationship between the appropriated land and the sea as the possibility of expansion and colonisation marks the tension of an orderly human existence in *nomos*. But the appropriation of land, the "great historical event", is the *archē* (*Ur-grund*) in which space and law originally come together as localisation and order.[49]

In Schmitt's less overtly metaphysical texts, he develops his notion of space into the spatial concept of *Großraum* and a theory of sovereign empires (*Reiche*) at peace within an international legal order (*Völkerrecht*).[50] The order of *nomos* is, then, unauthentic in a Heideggerian sense in that the pacific stability of a world of friendly or hostile "imperial spaces" (*Großräume*) is motivated by the inclination to conform to the familiarity of a shared and meaningful world or, in Schmitt's own terms, to the sovereignty of disparate political entities.

Nomos requires a global conception of the world in which the domains outside the limits of the *polis* are recognised as hostile territories. This structure is first conceived in Roman law, whereas the mythical and cosmopolitan character of a Greek *ius gentium* is apparent in the way in which the exterior is configured as a derivation of the *polis*.[51] In other words, the *cosmos* mimes the

[46] Schmitt, *Der Nomos der Erde*, pp. 13–14.

[47] *Ibid.*, p. 40. Cf. Agamben, *Homo sacer*, pp. 23–37.

[48] Cf. Cacciari, *Icone della Legge*, pp. 46–48.

[49] Schmitt, *Der Nomos der Erde*, pp. 15–17. In much a similar vein, Hegel identifies soil (*Boden*) with family and sea with commerce but, unlike Schmitt, understands colonisation as a means (*Mittel*), not as a constitutive appropriation through which order is established. Hegel, *Vorlesungen über Rechtsphilosophie 1818–1831*, pp. 514–515 (§ 203), 612 (§ 247), and 614 (§ 248).

[50] On the difference between *Raum* and *Großraum*, see Schmitt, "Völkerrechtliche Großraumordnung", in Schmitt, *Staat, Großraum, Nomos*, pp. 314–320. On *Großraum* and *nomos*, see Mehring, *Pathetisches Denken*, pp. 194–209. See also Kaiser, "Europäisches Großraumdenken—Die Steigerung geschichtlicher Größen als Rechtsproblem", in Barion et al (eds), *Epirrhosis*, pp. 529–548 at pp. 529–535.

[51] Schmitt, *Der Nomos der Erde*, p. 20.

structural design of the Greek *polis*. The oppositional structure of land and sea is fully established only during the colonial era of the seventeenth and eighteenth centuries.[52] This is what Schmitt understands as the European *ius publicum* in which the distinction between land and sea represents the tense and orderly characteristics of *nomos*.

In its epochal successions, the order of *nomos* is eventually extended from a global conception of the world in which the distinction between land and sea sustains the required tension to a planetary conception of the world. A planetary conception is, of course, established from an aerial position, that is, by appropriating the element of air. And, finally, fire—in the 1930s, Schmitt still associates fire with the rocket-engine—represents the ultimate nuclear threat of a world submitted to technology.

The epochal successions of new *nomoi* that appropriate the elements one by one will eventually conclude in a closure of the world, in an all-encompassing existence that annuls the original distinction between land and sea fundamental in relation to the terrain existence of man. Schmitt's position *vis-à-vis* this "mondialisation"[53] of the world is, however, ambivalent. On the one hand, it marks the end of the old European *ius publicum*, a fact that Schmitt can only acknowledge with regretful nostalgia. And yet:

> "The old *nomos* retreats voluntarily and with it a whole system of surpassing measures, norms and relationships. But what is to come is, however, not merely measurelessness or a *nomos*-hostile nothing. Even in the embittered spheres of old and new forces, just measures are born and meaningful proportions are founded".[54]

All epochal *nomoi* are established in a three-fold process that, according to Schmitt, corresponds with the three dimensions of the Greek verb *nemein*. First, there is the appropriation of the land (*Nahme*), secondly, the distribution (*Teilen*) and the order that is thus established, and, lastly, the grazing or the pasturing (*Weiden*), the exploitation of the product of the land.[55] Schmitt's austere critique against the conventions of the science of law is that the tradition has forgotten the original appropriation by consistently mistranslating *nomos* as rule or law, as order without foundation:

> "In its original sense, . . . *nomos* is the full immediacy of a juridical force that is not mediated by laws; it is a constitutive historical event, an act of *legitimacy* [*Legitimität*] that makes the legality [*Legalität*] of mere laws meaningful in general".[56]

[52] *Ibid.*, p. 24.

[53] Cf. Nancy, *Le sens du monde*, pp. 13–20.

[54] Schmitt, *Land und Meer*, p. 107.

[55] Schmitt, "Nehmen/Teilen/Weiden," in Schmitt, *Verfassungsrechtliche Aufsätze*, pp. 489–504 at pp. 490–492.

[56] Schmitt, *Der Nomos der Erde*, p. 42. For Schmitt, this neglect has brought about momentous political consequences: "From the perspective of constitutional theory, the strongest motive of all tendencies towards *auctoritas* . . . originates directly from the fact that, at present, the only recognised system of justification left is referendary legitimacy [*plebiszitäre Legitimität*]": Schmitt, *Legalität und Legitimität*, p. 93.

The appropriation of land is the decision that constitutes all *nomoi*, but because an epochal appropriation necessarily implies both a position from which the appropriation is effectuated and an object to be appropriated, the *Nahme* inherent in the subsequent epochal *nomoi* is already preceded by the distinction between land and sea.[57] The *Ur-akte* would, then, be the original appropriation of land that localises man into his terrain existence. In this original appropriation, the orderly and meaningful nature of the world that man inhabits is literally "grounded".

V

It seems that the philosophical tradition that studies law as an individual existent usually tends to understand law either as evidence of the social nature of human existence or as a normative yardstick that measures human conduct. Both approaches, however, are indications of a more or less scientific and reflective stance that, according to Heidegger, cannot account for man's primordial and original experience of law. The question must be posed once again: what does Heidegger have to offer the philosophy of law? As an equipmental being, law directs our everyday comportment in a transparent way that upholds the meaningful and orderly experience of a world shared with other human beings. This meaningful order must, however, be somehow grounded. This grounding is what Schmitt understands as the original appropriation of land, as the *localisation that together with order accounts for the original experience of law.*

For Schmitt, orderly human existence is the tension between land and sea. But this tense terrain existence already constitutes a spatial order of sorts. Localisation as the original appropriation of land must necessarily take place before any order is established, before the being that appropriates couples itself with what is appropriable in terrain existence or, in other words, before the object of an original desire is recognised. How can such an original desire "make sense"? Within the rapport of the world, Jean-Luc Nancy identifies sense as the tension between desire and donation.[58] For sense to remain a rapport, that is, before the desired object is recognised, sense cannot be determined either as the realisation of the relationship or its invalidation. Desire cannot indicate the object of the donation that must necessarily remain unknown both to the donator and the donatory:

> "The appropriation of the donation itself and the donation of the inappropriable itself configures the original chiasm of philosophy—and of sense".[59]

[57] Cf. Schmitt, *Der Begriff des Politischen*, pp. 26–28. On Schmitt's decisionism and the "concrete order" of *nomos*, see von Krockow, *Die Entscheidung*, pp. 94–106.

[58] Nancy, *Le sens du monde*, pp. 86–87.

[59] *Ibid.*, p. 87 (emphases deleted). On the rapport and the *polis*, see also Lacoue-Labarthe and Nancy, "Ouverture", in Balibar et al, *Rejouer le politique*, pp. 11–28 at pp. 24–26, and Lacoue-Labarthe and Nancy, "Le 'retrait' du politique", in Kambouchner et al, *Le retrait du politique*, pp. 183–200 at p. 197.

Sense is the *agathon* offered in accordance with the excess of its excellence. Desire and donation are *offered* to each other, sacrificed. They are left at the discretion of a decision the agent of which can be neither desiring nor donator, but only existent.[60] It would seem, however, that the allegedly original appropriation of Schmitt's philosophy of *nomos* is preceded by something even more anterior, for:

> "No man can give, divide and distribute without appropriating. Only a god that creates the world from nothing can give and distribute without appropriating".[61]

Any human donation is the distribution or the re-distribution of something that has already been appropriated; man cannot donate but can only appropriate and distribute. But as man appropriates (*Nahme*), he also names (*Name*) by claiming a piece of land as his own or by denominating an heir or a spouse either by assigning or accepting a name.[62] As *Landnahme*, then, the original appropriation of land necessarily includes a recognition and an acknowledgement of what has been given. When man claims land as his locality in a seemingly original appropriation, a donation is concurrently accepted: land "is", "it gives" (*es gibt*) land.

But in such a donation, both the gift and the donator have also been recognised. In its privileged giftedness to donate by creating *ex nihilo*, a divinity confers man his terrain locality, that is, his original aptitude to appropriate the appropriable. The decision is, then, not only the original and constitutive appropriation of land in *nomos*, but also the acknowledgement of a divine donator and of the endowment of existence.

Such a decisionism does not even need a negative theology in order to restate its onto-theological foundations.

[60] Nancy, *Le sens du monde*, p. 88.

[61] Schmitt, "Nomos—Nahme—Name," in Schmitt, *Staat, Großraum, Nomos*, pp. 573–591 at p. 581.

[62] *Ibid.*, pp. 583–584.

4

Right Things to Come

> "The event [*Ereignis*] is *the* law [*Gesetz*] in so far as it gathers mortals into the appropriateness of their essence and there holds them."
>
> Martin Heidegger

> "the law [*loi*] is itself a kind of place, a *topos* and a taking place."
>
> Jacques Derrida

I

In the previous chapter, I attempted to show how the philosophy of law that thinks of law as equipment has confronted a problem that is characteristic of its ambitious nature. Even if law localises and orders Dasein's existence within the world, Being-in-the-world with other Dasein, that is, Being-with, does *not* involve authentic Being. Dasein is still caught in the unauthenticity of fallenness, in its everyday dwelling and its mundane chores. The philosophy of law has consistently refused to reduce law to a simple entity equatable with a shovel, and in doing so, it has had to find other paths of thinking in order to give law a meaning in relation to what is considered the true Being of Dasein. Something, then, seems to be missing in the tool-analysis: a more profound understanding of law as an ingredient of the world and of the thinking creature that inhabits it.[1]

But as I have mentioned before, Heidegger does not necessarily understand unauthenticity as a pejorative mode of Being. For the most part, Dasein spends its life absorbed in its everyday activities and, indeed, *must* do so. But the profundity that the philosophy of law strives for—we are, once again, talking about a "desire to see"—is evident in the serenity of the neighbouring worlds that law touches upon: morals, ethics, politics, and so on. Are, then, the normative aspects of Dasein's Being merely ways in which it copes with the everyday? Or does Dasein's true existence reside in areas that a Heideggerian analysis would, strictly speaking, regard as either inconsequential or secondary? To overcome these difficulties, the philosophy of law situates Dasein's true existence into the *social world* and must, subsequently, substitute the ontological difference distinguishing Being from beings with a more existential tone. Arthur Kaufmann, for instance, maintains the difference but modifies the register in which the philosophy of law is articulated in order to better serve the requirements of his tradition:

[1] See, e.g., Henkel, *Einführung in die Rechtsphilosophie*, pp. 172–183.

> "for all ontology, in particular for the ontology of law, the difference between essence and existence is primary, whereas the difference between Being and beings is only significant to the extent that it allows to bring into light the transcendental background of ontological questions".[2]

Hence, the *ontological question* of the philosophy of law is usually formulated as an issue of *existence*. A preliminary variant of such a question would understand law as a sign that guides Dasein in its everyday activities. It has, for example, been argued that because law must necessarily be connected to Dasein's authentic mode of Being, it cannot merely be available equipment such as a shovel but, indeed, a signal, a meaningful sign that directs Dasein's comportment within the parameters of a specific order.[3] As a sign, law services Dasein as an indicator that points out the background against which the world appears as meaningful. In most Continental languages, this aspect of indication can be illuminated by analysing one of the ways in which the word "right" (*Recht*, *droit*, *diritto*, *derecho*) is used in association with law: law must necessarily also be "right", only "right law" is law.[4]

Right is an equipmental being the in-order-to of which is the communication of Dasein's understanding of law as "right", "correct", "true", and so on. Its for-the-sake-of-which is the specification of Dasein's locality and order within the world as right, that is, the structuring of Dasein's orderly world into a correct social existence. How does this specification take place?

In the previous chapter, I used the example of someone purchasing a paper at the newsstand to indicate the transparent way in which Dasein uses law as a tool. I will now take the example one step further: how can we understand the claim that this is not only what one does, but that it is also "right" and "correct" that one should pay for the paper? How can we account for the "rightness" of law?

For Heidegger, there are beings that do not function merely as equipment that Dasein uses in its everyday activities but that, at the same time, serve as indicators revealing their mode of Being and the referential context in which they function. Heidegger calls such beings signs (*Zeichen*). In its functioning, a sign points out the shared background in relation to which Dasein understands it, that is, the world. A legal sign proper such as, for example, the lined asphalt of a crosswalk is not merely a representational relationship between, say, a painted image on the asphalt surface and a legally defined place to cross the street. Like all beings, a crosswalk sign is, of course, equipment serviceable in, for example, guiding a pedestrian amidst the rush of the metropolis. But, at the same time, the sign must also be enclosed in an involvement totality in which it appears as

[2] Kaufmann, "Die ontologische Struktur des Rechts", in Kaufmann, *Rechtsphilosophie im Wandel*, pp. 104–134 at p. 121.

[3] Wolf, "Rechtsphilosophie", in Wolf, *Rechtsphilosophische Studien*, pp. 69–82 at p. 72.

[4] I have previously indicated that I prefer to use the word "correct" (*richtig*) in such instances because the English language equates "right" primarily with subjective privileges or morality. This is, however, not the case here. I hope that the reader will bear this in mind.

meaningful for Dasein: "crosswalk", "danger", "passage", "traffic", and so on. In its functioning, a sign points out this totality. For Heidegger, then, a sign does not only point to an other being and is not a representational relationship between the two. The working of signs, that is, their use in Dasein's everyday activities and their indicative function, presupposes a shared understanding of the world which the sign simultaneously reveals.[5] The sign communicates the involvement totality to, for example, both driver and pedestrian.

The attribute that right as a sign predicates to the involvement totality of law has, however, no specific function in itself. If right is not serviceable as equipment like other tools, how can Dasein understand, interpret or use it in the world? Understanding right is understanding the involvement totality of law that the sign reveals *as* right. For Heidegger, any such understanding is articulated in an assertion (*Aussage*). An assertion is a specific mode of sign with which Dasein assigns predicates to beings. Even though predicates such as natural attributes are not in themselves serviceable as equipment, assertive understanding that, for example, "law is right" or, in other words, that the involvement totality of law is right, is interpretation that must necessarily be grounded in Dasein's everyday understanding of the world. Understanding right requires the use of a sign as equipment asserting that the involvement totality of law is right.[6]

Dasein articulates the meaning (*Sinn*) of the assertion by using it, that is, by asserting that the involvement totality of law is right. The meaning of an assertion is, however, not understood as semantic signification. It is, quite simply, that the sign in question is, indeed, the given assertion or, in our case, the assertion that is used as equipment to designate that the involvement totality of law is right. An "incorrect" interpretation of an assertion is, then, to use the sign in a wrong way. With assertions, Dasein can, for example, allude to the binding character of law, its essence as power, and so on, but this is not the meaning of right as an assertion. Assertive signs that indicate to legal predicates such as efficacy, power or justice all have meanings in their own right, so to speak, but they cannot contest the meaning of right.[7]

By asserting that law is right, Dasein points out the involvement totality of law without having to use law as conventional equipment. The possibility of using is, nevertheless, always latent. Asserting about law alleges that it is serviceable as equipment. The assertion indicates that it is, indeed, right and correct to keep law intact by, for example, paying for the paper at the newsstand even when we are not involved in the practice of purchasing one. With an assertive sign, Dasein indicates or points out law without actually using it for its designated purpose, that is, keeping it intact. The assertion does, however, communicate the understanding that in order to achieve this purpose, we must use law in a particular way. Through assertions, Dasein shares its understanding of

5 Heidegger, *Sein und Zeit*, pp. 76–79 (§ 17).
6 *Ibid.*, pp. 153–154 (§ 33).
7 *Ibid.*, p. 151 (§ 32).

the world in which it dwells with other Dasein. This communicative function of assertive signs can be analysed using the same practical framework as with other serviceable beings that Dasein uses.

Right is, however, not a *theoretical* assertion predicating law with an isolated and occurrent property such as "rightness" that is dissociated from Dasein's practical involvement in the world. *An assertion is a derivative mode of interpretation that presupposes an actual or possible disturbance in Dasein's purposive comportment with law.* By merely keeping law intact, Dasein is unable to grasp the involvement totality in which law functions or, in other words, the world to which both Dasein and law belong. In its availability, law would remain transparent in a way that would inhibit any form of communicative thinking. In order to share its understanding of law and, consequently, to uphold the orderly world that is necessary for its Being-with, Dasein can use right as a sign to assert that law must be kept intact in a specific way. Only if it is right to keep law intact or, in other terms, only if law is kept intact because it is right to do so, can Dasein realise its purposive involvement within the referential whole of law. In plain terms, only right law can be law.

As a sign, right functions within the general structure of assertions in three ways.[8] First, it indicates to or points out (*Aufzeigung*) a shared context or a referential totality in which law appears as meaningful for Dasein. This pointing-out is, however, motivated. Law may involve a deficiency that can obstruct Dasein from achieving what it has set out to accomplish. We can also keep law intact by, for instance, paying for the paper merely out of generosity or fear of punishment. But only if we pay because it is right to do so, can the transaction involve true law and achieve the purpose we set out to accomplish, that is, keep law and the orderly world it founds intact. In Heideggerian terms, assertions make manifest a shared problem.

Secondly, the assertion singles out law from a nexus of available equipment and, through predication (*Prädikation*), indicates to a specific aspect: in order for law to be law, that is, to be serviceable to Dasein as law, it must also be right. In its primordial mode of Being, Dasein encounters law as available equipment. But in order to function properly, law must also possess certain qualities or aspects that can at will be pointed out with assertions. Just as a shovel must possess certain aspects of solidity and endurance in order to function properly in the digging of ditches, law must also be right. We may, for instance, also pay for the paper because we only feel that law obliges us to do so, but with the assertion we wish to differentiate one specific aspect—"rightness"—that makes law what it is. In other words, law can exist with or without its obliging power but not without "rightness".

Thirdly, the assertion functions as communication (*Mitteilung*) within Dasein's purposive involvement in the world sharing a Being-towards (*Sein-zu*) in relation to what has been pointed out and predicated. Buying papers at the

[8] *Ibid.*, pp. 154–157 (§ 33).

newsstand, an activity any Dasein can take up, involves a specific law-related problem that we have first specified and now wish to communicate. We have first pointed out the complex involvement totality of law that is involved in the simple act of purchasing a paper, and then we have emphasised a specific aspect that is necessary in the functioning of law, namely, "rightness". We now wish to communicate all this in order to uphold right law in order to secure the possibility of a shared world.

Can Dasein, then, understand "rightness" independently as an occurrent property isolated from the everyday use of law? In other words, can Dasein decontextualise law from its practical involvement in the world, postulate context-free properties such as "rightness", and thematise all this into, for example, a theory? Heidegger's answer is, of course, affirmative. Dasein *can* thematise its world with occurrent properties, but even such thematisation must necessarily take place in a shared world that "always already" precedes theoretical reflection; theory is an impoverished form of hermeneutic interpretation. Occurrentness is perceivable but, for Heidegger, intentional states such as perception must necessarily also involve Dasein's practical understanding of the world. To perceive right is to perceive that *something* is right. Therefore, Dasein's understanding of right is necessarily dependent on the use of an assertion that predicates "rightness" to law.

But even if right could be explained as an assertive sign that helps us communicate an essential feature of law, Dasein's relationship with the world remains unauthentic. The rapport between man and right law is still a matter of mundane and everyday coping, sharing a meaningful world with other Dasein. The tradition of the philosophy of law cannot accept the banality that such an account confers to law; even right law is still too much like a hefty shovel. In order to avoid the fate of becoming such a philosophy of the commonplace, the philosophy of law that is inspired by Heidegger attempts to develop the issue of Being-with into a mode of authentic existence. This approach has developed into a Continental European school of thinking that can well be called the existential philosophy of law.

II

By far the most elegant attempt to develop an existential interpretation of Heidegger's Dasein analytics in relation to law is Werner Maihofer's unfortunately short-lived elaboration of the social premises of Being-with from the mid-1950s. Maihofer's existential philosophy of law, comprising of only two short books and a handful of articles, addresses the relationship between Dasein's Being-in-the-world and a specific mode of juridical existence: Being-in-the-law (*im-Recht-Sein*).[9] This formulation indicates that Maihofer understands law

[9] Once again, the English language fails us here. *Im-Recht-sein*, literally "Being-in-the-right", also means "doing the right thing", that one's actions are ethically correct.

primarily as an order in which Dasein exists. The order structures Dasein's existence in a disclosure with other Dasein. Although Maihofer follows Heidegger in terminology and analysis, there is a clear indication of the influence of, for instance, Jaspers: the ontology of law is understood in terms of existential philosophy.

The turn to existential analysis is also worked out in detail. Maihofer refers to Heidegger's writings on *dikē* as a conclusive order of human existence and infers that law must somehow be an expression of the authenticity of Being. It is, however, impossible to find a corresponding notion between Dasein's unauthentic relations with other Dasein in its everyday existence and the authenticity of *dikē*. Dasein's Being-in-the-world must, then, include an authentic aspect which can be found in the social mode of its Being. Therefore, Maihofer concludes, the ontology of law must necessarily be existential. Being-with cannot be restricted to unauthentic Being under the conforming influence of the "one".

Maihofer's reservations *vis-à-vis* Heidegger are rather obvious. He gives priority to the domain of the public stating that, within the social, there are necessarily modes of Being-with that do not belong to the unauthentic. Authentic Being can also exist as social human Being that is not Being-self (*Selbstsein*) but, rather, Being-as (*Alssein*), that is, existence in the world with the other "as" something.[10] Here Maihofer's existential philosophy of law is alarmingly close to an instrumentalism that would invalidate his very aim. In the world, Dasein understands beings as fit for specific jobs. Heidegger states that Dasein comes across a hammer as (*als*) a hammer, and this "indication 'fit for' [*Dienstlichkeit zu*] is, therefore, an ontologico-categorical characteristic of the equipment *as* equipment".[11] For Maihofer, then, Dasein encounters other Dasein in the same way as it comes across equipment "fit for" specific purposes, and for Heidegger, this would indicate, for instance, the way in which Dasein reads literature or appreciates art.

But for Maihofer, Being-as refers to the correlative and reciprocal existential relations between Dasein engaged in a world that they share. One exists "as" a newspaper dealer for the other just as the other exists "as" a customer for the keeper of the newsstand. These existential relations are not inferred from juridico-economical institutions such as commerce or contract. They constitute, in an original way, the comportment of Dasein within its world. They are *existential roles which form the basis of law's ontological existence*. Such an explanation would only amount to a descriptive account of how individual human beings relate to each other in a social space if Maihofer did not attempt to establish the way in which such an original order also constitutes Dasein in relation to the other. Within the order of law that this existential ontology elaborates, Dasein is engaged in interdependent relationships with others: the dealer does not exist without his customer, and vice versa. Such interdependency creates

[10] Maihofer, *Recht und Sein*, p. 114, and Maihofer, *Vom Sinn menschlicher Ordnung*, pp. 47–52. See also Thyssen, "Zur Rechtsphilosophie des Als-seins".

[11] Heidegger, *Sein und Zeit*, p. 73 (§ 17).

mutual expectations and, with them, the possibility to anticipate the interests of one another.[12] This possibility constitutes the normative aspect of law and, simultaneously, the ethical quality of human existence. As Dasein is cast into the world, it is also cast into the order of law. In Being-in-the-law, then, ontology and ethics come together as social existence:

> "*ought* is not the opposite of *is*, but the *forerunning projection* [*Vorausentwurf*] *of Being* itself. Not into an 'other' world, a 'superworld' of ideas and values, but focused into the always *futural* [*zukünftig*] *authenticity* of the *Being* of beings that is *to-come* [*zu-kommen*] in 'this' world and is seen here in the *pro-jection*. Therefore, 'worlds' do not separate is and ought from each other, *ontology* and *ethics* are not 'indifferent' in relation to one another. On the contrary, *individual ethics* and *social ethics* are both attempts to indicate in advance [*Vor-zeichnung*] to man's projection into the authenticity of his Being, of *Being-self* as well as of *Being-as*".[13]

In order to dissociate himself from the dangers of the functionalism that is inherent in his earlier analyses, Maihofer later develops his existential philosophy of law by elaborating the difference between the unauthenticity of Being-with and the co-existence of Dasein as persons. Dasein is a co-existential relation in which the question of justice must necessarily arise. A *persona* is not only a participant in the discourse of justice, but also an essential (*wesentlich*) phenomenon in the ontological relations that constitute what is called normative reality. Dasein has, then, also a juridical aspect to it that is related to the world surrounding it, to its *Umwelt*.[14] Dasein's relationship with available equipment is not only characterised by functional availability, but also by a specific enjoining order (*Verfügbarkeit*). Different persons relate to equipment in different ways, and as Dasein, a person does not only relate to equipment in its own surrounding world, but also in another strange setting. This designates the basic difference between Dasein and person: for the person, the surrounding existential world encompasses "my" availableness and enjoining order as well as "yours". This difference extends from the level of Being-human and the social level of Being-as all the way through to the person's level of Being-self. The ontological relationships between persons constitute the heuristic horizon through which Dasein interprets its own Being. It furnishes the foundation of both normative discourse and the factual situations of justice.[15] The key to the understanding of the Being-with of persons is, then, relation, not as a category, but as a scheme of co-existence.[16]

In his early work on law, Nicos Poulantzas criticises Maihofer for ignoring the basic claims of French existentialism in his analysis. Maihofer attempts to

[12] Maihofer, *Recht und Sein*, p. 23; Maihofer, *Vom Sinn menschlicher Ordnung*, pp. 86–89.

[13] Maihofer, *Recht und Sein*, p. 122, n. 121.

[14] Maihofer, "Recht und Personalität", in Haft et al (eds), *Strafgerechtigkeit*, pp. 219–248 at pp. 228–231.

[15] *Ibid.*, pp. 231–237.

[16] *Ibid.*, pp. 246–248. Cf. Maihofer, "Anthropologie der Koexistenz", in Hollerbach et al (eds), *Mensch und Recht*, pp. 162–211 at pp. 166–167.

constitute the authenticity of the social domain, but he allegedly fails to acknowledge the only ontological given that can make any such authenticity possible, namely, freedom. In order to assess the expectations of the other, Dasein must first acknowledge its own freedom.[17] A more "existentialist" version of Dasein's social existence is also offered by Charles Donius. His original point of departure is a phenomenological analysis of law, but with the help of Heidegger, Donius wishes to furnish his phenomenology with an existential tone. The philosophy of law is directed by the concept of history which is the true history of man as the unity of past, present and future. History is meaningful as sense because it is the locality where human Being flourishes and where it communicates with the other. The science of law that is sustained by the tradition is insufficient because, in its temporal quality, it is necessarily posterior in relation to the phenomenon that it studies. Only a philosophical perspective to law can supply a proper justification for the science of law:

> "Law [*Droit*], the history of Law and the philosophy of Law coincide because they are concurrent . . . the philosophy of Law is commentary to Law that *temporalises* itself and to history that *legalises* itself".[18]

Donius criticises Maihofer of a certain formalism that would call for a radicalisation of the existential preconditions on which his philosophy of law is founded. The social objective of the philosophy of law, Donius concludes, is to indicate the philosophical and the historical continuity of juridical institutions and their sense.[19]

Erich Fechner's point of departure is also the problematic question concerning the unauthenticity of law. As equipment, law operates merely as a functional entity without any essential connection to human existence as such. Therefore, the ordering aspect of law is juxtaposed with Dasein's possibility of Being.[20] The first question concerns the specific way in which law "is", its *Seinsweise*. Law must necessarily be more than equipment or a mere sign, but the meaning of this further dimension must be worked out. Law is language that serves Dasein in its understanding of the world of equipment. But as the Being of language is that of Dasein itself (*daseinsmäßig*), the Being of law must also correspond with Dasein's own mode of Being.[21] Law operates in the social world of the *Mitwelt*.[22] There is, then, an exterior relationship between law and existence. This constitutes the mediate sense of law: law furnishes "protection and boundaries for the space in which Dasein (as possible existence) can announce itself".[23]

17 Poulantzas, "Notes sur la phénoménologie et l'existentialisme juridiques", pp. 229–235. Cf. Poulantzas, *Nature des choses*, pp. 116–131.

18 Donius, "Existentialisme, phénoménologie et philosophie du droit", p. 228.

19 *Ibid.*, pp. 229–231.

20 Fechner, *Rechtsphilosophie*, pp. 227–228.

21 *Ibid.*, pp. 230–231.

22 "Dasein's world is a world-with [*Mitwelt*]. Being-in is *Being-with* others. Dasein's innerworldly Being-in-itself is Being-there-with [*Mitdasein*]": Heidegger, *Sein und Zeit*, p. 118 (§ 26).

23 Fechner, *Rechtsphilosophie*, p. 233.

But there is also a more immediate sense to law, and this is where Fechner's Jaspersian influences are most obvious. Law involves an existential choice: law is Dasein's lot. It marks the dividing line between a two-fold possibility: to be either cast into the world of unauthenticity, or to push forward to authentic Being. Dasein can acknowledge the world in an indifferent manner, but it can also recognise it as decisively important. Existence emerges as a reality in the tension between these two choices. If Fechner has taken such a point of departure, it is not hard to understand why he regards Heidegger's philosophy as "mere nihilism".[24] For Fechner, freedom is not an attribute of man, but rather vice versa: freedom or, in other words, ek-sistent Dasein, occupies man. If Dasein is viewed from this existential perspective, true law is a bond with the enclosure of Being. Law is the announcement of Being in Dasein that "is".[25]

III

Regardless of its sources of inspiration, an existential account of law reduces the radicality of Heidegger's philosophy into a scheme of the human condition as social existence in the order of Being-with. Gadamer emphasises that:

> " 'Being-with' does not mean the Being-with-one-another of two subjects, but an original manner of Being-us. It does not complement I through a Thou, but embraces it in a primary togetherness'.[26]

For my purposes, the relationship between law and Dasein's authentic mode of Being remains open. An ontological account of law is possible only if the question of Being is itself examined as a possibility of Dasein's authenticity.[27] But because law seems to be situated in the surrounding social world that can only account for Dasein's unauthentic Being, the more profound question concerning law and authenticity remains to be elaborated. As we have seen, one response would be to deny the unauthentic nature of Dasein's social world, a route that Maihofer and others seem to follow with the help of existential philosophy, a question that Jean-Luc Nancy—much later and without necessary implications for the philosophy of law—takes up by radicalising Heidegger's notion of Being-with.[28] Regardless of what route is taken, such responses seem to insist on the relationship between law and the domain of the social. Another possible route would be to develop a *fundamental ontology of law*: law is somehow more directly related to the question of Being. Law is not equipment that

[24] Fechner, *Rechtsphilosophie*, p. 254. Cf. Rosenmayr, "Gesellschaftsbild und Kulturkritik Martin Heideggers".

[25] Fechner, *Rechtsphilosophie*, p. 256.

[26] Gadamer, "Existentialismus und Existenzphilosophie", in Gadamer, *Neuere Philosophie I. Hegel—Husserl—Heidegger*, pp. 175–185, at p. 184.

[27] Heidegger, *Sein und Zeit*, pp. 13–14 (§ 4).

[28] Cf. Nancy, *La communauté désœuvrée*, pp. 220–225. On Nancy's position *vis-à-vis* Heidegger in general, see, e.g., Nancy, *L'expérience de la liberté*, pp. 51–63.

Dasein uses while it dwells in its world but, rather, a structural component of Being itself.

Such an approach is suggested in Heidegger's reading of *dikē* in the fragment of Anaximander of Miletus. Things present, things that linger in the while of their presence, are "out of joint": in presence, things are not right, they are "incorrect" or *adikon*. On the other hand, *dikē* as jointure belongs to Being understood as presencing, as things coming into their while only to withdraw again. *Dikē* is, then, the order that conjoins two absences to presence surmounting the disorder of things present. The while in which things linger as what they are is a transitory moment related to a future that approaches from what has not yet come to be or past away and remains, then, to come.[29]

Within critical legal scholarship, there is a clear temptation—perhaps triggered by Derrida's reading of Heidegger's text[30]—to work out the order of *dikē* into a juridico-moral metaphysics of justice, as a just future realisable with the help of juridical technology, that is, with critical legal policies. In my mind, this would, however, repeat the error of existential readings of Heidegger: Dasein as human Being is understood as the social existence of the *zōon politikon*. But, as Heidegger himself points out in several places, "[i]f we translate *dikē* as 'justice' and understand it in a juridico-moral way, the word loses its grounding metaphysical content".[31]

Among the few attempts within the philosophy of law to conceive of a metaphysical understanding of *dikē* is the work of Erik Wolf.[32] For Wolf, an ontology of law (*Rechtsontologie*) addresses the relationship between law and Being: Is law? Does law exist? How does law relate to Being? A preliminary answer to the *Seinsfrage* of law is offered by the various modes of ontic inquiry into law understood as a being—positivism, rationalism, voluntarism, phenomenology, and so on—but, as the preliminary introduction of *Sein und Zeit* will indicate, an ontic inquiry is unable to attain the Dasein of law, that is, the specific way in which law appears for Dasein. The point of departure of the ontology of law is, then, the ontological difference, the inconvertibility of Being-right (*Rechtsein*) and law as a being (*Rechtseiende*). Wolf claims that law is neither an unauthentic aspect of some other being nor a deficient mode of Being. Its essence (*Wesen*) is not located in the domain of the public; it unfolds (*es west*) in Being-with and

[29] Heidegger, *Holzwege*, pp. 329–332 and 352–361. On *dikē*, see also Heidegger, *Hölderlins Hymnen "Germanien" und "Der Rhein"*, pp. 123–129, and Heidegger, *Einführung in die Metaphysik*, pp. 167–170 and 174–176.

[30] Cf. Derrida, *Spectres de Marx*, pp. 55–57.

[31] Heidegger, *Einführung in die Metaphysik*, p. 169. For similar reasons, I find Robert Bernasconi's "ethical" assessment of *dikē* and justice (*Gerechtigkeit*) in Heidegger captivating and, yet, paradoxical. See Bernasconi, "Justice and the Twilight Zone of Morality, in Bernasconi, *Heidegger in Question*, pp. 40–55.

[32] Wolf, "Rechtsphilosophie", in Wolf, *Rechtsphilosophische Studien*, pp. 64–82, at pp. 71–72. Wolf was Heidegger's colleague during the strenuous years at Freiburg. As dean of the Faculty of Law during Heidegger's rectorship, he also shares with Heidegger a debatable relation to the Nazi government before the Second World War.

Being-for which are preconditions of authentic Being-self.[33] Law is not merely available equipment that Dasein manipulates isolated from other Dasein but, rather, assignment (*Weisung*).[34]

Wolf founds his fundamental ontology of law on two short citations from early Heidegger.[35] The first is from Heidegger's reading of Nietzsche's affirmation on the death of God in *Holzwege*, and Wolf contends that the following passage reveals Heidegger's determination of justice:

> "The just is that which is in conformity with right [*das Rechte*]; but what is right is determined from what, for beings, is to be [*was als Seiendes seiend ist*]".[36]

In other words, it is a question concerning a particular futural sense of Being. A few lines above the quoted passage, Heidegger reminds us that, for Nietzsche, justice is not primarily the determination of the ethical and juridical domains. The thinking of justice and right commences from the Being of beings.[37] With the determination of right in the Being of beings, Wolf couples Heidegger's notion of the necessary relationship between truth and Dasein:

> " 'There is' [*es gibt*] Being—not beings—only in so far as truth is. And truth *is* only in so far as and as long as Dasein is. Being and truth 'are' equiprimordial".[38]

From these passages, Wolf concludes that the truth of law can only be revealed in its mode of Being (*Rechtsdasein*). The truth of law as a being is true justice that is determined in accordance with right. Right, on the other hand, is determined from whatever is to be right in law understood as a being, while the latter is, finally, determined from Being. These sentences are neither circular nor elements of a chain of rational thought but, rather, road marks that assign the direction of thinking.

Wolf's reading of *dikē* involves three questions. The philosophical question addresses the dialectical unity of historicality (*Geschichtlichkeit*) and truth; the poetic question addresses the way in which poesy brings something of the essence of truth into the clearing; and, finally, the historical question addresses how this revelation has been brought to its conclusion in an original and compelling way in the thinking and the poetising of the early Greeks. A disciplined historical inquiry is but escape from the present, whereas historicality is the essence of the ever-present spirit. As law exists historically in the way of a spiritual Dasein and, as part of history, is only comprehensible as spirit, the essence

[33] I hesitate to translate *Wesen* as essence and, thus, participate in a reduction of Wolf's ontology to naive essentialism. The old German verb *wesen* that is also frequently used by Heidegger has usually been translated as "to occur essentially" and "to come to be and unfold".

[34] "In Greek, to assign [*zuweisen*] is *nemein. Nomos* is not only law but more originally the assignment [*Zuweisung*] contained in the dispensation of Being. Only the assignment is capable of conjoining man into Being. Only conjoining is capable of supporting and binding. Otherwise all law remains merely a fabrication of human reason": Heidegger, *Wegmarken*, pp. 360–361.

[35] Wolf, "Rechtsphilosophie", p. 72.

[36] Heidegger, *Holzwege*, p. 247.

[37] Cf. Schürmann, *Le principe d'anarchie*, pp. 233–236.

[38] Heidegger, *Sein und Zeit*, p. 304 (§ 44).

of law is its historicality. Spirit can be and become only what it originally was. The essence that appears as law is the same at any given moment in history and must be comprehended as meaningful in relation to Being-with-another and Being-for-another. History is not, then, what has come about, it is what comes to be. This takes place in the event (*Ereignis*), the ever-present, the eternal Being of ephemeral beings.[39]

The cultural value of Antiquity is social and ethical in the sense that it involves an obligation to regard the essential and to waive the arbitrary. This obligation concerns primarily the duties of everyday Dasein of which one is the sheltering (*Hut*) and the attendance of law. Wolf responds to this obligation by observing what the early Greeks brought into the clearing as the essence of law. The image of Antiquity so observed is the origin (*archē*), the uncovering of the lasting and primordial essence in which pre-Christian man became himself in his encounter with the gods and the cosmos. In the spiritual world of the early Greeks, the human spirit comes to be in its historical truth. The historical unity of the spiritual attempts to convey the essence of Being-in-the-world into appearance are determined from historical Dasein and indicate back to it. The determination of the historical truth of Being-in-the-world in the thinking and the poetising of pre-Socratic Greece necessarily precedes any Platonic or Aristotelian understanding of law as an idea or a category; truth (*alētheia*) is the primordial uncovering of Being-right.[40]

IV

Wolf's fundamental ontology of law is mainly built on three words which he reads and interprets from Homeric poetry. First, *themistes* is the ordering aspect of law; it is the rectifying or corrective assignment with which the gods or their human envoys address Dasein's world.[41] Secondly, the order so stipulated is *themis*: "*so gilt es*", "it is so ordered". This does not concern the social sphere of human existence—*themis* is neither natural law nor political order—but an assertion on Dasein that is "in the law". To exist within the order of *themis* is essential Being, to be "in the law" as that which it is.[42] Thirdly, *dikē* is neither law nor rule as it is usually translated. It is appeal and solicitation, the demand for and the allotment of essential Being as what comes to be (*Zukommende*). *Dikē* is, then, the coming into the order of *themis* in the assignment of *themistes*.[43]

The verb *zukommen* on which Wolf structures his whole interpretation of *dikē* indicates how law is related to the temporality of Being. The temporal

[39] Wolf, *Griechisches Rechtsdenken I*, pp. 9–12.
[40] *Ibid.*, pp. 14–18.
[41] *Ibid.*, pp. 72–76.
[42] *Ibid.*, pp. 76–84.
[43] *Ibid.*, pp. 107–112.

mode of law is the future (*Zukunft*), the *à-venir*, the *advent* or the coming into Being of beings. Heidegger interprets *dikē* as the order of Being; for Wolf, however, it is the "right" of Being. To be "in the law" is right as the advent of the Being of all beings, their coming into Being. Beings cannot be thought without *dikē*; the wrong is the unessential, that is, not coming into Being.

Wolf seems to combine together two different aspects in Heidegger's philosophy. On the one hand, he seems to agree with Heidegger's interpretation in which *dikē* translates into order (*Fug*), but continues to make a reservation:

> "although it [Heidegger's translation] touches upon the essential of the matter, it does not say clearly enough what *dikē* 'conjoins', namely the allotment of what is to come, the claim to what is to come, and what is to come as each's ownmost future"[44].

In Heidegger, the verb *zukommen* employed by Wolf throughout his fundamental ontology of law can be found in the Marburg lectures on temporality from 1927. Of the three *ekstasis* of original temporality (*Zeitlichkeit*), Heidegger gives priority to the future:

> "Dasein understands itself by way of its ownmost peculiar capacity to be [*Seinkönnen*] of which it is expectant. In thus comporting toward its ownmost peculiar capacity to be, *it is ahead of itself*. Expecting a possibility, I come from this possibility toward that which I myself am. Dasein, expecting its ability to be, *comes toward itself*. In this coming-toward-itself [*Auf-sich-zukommen*], Dasein is *futural* [*zukünftig*] in an original sense".[45]

This is where Wolf decisively parts with Heidegger. He emphasises that Dasein's futural mode of Being must include a particular faith. While Dasein is expectant of its capacity to be, it is also tainted with a guilt (*Schuld*). This guilt is an indication of a fore-order of Being-in-the-wrong (*Im-Unrecht-sein*), a fundamentally wrongful or "incorrect" mode of Being that constitutes Dasein's mundane existence. In this unauthenticity, Dasein can only expect a right to come. The faith that Dasein invests into its expectant mode of existence and the guilt that follows thereof together imply a debt for an original donation.[46] All that Dasein has been given in this original gift of Being is the possibility of a right to come for which Dasein, in its guilt, is in debt. In the fore-order of the wrong or, in other words, in its "normal" and worldly existence, Dasein has access to the expected right to come only as a calling that constitutes Dasein's ability to respond, its response-ability. True right of which Dasein can only be expectant is the final revelation of beings that come to be as what they essentially are. Only this true right can deliver Dasein from the fore-order of the wrong in which

[44] Wolf, *Griechisches Rechtsdenken I*, p. 288. Here Wolf refers to Heidegger's Freiburg lectures on Parmenides from 1942/1943. See Heidegger, *Parmenides*, pp. 135–140.

[45] Heidegger, *Die Grundprobleme der Phänomenologie*, pp. 374–375. Cf. Heidegger, *Sein und Zeit*, p. 436 (§ 65): "The primary phenomenon of original and authentic temporality is the future".

[46] "The truth of Being donates the duration [*Halt*] for all that is concealed [*Verhalten*]": Heidegger, *Wegmarken*, p. 361. Agamben states that man is originally in debt only because his ownmost Being is to exist as his possibility and potentiality (*potenza*): Agamben, *La communità che viene*, pp. 30–31.

Dasein dwells in its worldly existence. Every attempt to rectify the world is only a technology that concurrently marks a resignation from the future to come, that is, from true right. If, then, Dasein evokes an apparent right into the light of day, it also turns away from and rejects its ownmost essence.[47]

Wolf's reservations concerning the juridical technology referred to above are, however, not nihilistic. Dasein responds to the call of the right to come of which it is expectant by maintaining (*Haltung*) the possibility of Being-in-the-law. When the other is allowed to come into the right or, in other words, when Dasein maintains the possibility of the other to come to be as what it essentially is, what is to come as Dasein's ownmost future and, consequently, the Being-in-the-law that lies beyond Dasein's worldly existence in the wrong, approaches and comes forward. But maintaining is not rectifying non-rights, it is not righting wrongs. It is merely the devout awaiting of what is to come. If Dasein does not await, it presumes either to have right already at its disposal or to be able to posit it. For Wolf, the hubris of such juridical technology is the jointure (*Fügung*) of the wrong in which Dasein can only evade (*entkommen*) what is essentially to come (*zukommen*).[48]

Dasein's finite nature is conclusively revealed in the decision (*Entscheidung*). The locality of such a decision is a juridical court (*Gericht*). Because Dasein is primordially responsible—Dasein is able to respond to the call of true right—the court must not be adjourned. Wolf argues that, in this metaphysical court of law, men, heroes and gods must all alike decide what is to come (*dikē*) and what is not (*adikia*).[49] But all that Dasein can recognise as right is merely temporary, not what is finally to come, for true right is always futural (*zukünftig*) and postponed. Even if the present reign of monsters and demons is not final, only the court of God can decisively rule the essence of Dasein as true right and annul the nothingness of Dasein's worldly existence in the wrong. The court of God, however, also involves an element of mercy in that it also embodies the promise of a future to come for everything that dwells evading in the fore-order of the wrong. This promise is the call to which Dasein can respond by maintaining the possibility of Being-in-the-law. But only what is to come as true right can liberate Dasein from its temporal existence as *persona*. In its supra-temporal and infinite mode of Being, Dasein will finally be delivered from the wrong.[50]

Right and wrong, the finite and the infinite, are, then, indispensably bound together; the wrong also has its jointure. Even when philosophy addresses right in a question, what is to come is unthinkable without the wrong that evades the decisive coming. Evading right reveals an opening and renders a brief view (*Blick*) of what is to come. On the other hand, if right appears as self-evident, truth conceals itself. Being and the true right to come are unveiled only where a self-evident world is questioned. For Wolf, the insistence of this worthy

[47] Wolf, *Vom Wesen des Rechts in deutscher Dichtung*, pp. 335–337.
[48] *Ibid.*, p. 283.
[49] *Ibid.*, p. 229.
[50] *Ibid.*, p. 259.

question constitutes the dialectics of incertitude (*Fragwürdigkeit*) and necessity (*Notwendigkeit*) without which a philosophy of law would be impossible.[51]

The ability to respond by maintaining the possibility of Being-in-the-law is also Dasein's correct (*richtig*) mode of Being. In language, this correctness is effected through assignment (*Weisung*). Even if Dasein's fate is to dwell in the fore-order of the wrong, it would be correct to let things into the right, that is, to allow them to come to be as what they essentially are. Dasein can achieve this only by abstaining from the realisation of right. In correctness, Dasein acknowledges that it is not in the right and retains from knowing what is to come and what its consequent lot will be. Nor does Dasein possess right; in correctness, Dasein waives any right to facilitate in the present what is to come in the future. Lastly, in correctness, Dasein does not posit right. It refrains from realising right in any conclusive way because juridical technology cannot release Dasein from its original debt. In other words, Dasein must yield to its own finitude. Dasein is attuned (*Bestimmung*) to go its way in the fore-order of the wrong and to respond to the call of right within its ability to maintain. But Dasein's worldly way (*Gang*) is also a passage beyond (*Übergang*) where it may encounter the prospect of experiencing its futural essence to come, that is, true right.[52]

In an encyclopedia entrance on the philosophy of law from 1961, Wolf attempts to gather together his notion of right as what is to come.[53] This short and dense passage commences with the assertion that there "are" (*es gibt*, *il y a*) right beings in the world (*hē gar dikē esti*). Right beings that are just in truth are right things (*rechte Dinge*, *ta dikaia*). Beings that are truly just are in accordance with right (*kata to dikaion*), they are appropriate. To be right does not add an additional quality to beings, nor does it involve an ethical evaluation. If a being is "right", it is merely what it is or, in other words, the thing it is. It is, then, a right thing (*to dikaion*), and a righteous man being (*ho dikaios*) corresponds (*entsprechen*) with rightness by articulating (*aussprechen*) the ontological essence of right beings (*ho logos dikanikos*). This articulation takes place in the right word (*dikaios logos*). The corresponding is, then, what is in accordance with right (*to dikaiōma*), and accordance with right (*hē dikaiotēs*) determines all that is just in right beings.

If right beings are determined from Being, then Being is to come to right beings. In other words, right beings will come to be (*hē dikē*). What is to come to beings is their ownmost (*to heauton*), and the ownmost that is to come to beings is the temporal mode of to come (*dikaiōs*). In such a temporality, beings are in the right (*endikos*). Therefore, beings that are to come to be are truly to come or, in other words, right (*to dikaion*). Coming to be takes place in justice (*dikaiosunē*) which articulates itself in appropriate speech (*ta dikaia legein*).

[51] Wolf, *Vom Wesen des Rechts in deutscher Dichtung*, p. 211. See also Wolf, "Fragwürdigkeit und Notwendigkeit geschichtlicher Rechtsphilosophie", in Würtenberger (ed.), *Quaestiones et responsa*, pp. 31–41.

[52] Wolf, *Vom Wesen des Rechts in deutscher Dichtung*, pp. 337–338.

[53] Wolf, "Rechtsphilosophie", pp. 72–73.

What is always to come to right beings is the supreme right that is to come (*to dikaiotaton*).

But what is to come also evades (*entkommen*) the other (*to adikon*). In the wrong (*adikos*), what is not to come (*hē adikia*) takes place and allows the evasion of what is to come (*adikein*). On the other hand, what is to come is acquired (*dikēn dounai*) by letting what is to come take place (*dikēn didonai*). All that is to come is firmly posited (*themisteuein*) in corresponding and corrective judgement (*themiton*). What is firmly posited (*thesmos*) is the ground from which corrective judgements (*themistes*) affirm (*zusprechen*) what is to come as correspondence. It is the grounding (*archē*), the joining (*tuchē*), and the binding (*anagkē*) of Being-right (*themis einai*).

V

Wolf's fundamental ontology of right is, no doubt, prone to the critique of rigorous readings on many levels. Even if the philosophy of law was willing to accept the metaphysical presumptions on which Wolf's enigmatic thinking is founded, its complexity and peculiarity in relation to the juridical culture as it is usually understood cause resistance. For my part, the merits of Wolf's thinking are not to be found in the way he regards law as a part of the social order, but in the way he understands philosophy. *A philosophy of law is not an ontic or a regional investigation into an entity called "law", but an inquiry concerning the juridical moment of metaphysics itself*, about what I have previously called "correctness". Correctness depicts the peculiar way in which Dasein addresses Being with the idioms of law. "*Ein rechter Mensch*", "*ein richtiger Mensch*": a human being that is "correct", "real", "true". The ultimate right, that is, the future of right things to come understood as, perhaps, justice, remains ultimately a matter for the courts of the divinities. Correctness is man's response to the call of the ultimate right.

But Wolf's metaphysical account of law is of a rather distinct character. In addition to the more or less obvious pitfalls of metaphysical thinking, that is, the dubious archaeology of Greek origins, the hantology of the spiritual Dasein, the eschatology of deliverance, and so on, Wolf cannot purge himself from the double bind of right and Being. Instead of continuing his analysis by way of elaborating on the relationship between right and the temporality of the future, he seems to retreat anticipating the devastating consequences of a destruction that is taken to its conclusion.

For Wolf, then, *dikē* as what is to come is not only Being-right, but also the right *to* Being of all beings. Such a right can only be thought from a juridico-moral metaphysics that precedes and determines the foundations of the *Seinsfrage*. The interplay between Being-right and the pre-ontological right to Being suggest a translation of *Zukommende* as *due* rather than as the advent. Right is not only due as the temporality of the advent, but also as an event that will come to take place according to a rightful necessity. As the due of all beings, such a right to Being reaffirms the onto-theological ground that a fundamental ontology of right was set to destruct.

We return to the insistent question: is a philosophy of law after Heidegger possible? Perhaps aware of the strained paradoxes in his affiliation with Heidegger, Wolf dedicates his later years to the elaboration of theological issues related to law. His writings on justice and the other as the neighbour, inspired by the theology of Karl Barth,[54] resonate curiously with much of what is currently done in critical legal scholarship on law and Levinas. The danger that lies in such undertakings is that an ethics that is simply deemed and declared "pre-ontological" will be understood merely as a haven of retreat, as a withdrawal from the fundamental questions concerning the possibility and impossibility of law, right and justice.

[54] Wolf, *Recht des Nächsten.* I shall return to Wolf's theology of law in the final chapter of this book.

5

A Peculiar Economy

"All understanding, all knowledge, however limited and 'scientific', presupposes a frame of reference; it presupposes a horizon, a comprehensive view within which understanding and knowing take place. Only such a comprehensive vision makes possible any seeing, any observation, any orientation. The comprehensive view of the whole cannot be validated by reasoning, since it is the basis of all reasoning."

Leo Strauss

I

Throughout the foregoing chapters, I have argued that contemporary critical legal scholarship has implicated itself in Heidegger's philosophy while being more or less unaware of previous engagements that have taken place within the philosophy of law. Critical legal scholarship, rather uninterested in either phenomenological or existential accounts of law, has found Heidegger mainly through the philosophy of Jacques Derrida. Although the relationship between Heidegger's "destruction" and Derrida's "deconstruction" is well known even in juridical circles, the finalistic nature of the critical jurist's enterprise has conditioned the way in which both Heidegger and Derrida have been read and understood. My argument has maintained that any *philosophy* of law must necessarily be a metaphysics, and I have tried to depict my own version of such an undertaking through the notion of "correctness". Along the way, however, my reservations concerning critical legal scholarship and its appropriation of either Heidegger or Derrida have remained laconic and undocumented. It is now time to return to critical legal scholarship and, in the form of an excursion, inspect in more detail the issue concerning its possible philosophical implications.

The *critical question* of the philosophy of law addresses the possibility of a metaphysical account of law as departure from the tradition of Occidental thinking. Can the philosophy of law as metaphysics be critical? How can the "destruction" or the "deconstruction" of the philosophical tradition imply criticism in the sense that critical legal scholarship seems to understand it? Can the "deconstruction of dominant legal structures", as one of the proverbial expressions of critical legal scholarship would have it, be utilised in a "politics of empowerment"? One of the intricacies involved here is to retrace some of the grounds for such an understanding of, indeed, practically everything that comes under the banner of "Continental philosophy" despite the numerous reservations and cautions that have been presented.

A preliminary remark can be made: critical legal scholarship was—and is—primarily an Anglo-American phenomenon. This also involves a particular understanding of "Continental philosophy", an understanding that is at the core of numerous trans-Atlantic debates within philosophy proper. But because virtually no such thing as "critical Continental philosophy of law" exists, the "paradigm" of critical legal scholarship is essentially founded on an Anglo-American emphasis on the centrality of social issues relating to law. As an attempt to appropriate and to rectify the misfortunes of human existence, legal deconstruction, for instance, is primarily understood as the critique of the social domain.

In this chapter, I will attempt to address the possibility of such a critique through the notion of tradition. I will first indicate how this notion has come to be as significant as it is for "Continental" jurisprudence through the hermeneutics of Hans-Georg Gadamer. The key to understanding Gadamer's allegedly conservative appraisal of tradition is the consideration that he gives to Dasein as historicality, a theme that has also been touched upon in the previous chapter. My claim, however, is that even Gadamer finds himself obliged to scientifically "found" the thinking of historicality—yet another trace of neo-Kantianism—and he does this by positing the hermeneut into a critical relationship *vis-à-vis* the philosophy of the Enlightenment. Gadamer's "conservatism" is not, then, in his emphatic assessment of tradition, but in his insistence to establish hermeneutics as a science and in the consequent revocation of historicality itself.

Like its more traditional counterpart, critical legal scholarship will readily acknowledge the significance of Gadamer's philosophical hermeneutics in any understanding of a "Continental" philosophy of law. This involves both Gadamer's relationship with Heidegger and the affinity between the "textual strategies" of deconstruction and the hermeneutic interpretation of juridical texts. But one of the essential turns that critical legal scholarship takes here signals an intentional departure from the notion of tradition that Gadamer is claimed to cherish. Deconstruction, then, is a critical rejection of the juridical tradition that Gadamer's hermeneutics must seemingly advocate. I will try to indicate how this understanding of Gadamer is rearticulated into the possibility of deconstruction as critical legal scholarship and why such an understanding remains problematic.

II

When Rodolphe Gasché presents his reservations concerning the status of deconstruction as critique, he is, in fact, confronting critically a tradition to which he himself somehow belongs: "deconstruction in America".[1] The core of

[1] Cf. Derrida, *Mémoires pour Paul de Man*, pp. 37–38.

his argument is simple enough: deconstruction is presumed to be critical because it departs from the philosophical tradition in a radical manner. However, digression from a tradition cannot be reduced to critique, and the complex relationship between deconstruction and critique cannot be exhausted by simply referring to a departure from the philosophical tradition. Even in its singularity, deconstruction maintains a curious relationship with the tradition, and the pith of this relationship cannot be depicted as critical. Therefore, deconstruction is not critique.[2]

Even the jurist found deconstruction "in America" where it was primarily understood as a mode of social criticism. Within critical legal scholarship, the term "deconstruction" came to be used to describe a theory of interpretation with which juridical texts are close-read emphasising and emancipating meanings that the legal tradition has silenced.[3] The tradition, it is said, speaks the tongue of the white European male, and the inadvertent repetition of this language merely renews and enhances the fundamental legal structures of Occidental society. For the scholar of law, then, deconstruction is first and foremost a textual strategy that enables the other to speak and to recount its tale.

But regardless of Gasché's reservations, critical legal scholarship seems to think that Derrida himself has somehow authorised the emancipatory project by taking part—especially in his text *Force de loi*—in the discussion concerning deconstruction and the critique of law.[4] It should, however, be noted that even Derrida cautions about the dangers of identifying the philosophy of deconstruction with the project of critical legal scholarship,[5] and with reference to critique, Gasché has restated and clarified this caution.[6]

What are, then, the central arguments here? Gasché is himself in the odd position of having to articulate his cautioning statement as, indeed, a critique of "deconstruction in America", as a critical account of the philosophy of deconstruction that is understood as either "play" and "game" or "theory". Even if the core of Gasché's argument is addressed to the sciences of literature—or, to be

[2] Gasché, *The Tain of the Mirror*, p. 125. Gasché, "The Law of Tradition," in Gasché, *Inventions of Difference*, pp. 58–81, at p. 59. On the Heideggerian "tradition" of deconstruction in general, see Gasché, *The Tain of the Mirror*, pp. 109–111. Cf. Rapaport, *Heidegger and Derrida*, pp. 79–96. On the problems of situating Heidegger within the—especially Hegelian—tradition, see Marx, *Heidegger und die Tradition*.

[3] "Like psychoanalysis, deconstructive readings of texts offer the possibility of emancipation from customary ways of thinking. Deconstruction operates by a momentary reversal of privileging. This reversal alters our view of the privileging, just as the act of uncovering repressed material liberates the psychoanalytic patient": Balkin, "Deconstructive Practice and Legal Theory", 765–766. On the political implications of "deconstructive emancipation", see, e.g., Fish, *Doing What Comes Naturally*, pp. 494–496, and Rosenfeld, "Deconstruction and Legal Interpretation: Conflict, Indeterminacy and the Temptations of New Legal Formalism," in Cornell et al (eds), *Deconstruction and the Possibility of Justice*, pp. 152–210.

[4] According to Bennington's "authorised" general presentation, *Force de loi* and the debate it engendered "emphasised in an important way the rapid progress of 'deconstructive' research within the philosophy of law and legal theory (*critical legal studies*) in the United States": Bennington and Derrida, *Jacques Derrida*, p. 308.

[5] Derrida, *Force de loi*, pp. 24–26.

[6] Gasché, "On Critique, Hypercriticism, and Deconstruction: The Case of Benjamin".

more specific, to "literary criticism"—his observations have apparent analogies with critical legal scholarship, as well. How, then, is deconstruction understood as critical legal scholarship?

On the one hand, we have the *gaya scienza* referred to before that, with the help of more or less free association, explores the pristine reservoirs of signification and meaning by exploiting the interpretative possibilities that the term "play" seems to grant. The verbal play of legal scholarship, unleashed from the restrictive chains of scientific thought and method, is critical in as much as it is founded on an intentional confrontation with the tradition of the Enlightenment that has allegedly exhausted its philosophical and social impetus. In this sense, play is a critical and radical departure from what the tradition has come to know as modern law.

The other deconstructive variant of critical legal scholarship founds itself on the notion of "theory". Deconstruction is here understood as a theoretical meta-level enabling the posing of general questions that have been taken up in philosophy within the domain of a regional science such as law.[7] Here, once again, the basic tone of the enterprise is critical to the extent that the "theory" of deconstruction justifies the questioning of basic concepts and notions such as subjectivity within a distinctly juridical context. "Play" and "theory" are, then, the two peculiarities that also characterise "legal deconstruction in America".

What does, then, Gasché's caution concern? He seems to claim rather bluntly that a playful, more or less freely associating deconstruction is founded on an unfamiliarity with philosophical issues and the inability to recognise a distinct tradition to which deconstruction belongs with its perspectives and methods.[8] Gasché's claim has sometimes been deemed as an attempt to domesticate deconstruction: after it has been situated within a tradition, this philosophy, once immune to the dictates of method, loses its radical possibilities. The problem concerning the other variant of "deconstruction in America" is that a theoretically founded criticism is unable to deal with its own presuppositions:

> "Derrida's philosophical work can be turned into a theory to be applied to the regional science of literary criticism as well as to the literature it deals with, without the categories of literature and criticism (and the institutions supporting them) being put into question".[9]

Deconstruction, as it has been adopted by critical legal scholarship, is a critique that is based on the possibility of a pure difference.[10] Both as "play" and

[7] On an "applicable" deconstructive theory in juridical interpretation, see, e.g., Norris, "Suspended Sentences: Textual Theory and the Law", in Norris, *The Contest of Faculties*, pp. 167–192. See also Norris, "Against a New Pragmatism: Law, Deconstruction and the Interests of Theory", in Norris, *Paul de Man*, pp. 125–148.

[8] Gasché, *The Tain of the Mirror*, p. 123.

[9] Gasché, "Deconstruction as Criticism," in Gasché, *Inventions of Difference*, pp. 22–57, at p. 25.

[10] Balkin, for instance, argues for a "rational" juridical deconstruction that would operate with normative choices. Balkin, "Understanding Legal Understanding", 124–126.

as "theory", deconstruction in law is the analysis of oppositional structures that are close-read from juridical texts. After the repressed other of the oppositional pair has been identified—it can be, for instance, the "black" of colonial language or a "rhetorics" silenced by modern scientific thinking—critical legal scholarship "empowers" the other by graciously granting it the possibility to articulate itself. This "politics of empowerment" is executed by reversing the oppositional pair.

However, a reversal founded on the idea of emancipation either reduces deconstruction to a structural critique that merely restates the original oppositional pair—white/black is, for example, "deconstructed" into black/white—or, as in the case of a "rhetorics" that supposedly overcomes the traditional distinction between science and art, dialectically annuls the original pair with the foundation that is offered in the new critical concept.[11] But deconstruction is not a movement from one concept to another within an oppositional pair, nor is it a form of dialectical critique. The "infrastructure" with which the relationship between concepts is accounted for will establish that deconstruction does not concern "concepts" to begin with.[12]

Leaving the issues of individual "deconstructions" aside, the oppositional pair that critical legal scholarship must time and time again return to is, of course, the relationship between tradition and critique. If the privilege that is granted to critique in the reversal empowers the other to have its say, then the critical legal scholar can be understood as an "advocate" speaking on behalf of the other. But the competence to speak for an other can only be acquired by first granting critique its privilege over tradition in the original reversal. The figure of the critical advocate seems to hold within itself a more general problem concerning the legal scholar and tradition: tradition binds the scholar in a way that makes a comprehensive criticism impossible. A critic of law could, then, only be a restorer of tradition.

The intersection of tradition and critique is also one of the principal sites where critical legal scholarship with its understanding of "deconstruction in America" must negotiate its uneasy affiliation with the philosophical hermeneutics of Gadamer, a "Continental" school of thought that conditions both the understanding of deconstruction and its critique.[13] On the one hand, hermeneutics is often used as a generic term to emphasise the dangers of politically motivated interpretations. An influential participant in this debate is Richard Rorty,

[11] Gasché, *The Tain of the Mirror*, p. 142; Gasché, "Deconstruction as Criticism", n. 9 above, p. 26.

[12] Gasché, *The Tain of the Mirror*, p. 165; Gasché, "Deconstruction as Criticism", n. 9 above, p. 39.

[13] Gadamer is here an important figure for numerous reasons. In addition to the centrality of tradition and authority in Gadamer's own project, philosophical hermeneutics has played an important role in the development of Continental theories of legal interpretation. The infatuation of the juridical sciences with Gadamer is partly due to vanity: Gadamer grants the juridical sciences themselves a central role in the development of all interpretative sciences. Gadamer, *Hermeneutik I. Wahrheit und Methode*, pp. 334–336. See also Gadamer, "Text und Interpretation," in Gadamer, *Hermeneutik II. Wahrheit und Methode*, pp. 330–360 at pp. 345–346.

who originally presents his critical review of Continental philosophy as "hermeneutics" in *Philosophy and the Mirror of Nature*. For the Rorty of the period, it is clear that Derrida and his followers represent what Rorty calls "edifying philosophers" whose "abnormal" and "reactive" "protests":

> "make it as difficult as possible to take their thought as expressing views on traditional philosophical problems, or as making constructive proposals for philosophy as a cooperative and progressive discipline".[14]

But viewed from the perspective of critical legal scholarship and its understanding of deconstruction, hermeneutics is also a conservative theory of interpretation that, without proper justification, underscores the significance of tradition. Paul Ricœur, for instance, criticises this Romanticist remainder of hermeneutics and attempts to elaborate a dialectic of the recollection of tradition that hermeneutics involves and the anticipation of liberation advocated by critique.[15]

Hermeneutics is, then, both edifying and conservative, both "critical" and "traditional". But how does Gadamer perceive the relationship between tradition and critique?

III

Gadamer's central argument claims that belonging to the tradition is a condition of all understanding,[16] but the uncompromising belief of modern science in the power of critique seems to prevent this. Even if Gadamer is in debt to Heidegger for the general question of belonging to the tradition, he also remembers to emphasise the difference. For Heidegger, the fore-structures that enable understanding are of interest only in so far as they contribute to the *Seinsfrage* of a fundamental ontology. The tradition of philosophical hermeneutics, on the other hand, is related to the conditions of a notion of understanding that has been relieved of the demand of scientific objectivity.[17]

Gadamer maintains, then, that tradition is first and foremost a question concerning the epistemological justification of the human sciences in the era of

[14] Rorty, *Philosophy and the Mirror of Nature*, pp. 368 and 377. On Continental philosophy, see Rorty, "Philosophy in America Today", in Rorty, *Consequences of Pragmatism*, pp. 211–230 at pp. 223–227. On Rorty's reading of Gasché on Derrida, see Rorty, "Is Derrida a Transcendental Philosopher?", in Rorty, *Essays on Heidegger and Others*, pp. 119–128. For a reply, see Critchley, "Deconstruction and Pragmatism—Is Derrida a Private Ironist or a Public Liberal", in Mouffe (ed.), *Deconstruction and Pragmatism*, pp. 19–40. On the tension between hermeneutic interpretation and the *Rechtsstaat*, see Dallmayr, "Hermeneutics and the Rule of Law", in Cornell et al (eds), *Deconstruction and the Possibility of Justice*, pp. 283–304.

[15] Ricœur, "Herméneutique et critique des idéologies," in Ricœur, *Du texte à l'action*, pp. 333–377, on Gadamer especially pp. 335–351.

[16] Gadamer, *Hermeneutik I. Wahrheit und Methode*, p. 295. This notion is reminiscent of what Leo Strauss calls "radical historicism": Strauss, *Natural Right and History*, pp. 26–28.

[17] Gadamer, *Hermeneutik I. Wahrheit und Methode*, p. 270. Cf. Heidegger, *Sein und Zeit*, pp. 150–151 (§ 32).

modern science and critique. In hermeneutical understanding, the text to be interpreted presents itself to the interpreter as a projection (*Entwurf*) that begins to take shape as soon as the text appears to make sense. This preliminary sense would, then, have something to do with the way in which the text emerges as worthy of interpretation, and within this sensible projection the interpreter approaches the text with specific expectations.[18] As the interpreter's understanding of the text proceeds, these continually changing expectations bind him to the tradition.[19]

Belonging to tradition produces expectations that are, in fact, essential prejudices (*Vorurteile*) that the interpreter shares with his peers. In other words, the interpreter can acquire an understanding relationship with the text only after he has uncovered the tradition in the community of prejudices. The text presents itself as concurrently familiar and strange, and such a contradictory experience arises from the language with which the text addresses the interpreter. The text is, then, historically determined by the distance of time, but it is also part of a familiar tradition that reaches towards the present, and the area that is left between familiarity and strangeness is the true place of a philosophical hermeneutics.[20] The paradox of the interim is one of the cornerstones on which Gadamer builds his project.

But as historical research has indicated, time is not an abyss that separates the interpreter from the text; it is a productive element that enables the evaluation of his prejudices. We may, to put it in another way, claim that temporal distance is the precondition of critical knowledge. Such critique would, however, require consistency: knowledge can be critically objective only if the temporal distance that separates the interpreter from the text remains constant. This is not the case, for interpretation effects the distance. From his remote position, the interpreter must evaluate his expectations by distinguishing true prejudices from false ones. The truthfulness of a prejudice must, however, be postponed to the future, for regardless of the distance that a critical evaluation requires, the tradition addresses the interpreter in a way that Gadamer depicts as "arousing" (*reizen*). Even if the critical evaluation of prejudices is possible from the distance that the historical sciences provide the interpreter with, the timeless truths of the human sciences call for a suspension of the evaluation into the future. Structurally Gadamer regards this suspended evaluation as a question.[21]

But why suspend? In the text, the interpreter is addressed by the voice of the other, and if this voice is not heard, the possibility of erring cannot be accommodated with the interpreter's expectations. The task of a philosophical hermeneutics is, then, to question things, to suspend the hasty evaluation of prejudices in accordance with the structure of the question. Even if an interpreter, sensitive to the otherness of the text and wishing to understand, were to

[18] Gadamer, *Hermeneutik I. Wahrheit und Methode*, pp. 271–272.
[19] *Ibid.*, pp. 298–299.
[20] *Ibid.*, p. 300.
[21] *Ibid.*, pp. 302–304.

allow the text to speak freely for itself, the temporal distance will not disappear. The text is left to introduce itself in its otherness, and the timeless truths that emerge from the tradition will be juxtaposed against the interpreter's prejudices. The tradition that arouses the interpreter must, then, not be restrained. Quite the contrary, all obstacles that inhibit its understanding must be eliminated. If this is not done, the interpretation of the text will be guided only by misconstrued prejudices.[22]

If Gadamer deems the central task of his philosophical hermeneutics as the discerning of true prejudices from false ones, the major obstacle in the understanding of the tradition is the forthright contention against prejudices inscribed into the philosophy of the Enlightenment.[23] The enlightened mind regards all prejudices as false and groundless dogmas that have not been tried with the critique of reason. The text of a written tradition embodies an authority that must be critically verified, and the prejudices that are essential as far as belonging to the tradition is concerned are conveyed to the interpreter through and in this authority. However, the philosophy of the Enlightenment cannot accept authority as such and evaluates everything from reason. Tradition cannot be truthful if only reason can prescribe what is true and what is not.[24]

If the authority of the tradition is understood as the lack of reason or as irrationality, tradition and reason are incompatible as an irreconcilable contradiction. Critique and the authoritative position that Gadamer conveys to tradition would, then, also be incompatible, and critique would, accordingly, have to be understood as a rational departure from a prejudiced tradition. But for Gadamer, the identification of prejudice and irrationalism is itself a prejudice—a "prejudice against prejudice"—according to which all prejudices have already been tried and submitted to the light of reason. Such a claim could only be acceptable with regard to ungrounded prejudices, for Gadamer argues that epistemically productive prejudices are "legitimate" (*berechtigt*). Even if the distinction between belief founded on authority and the free use of reason was correct, the authority of tradition could, all the same, serve as a source of truth. The truth can only be established by evaluating the truthfulness of prejudices, and, for Gadamer, such an evaluation must inevitably be suspended. In other words, a question must be posed.

The tradition communicates its central prejudices onwards with an arousing authority that the interpreter must not suppress with reason. The arousal that the tradition produces does not, however, annul reason because the tradition that is maintained in understanding includes both history and the free use of reason. All historical changes grounded in reason, all "critical evaluations", also promote tradition. No critique can completely depart from the tradition that has been evaluated. In the historicality of promoted traditions, man is engaged between diverse traditions that do not produce knowledge (*Erkenntnis*) in the

[22] Gadamer, *Hermeneutik I. Wahrheit und Methode*, pp. 273–274.
[23] *Ibid.*, p. 275.
[24] *Ibid.*, pp. 276–277.

scientific sense of the word, but enable man to recognise himself (*sichwieder-erkennen*). In understanding, both what is to be interpreted and the tradition address the interpreter in a way in which the meaning both precedes the interpretation and persists after it.

Therefore, the opposition of tradition and critically assessed knowledge, of historicality (*Geschichtlichkeit*) and history (*Historie*), must be overcome. In a philosophical hermeneutics, the consequences of both a living tradition and critical knowledge must be reconciled, and in this reconciliation, Gadamer's task is to reevaluate the significance of prejudice that has already been dismissed by the Enlightenment.[25]

But Gadamer executes his reevaluation in quite a distinctive way. His premise is the critical position that the Enlightenment takes on prejudice. In other words, this is Gadamer's own assessment of the philosophy of reason. As a tradition, the Enlightenment, no doubt, arouses Gadamer in a certain way. But he is unwilling to accept the authority of this single tradition. He does not structure the relationship of the Enlightenment to prejudice into a question and, accordingly, also fails to suspend the evaluation of his own prejudice into the future. He does not *question* the Enlightenment but, instead, *posits* his philosophical hermeneutics into a critical position in relation to the Enlightenment with a gesture that unmistakably mimes a *law of reason*:

> "This is what a philosophical hermeneutics has attempted to critically assess [*kritisch einsetzen*]. We must demonstrate that the overcoming of all prejudices, this general demand of the Enlightenment, is itself a prejudice. Only its reevaluation will open the way for a proper understanding of finiteness that governs not only our human existence but also our historical consciousness".[26]

Is the Enlightenment not a tradition to which (even) Gadamer belongs? Is it not a tradition at all that should be treated with the same consideration as all traditions of the human sciences? Or is it, perhaps, a tradition, but one to which Gadamer's philosophical hermeneutics bears no relation? Or is it a tradition that a philosophical hermeneutics must simply discard? Initially the human sciences were juxtaposed with the Enlightenment, tradition with critique, but such a difference is only possible by taking distance in relation to both. But in the end, Gadamer is able to reconcile the tradition maintained by the human sciences with the critical demands of reason only by *positing* (*setzen*) them together with the legislative gesture of a critical epistemology.

Gadamer must reject the arousing potential of the Enlightenment because a true understanding of its prejudice against prejudices would eventually lead into an interminable decline—in Gadamer's case, we would already be dealing with a "prejudice against the prejudice against prejudices"—and such a decline would inevitably also prevent the *scientific* founding of a philosophical hermeneutics.

[25] *Ibid.*, pp. 281–290.
[26] *Ibid.*, p. 280.

My claim, then, is that Gadamer's alleged "conservatism" cannot be accounted for simply by referring to the way in which he recognises the historical nature of man requiring the recognition of tradition, but it is rather due to the *scientific position into which he posits the understanding of this historicality*. As an evaluation of the reason of the Enlightenment, Gadamer's understanding of tradition and, consequently, of historical man is, in the end, a critique of critique.

IV

The "conservative" nature of Gadamer's hermeneutics has, nevertheless, usually been attributed to the recognition of authority and the appraisal of tradition, and this has often offered the background against which the critical nature of deconstruction has also been argued for. John D. Caputo's assessment of a "radical hermeneutics" is, perhaps, not a particularly proficient interpretation of Derrida's philosophy, but it does serve as an exemplary illustration of this trait in "deconstruction in America". As such, it has also inspired the way in which critical legal scholarship has understood its deconstructive ventures. One of the central chapters of Caputo's book brings together the later Heidegger, Gadamer and Derrida under the title "Three Interpretations of Interpretation", but we are, in fact, only dealing with two. For Caputo's analysis is an attempt to illustrate how Gadamer emphasises the conservative aspects of the author of *Sein und Zeit*, while Derrida represents the radicality of the later Heidegger.

For Caputo, Gadamer's philosophical hermeneutics is a reactionary interpretation of the philosophy of early Heidegger because it reinstates philosophy back into the ranks of metaphysics. This claim requires that metaphysics, that is, Occidental philosophy, is understood as an authoritative tradition in the Gadamerian sense outlined above. In this sense, Caputo is a true representative of the Enlightenment in that he understands the authority of the tradition as a conservative force. For Gadamer, the general rejection of all authority would require that all prejudices arising from the tradition have already been evaluated and confirmed as false. Because of the problematic nature of such a position, Gadamer proposes to suspend evaluations and to try the truthfulness of prejudices, to question the authority of tradition. Caputo, on the other hand, cannot apply a suspensive questioning, because the overall rejection of authority serves as the critical justification of radical hermeneutics. Gadamer allegedly aspires to reconcile the horizons of thinking together and to—seemingly unnecessarily—prolong the life of tradition, and this can only be done by disregarding the hermeneutic (self-) criticism of the later Heidegger.[27]

For Caputo, the hermeneutics of Gadamer is, however, an ultimately liberal interpretation of a fundamentally conservative position. The necessity of flux

[27] Caputo, *Radical Hermeneutics*, pp. 5–6.

and play is recognised, but only to the extent that it does not interfere with the ageless truths of tradition. Philosophical hermeneutics and deconstruction are, then, portrayed as mirror-images,[28] and as such, deconstruction is depicted as the radical critique of both hermeneutics and the tradition it stands for. In addition, Caputo emphasises the primarily social nature of this critique, because, unlike Derrida, Gadamer does not display any interest in the interconnections between tradition, play and power. From the perspective of radical hermeneutics, deconstruction is social criticism because it takes place at the "market place".[29]

As a political orator, Derrida is consequently accorded a messianic role in radical hermeneutics. Deconstruction does not make hermeneutics unnecessary, it simply liberates its radical possibilities. Caputo formulates the deconstructive "interpretation of interpretation" by way of Derrida's early text on Edmond Jabès. The point of departure is two interpreting figures. The rabbi approaches texts as the holy scriptures, and his task is to relay onwards the tradition inscribed into the book. The poet, on the other hand, represents the playful interpreter whose readings have been liberated from the chains of tradition.[30] Gadamer is, of course, here the rabbi and Derrida the poet, although, in contradiction to this, it is clearly the latter that is praised as the high priest of radical hermeneutics.

Caputo claims that the task of the poet, that is, of the radical hermeneut, is to prevent the authority of tradition from enclosing the meanings of philosophical texts. Gadamer the rabbi emphasises such aspects of hermeneutics that aim to settle contradictions and to restore tradition, while Derrida's poetry releases the more radical and inevitably also more playful destructiveness of Heidegger's philosophy.[31] The poet's "interpretation of interpretation" that is also adopted by radical hermeneutics bears with it the freedom of play, and it lacks the hypocritical humility that is characteristic of rabbinic interpretations.[32]

But deconstruction can hardly adopt the messianic role that radical hermeneutics seems to have assigned it, for the attempt of the poet to depart from the book must take place within the book itself. Derrida claims that Jabès's poet can digress from the book only within the book itself because the world is inscribed into the book and not vice versa:

> "the book can only be menaced by nothing, by non-Being, by non-sense. If this menace were to come into *Being*, it would be—as in this case—acknowledged, said, domesticated. It would belong within the home and the book".[33]

When the wild savagery of the poet has been broken, he is also delivered into the household like the domestic animal whose relationship with the world is

[28] *Ibid.*, p. 115.
[29] *Ibid.*, pp. 112 and 193.
[30] Derrida, *L'écriture et la différence*, pp. 102–104.
[31] Caputo, *Radical Hermeneutics*, p. 118.
[32] *Ibid.*, pp. 116–117.
[33] Derrida, *L'écriture et la différence*, p. 114.

structured within a fairly simple economy. This is clearly what Caputo does to the poet.

Caputo is also concerned about the ethical implications of playful interpretations in much a similar way as the juridical critics of deconstruction.[34] He emphasises the common features of radical hermeneutics and the Enlightenment and continues to argue that, as criticism, playful deconstruction will not lead to irrationalism. It will, however, require the reformulation of the concept of reason, and in doing so, radical hermeneutics refers to a more original and authentic philosophy of reason. Rationality allegedly includes elements of both principle and play, and the latter must be protected from the dogmas of formal thinking: the formality of the principle of reason runs the risk of annulling the possibility of play.[35]

Science, action, art and beliefs all emerge from movement, an idea that is also aptly supported by the image of the radical hermeneut as poet. Caputo's dialectical account of reason takes place in and from contradiction, but it does not engender irrationalism. Quite the contrary, the dialectics of principle and play is the only sensible and reasonable account of rationality itself. From the perspective adopted by the radical hermeneut, a concept of reason that confines itself to principles cannot be a token of freedom. It is merely an instrument of discipline.[36]

But as a critic of Gadamer, Caputo himself takes a "reactionary" turn by restricting critique to the criticism of political institutions. The principle of reason is understood as the instrument of institutional authority, and the potential it represents is alarming. For Caputo, the original anti-authoritarian impetus of the Enlightenment has turned against itself. By accepting its own authority, reason represses an original freedom that only play can now liberate. Play is, then, not alien to "true" reason. Critique operating in the name of deconstruction reminds us that the condemnation of undesirable approaches as non-scientific inevitably also unveils the necessary connection between reason and power.[37]

By criticising the formality of the principle of reason and, respectively, by emphasising the essentially playful character of "true" reason, Caputo escorts radical hermeneutics to the market place where the figures of philosophy—Heidegger, Gadamer and Derrida, for instance—debate amongst themselves and with the tradition of Occidental philosophy. But at the market place, the radical hermeneut can but attempt to identify its political allies. The relationships between diverse thinkers and traditions are accounted for with a dual economy of criticism in which the radical possibilities of play have inevitably been domesticated and cultivated into a beast bearing the burden of progress.

[34] Especially in relation to hermeneutics, see Hoy, "Dworkin's Constructive Optimism v. Deconstructive Legal Nihilism", 326–337. See also Dallmayr, "Self and Other".

[35] Caputo, *Radical Hermeneutics*, p. 227.

[36] *Ibid.*, p. 211.

[37] *Ibid.*, p. 234.

And only as such can critical legal scholarship as a fundamentally emancipatory project identify deconstruction as its ally.

I have tried to indicate how both philosophical hermeneutics and radical hermeneutics claim to diverge from the philosophy of the Enlightenment, and yet, in their departures, find themselves restating some of its central premises. Gadamer commences by attempting to formulate an original position for the human sciences but must, in the end, secure this position with an almost neo-Kantian gesture of epistemological legislation. One prejudice cannot be questioned by suspending its evaluation, and that is the hermeneut's own position *vis-à-vis* the Enlightenment. Hence, we find Gadamer as a critic of critical philosophy. On the other hand, radical hermeneutics understands its enterprise primarily as the social criticism of political institutions and must, therefore, also subscribe to the enlightened doctrines of subjectivity and intentionality. The latter position is where we find critical legal scholarship today.

"Allegiance", that is, the way in which radical hermeneutics requires taking sides with allies, clearly refers to choice. Here we are at the core of Gasché's caution. For Derrida, deconstruction cannot be a choice between two "interpretations of interpretation". In addition to the notion of "choice" being historically poorly motivated, the common ground of the interpretations must be accounted for: the *différance* of the irreducible difference. Even if tradition is not compatible with its radical departures, both are lived simultaneously and brought together within a peculiar economy.[38] The question is how to account simultaneously for the universal disposition that is necessarily inherent in all philosophical thinking and the way in which this universality always emerges as a singular event.

If, as Gasché's caution seems to be implying, the only possible moment of "criticism" in deconstruction concerns the critical belief in the possibility of a pure difference,[39] even critical legal scholarship deconstructs (itself) in its radical singularity. Criticism attempts to rid itself of the stifling universality of tradition, but in the end it will find itself in a position where its own claim to universality encloses even the tradition criticised. And yet, such a critical appropriation of the tradition always takes place in a singular manner. Gasché reminds us that the relationship between deconstruction and the philosophical tradition does not concern the original wonder of metaphysics (*thaumazein*) or its recurrence at the advent of ever new traditions. It concerns the unforeseeable conditions of the event itself.[40] In its response, deconstruction accounts for these conditions by establishing a law:

> "that calculates (the incalculable) commerce between [universality and singularity]—by a law, consequently, that in a strange way is more universal than all universals, yet is at the same time singular".[41]

[38] Derrida, *L'écriture et la différence*, pp. 427–428.
[39] Gasché, "On Critique, Hypercriticism, and Deconstruction", 1115–1117.
[40] Gasché, "The Law of Tradition", n. 2 above, p. 80.
[41] *Ibid.*, p. 265, n. 44.

There is no tradition and its critique, but only traditions to which deconstruction as thinking responds. Responding must necessarily involve a responsibility to account for their commerce with dominating concepts.[42] Only after the aporetic law governing the economy of this commerce has been accounted for, can we even begin to realise what deconstruction can offer the jurist.

V

It is now time to gather the arguments of the first part of this book together into a single claim. One must bear in mind that even if the presentation of a condensed claim serves the demands of the potential reader, it also runs the risk of poor synthesising. I have committed myself to the innate tensions of juridical thinking, and the ultimate danger in such syntheses is the annulment of these tensions in, for instance, a misconstrued Hegelian *Aufhebung*. As I have continually emphasised, my main argument deals with the philosophy of law as thinking, not with law as it is usually understood in the jurisprudential sciences. What is the philosophy of law? Is the philosophy of law possible to begin with? What does thinking law involve? In the foregoing analyses, I have addressed these questions by turning the problem around and by inquiring into the possibility of a juridical moment in philosophy itself: *what is philosophy as juridical thinking?*

For Aristotle, one essential association between thinking (*nous*) and law is desire (*orexis*). He claims that thinking without desire is law (*nomos*). Desire corrupts thinking. It seems to represent the beastly dimension of man, the fact that man is rather a creation of the gods than the ultimate creator. I have demonstrated that the association between law and desire is not merely coincidental, for many law-related words of both Germanic and Latin origin stem from the same root as "desire": *Recht*, *Richtigkeit*, *rectum*, *directum*, and so on. Aristotle goes on to say that thinking as such, that is, thinking as law, is always right (*pas orthos*). In other words, thinking attains its noemic object as something that cannot be otherwise. I further attempted to establish that the inability to be otherwise is another expression for justice (*dikaiosunē*). If a being cannot be otherwise, it is also just (*dikaios*). Justice is, then, the ultimate end of Aristotle's "first philosophy" as metaphysics. It designates "beings as beings" (*on hē on*), a thing "as it was to be" (*to ti en einai*) or, to use the Heideggerian expression, the Being of beings (*Sein des Seiendes*).

Justice as the ultimate end of philosophical thinking constitutes, then, the primary causes and principles that Aristotle's "first philosophy" inquires into, that is, the divine origin of things. If justice is the characteristic of being always right and the corresponding inability of being otherwise, law constitutes the relation-

[42] Gasché, "The Law of Tradition", p. 81. For a convincing account of the political nature of deconstruction, see Beardsworth, *Derrida & the Political*.

ship that conveys thinking to justice. Law also represents the relationship between thinking and divinity because it by necessity eliminates the possibility of desire as a relay that would deliver justice to philosophy. However, desire as the *orexis tou eidenai* of Aristotle's metaphysics is attributed to man by nature. Philosophy involves an inherent desire that contradicts the possibility of realising justice in thinking through law. Justice, it seems, is a divine matter, but for thinking imbedded in desire—in fact, all human thinking—it must remain an irresolvable aporia, that is, a question.

Nevertheless, the question of justice continues to incite thinking even if it cannot be realised or objectified. It continues to animate man's desire to know as sense, that is, as the direction towards which man's desire to see aspires. As the sense of a thinking imbedded in desire—all human thinking—justice remains something that is forever delayed. It is something that Wolf, in his account of *dikē*, understood as the futural constitution of the event, as the advent "to come" (*Zukommende*). When justice as the ultimate end of thinking remains "to come", philosophy produces its own object of desire (*to orekton*). Aristotle called this the excellence of practical thinking (*prakton agathon*). Unlike justice, the excellence of practical thinking may be right or not, it can be otherwise. When justice as the ultimate end of thinking remains impossible—it is, in Lacanian terms, "real"—philosophy produces an imaginary object with which it attempts to come to terms with the foundational lack of human Being. In this decision, it produces something "correct" (*ein richtiges Ding*) that must stand in for the ultimate truth of justice. I attempted to characterise this decision through the epistemological undertakings of the neo-Kantian philosophers of law in establishing their discipline as a science.

The decision of correctness as "right" is, however, indispensable for human Being. In my readings of Heidegger, I wanted to display a structure according to which abiding by the law can be seen as a way in which Dasein, in its unauthentic mode of Being or, in other words, in its everyday involvement with equipmental beings and other Dasein, upholds a common world, a universe of familiarity and shared meanings without which this background would disintegrate into chaos. Such an interpretation of human existence as Being-in-the-world suggests that the world is understood as a spatial order. Furthermore, an orderly world as shared meanings must by definition also be somehow grounded. I attempted to designate its grounding in my reading of Schmitt and *nomos* as the unity of order (*Ordnung*) and localisation (*Ortung*). Schmitt understands Dasein's localisation into the spatial order of its world as the original appropriation of land, as the *Landnahme*. But even in this context, the decision of the original appropriation entails a sense. This sense could be found in Schmitt's—admittedly theological—notion of the donation.

The aporetic structure of law, that is, the question of the philosophy of law, is the undecidable difference—the différance*—accounting for the advent of justice and the decision of correctness. It is the indecision of philosophy as juridical thinking.*

Although my account of the philosophy of law seems to deny the possibility of understanding it as a social practice founded on critique—or at least on the "criticism" of critical legal scholarship—I have also consistently argued for a radicality that is peculiar to its nature. This radicality is not without social implications. However, what I do reject is an understanding of philosophical thinking as a technology that could be used either in the conceptual justification of existing social institutions—this is usually the claim of neo-Kantian legal theory and mainstream jurisprudence—or in the righting of social wrongs, however commendable such a critical politics may be. But a philosophy of law may contribute to the problematisation of accepted notions of the social and the political, to the understanding of justice as an aporetic encounter with the foundations of human existence. This is the theme of the second part of this book.

Part Two

Law and the Social

6

The Juridical Matrix

"[i]n opposition to the juridico-philosophical discourse that constructs itself around the problem of sovereignty and law, the discourse that interprets the permanent war in society is essentially politico-historical, an indeterminately critical and, at the same time, extremely mythical discourse in which truth functions as a weapon to gain partisan victory."

Michel Foucault

I

A more or less plausible anecdote tells us that when Michel Foucault died in 1984, the television newscaster did not dwell on the occasion with a long overview of the philosopher and his *œuvre*. Instead, she chose to reduce her commentary to a short passage from a literary programme called "Apostrophes" from years ago. Foucault had exceptionally agreed to take part in a televised panel discussion dedicated to the newly published first part of his history of sexuality. A participant in the debate asked Foucault to illuminate, with an example, the restraining discourse on sexuality that his book was about. Instead:

> Muzil [Foucault], in suit and tie, literally twisted with laughter at the very moment when he was expected to immortalise, as seriously as a pope, some regularity in this history of human behaviour the foundations of which he had already undermined".[1]

The critique that is commonly identified with Foucault's Nietzschean stance resonates in this laughter:

> "Hate must only be viable enough in order to lead to something, to a great joy, but not to the joy of ambivalence or hatred, but to the joy that arises from the desire to destroy what mutilates life".[2]

But this is not the Foucault that is familiar to law. When the influence of cultural theory had reached its summit within critical legal scholarship, Foucault was undoubtedly one of the most frequently cited thinkers contributing to the inter-disciplinary venture. Lately, however, the enthusiasm has diminished into what could be called a critical reservation. The core of the reservation seems to involve an alleged incompatibility between the object of critical legal

[1] Guibert, *À l'ami qui ne m'a pas sauvé la vie*, p. 35.
[2] Deleuze, *Foucault*, p. 31.

scholarship—law—and Foucault's conception of disciplinary power. Boaventura de Sousa Santos, to take an example, has claimed that Foucault, in his understanding of modernity, overlooks the deep interpenetrations between juridical power and disciplinary power.[3] The argument may well be an echo of old controversies about Foucault, but it may also be an indication of a more profound flaw in critical legal scholarship itself, namely, that *Foucault's understanding of law in relation to power-knowledge has never been taken to its limits.* Perhaps because such an undertaking does not necessarily involve promises of redemptive results for a troubled era, critical legal scholarship has, in its aspirations for social justice, chosen to concentrate on issues of a more practical nature. This is why the Nietzschean philosopher has remained a stranger.

But to retreat at this stage can also mean possibilities lost. In this chapter, my aim is to attempt at a rethinking and a reworking of Foucault's *philosophical* position in relation to law.[4] Far from insolently assuming to be able to confer a coherent theory of law, such an attempt can merely point out uncharted routes for the study of law within a power analytics, a theoretical project that the so-called mature Foucault of the mid-1970s later abandoned as infeasible. I will address two distinct and yet interconnected questions. First, what does Foucault mean by "juridical power", and how does he understand it in relation to disciplinary power? Secondly, how do juridical practices contribute to the production of truth within power-knowledge relations? Before even a precursory answer can be given, it is necessary to touch upon the way in which the bulk of critical legal scholarship seems to understand Foucault's work.

For many legal theorists, sociologists of law and criminologists, Foucault's contribution to the study of law centres on the criticism of social institutions: the mental asylum, the hospital, the prison, and so on. Even if such criticism, in order to be considered "Foucaultian", is obliged to elaborate on the affinities of the institutions with respective domains of science—psychiatry, clinical medicine, the criminal sciences—the relationship remains problematic. The criticism of social institutions is still all too often based on an unnecessarily rigid distinction between power and knowledge in which the institution is understood as a more or less centralised domain of power while science is reduced to, for instance, a "superstructure" or an "ideological state apparatus", in short, a supportive ideational representation in relation to the material basis of power.[5] In

[3] Santos, "Three Metaphors for a New Conception of Law", 570–571. Santos's claim is, no doubt, also theoretically contestable, but I refer to it merely to indicate an evaluative line of thought adopted recently in critical legal scholarship.

[4] I emphasise the word "philosophical" in order to indicate an admittedly problematic distinction between the philosophy of law and legal theory. The former is "apolitical" in the sense that it cannot be *a priori* committed to the social struggles that condition most of what is today known as critical legal theory. This position leads to a certain "Foucault-immanence" that only laboriously lends itself to social criticism.

[5] This is, for instance, the position that Garland must inevitably come to in order to present his critique of Foucault's notion of power. For Garland, the penal institutions represent the tactical moves of a power still identified with the state while knowledge is accorded a more ideological role. See, e.g., Garland, *Punishment and Welfare*, pp. 138–139.

such a setting, the criticism of institutions takes on a necessarily non-Foucaultian tone. *Surveiller et punir*, often understood as the key to Foucault's power analytics in a juridical environment, defines the materiality of the prison as a "technology of power", as a *logos* that defines the uses of power and, consequently, as a *knowledge* moulding the body regardless of the pacifying intonations of the philanthropic juridical tradition of legalism.[6]

In many law-related interpretations of Foucault, the position of law in relation to social institutions such as the prison would, therefore, seem to be elaborated in a more traditional manner than Foucault's theoretical premises suggest. According to, for example, Gilles Deleuze, the prison as well as penal law are *both situated in the domain of knowledge*. An historical formation includes both language and light:

> "Just as penal law as the form of expression defines the domain of the speakable (the utterances of deviance), the prison as a form of content defines the domain of the visible (the "panoptic" or, in other words, the domain where everything can at any given moment be seen without being seen)".[7]

Expression, content; utterable, visible; discursive, non-discursive; "words and things" as two distinct realms of knowledge.

The way in which legal interpretations recognise the dividing line between power and knowledge in the prison and penal law is restated by classifying Foucault's work into, on the one hand, an archaeological method devised for the analysis of discursive formations[8] and, on the other hand, a social criticism emphasising the pragmatism of politics. Jurisprudents and legal theorists accentuating the critical dimension have consistently complained about the vague nature of the object criticised. Foucault is said to be more interested in quasi-juridical practices—the prison, criminology, legal psychiatry—operating on the fringes of the domain than about law itself, and in doing so, Foucault allegedly disregards the emancipatory potential of law.[9] On the other hand, there is a temptation for critical social scientists and criminologists to expand their point of departure by, for instance, fusing penal law and the prison into a single practice of social control.

Two preliminary questions must, then, be elaborated. First, how does one, within a Foucaultian power analytics, understand law in relation to "words and things", in relation to the discursive and the non-discursive domains of knowledge? Even if a satisfactory answer can be given to the first question, a much more profound problem must still be confronted. Is a Foucaultian power analytics compatible with the study of law? Is a Foucaultian "philosophy of law" possible?

[6] Foucault, *Surveiller et punir*, p. 35.
[7] Deleuze, *Foucault*, p. 55.
[8] Foucault, *Les mots et les choses*; Foucault, *L'archéologie du savoir*.
[9] e.g., Habermas, *Der philosophische Diskurs der Moderne*, pp. 340–341. Cf. Hunt and Wickham, *Foucault and Law*, pp. 61–64.

II

In a paradoxical way, law occupies a central position in Foucault's work during the first half of the 1970s. But the centrality does not appear in a way that would be recognisable from the traditional perspectives of the philosophy of law. After having published his books on the archaeological method and the analysis of discursive formations, Foucault was appointed professor at the *Collège de France*. The chair that he occupied until his death had formerly been entitled "The History of Philosophical Thought". Six months prior to the nomination the chair was renamed "The History of Systems of Thought". Foucault held annually a series of lectures on the historical development of Occidental science and knowledge.[10] Foucault's next significant publication was *Surveiller et punir* in 1975.

The voluntary silence that lasted for over five years has often been interpreted as Foucault's desire to distance himself from the archaeological project, emphasising the centrality of the discursive domain. From this period, only the short reports that Foucault wrote about his teaching at the *Collège* have until recently been available. In these short texts, especially between 1970 and 1973, an ambitious undertaking seems to be taking shape.[11] Foucault is sketching outlines for a project the aim of which is to develop a morphology of the will to knowledge and, further, to situate the morphology into the history of systems of thought. In the project, archaeology represents a preliminary, empirical phase after which key concepts such as *connaissance*, knowledge (*savoir*) and, finally, the will to knowledge must be worked out philosophically.

For Foucault, philosophy gives but precursory remarks about the will to knowledge. The traditional model is basically Aristotelian as the *orexis tou eidenai* at the beginning of *Metaphysics* indicates. Through the senses, the will to knowledge is coupled with a pleasure that does not correspond to personal interests. According to the model, the unveiling of truth in sensory perception concurs with a non-utilitarian conception of pleasure. The terminal point of the model is the philosopher proper pursuing *connaissance* about the world only due to the pure pleasure involved in the unveiling of truth. By way of contrast, Foucault's own model is Nietzschean and is based on conflict. *Connaissance* is necessarily a product, and behind the production of *connaissance* operate instincts, desires, fears and the will to appropriate the world. Within the discourse on *connaissance*, truth is always produced as an effect preceded by an originary falsification introducing the difference between right and wrong.[12]

Elsewhere Foucault writes about the external history of truth. Truth is produced as an effect within numerous social domains. On the social level, we find

[10] On Foucault's conception of history, see, e.g., Veyne, "Foucault révolutionne l'histoire", in Veyne, *Comment on écrit l'histoire*, pp. 345–385.

[11] Foucault, *Résumé des cours 1970–1982*, pp. 9–15.

[12] Cf. Foucault, "La vérité et les formes juridiques", in Foucault, *Dits et écrits II*, pp. 543–550.

the rules of the game according to which specific forms of subjectivity, the domain of objects and the species of knowledge are born. An important example are the juridical practices in which correlations between man and truth are constructed.[13]

If law is to be situated within the domain of knowledge as Deleuze suggests, its relation to power remains enigmatic. For Foucault, the performance of power often takes on the metaphorical figure of war.[14] According to Hobbes, the destruction of the originary war is avoided as the sovereign obliges the battling counterparts to peace in the name of a common good, of the commonwealth. Law is the covenant of social tranquillity into which the prerequisites of decency have been prescribed. It is not war that founds society but its calculated avoidance. Foucault's conception of the radical immanence of power denies the possibility of any treaty:

> "We are, then, dealing with a political and historical discourse that refers to truth and law but also renders itself explicitly incompatible with juridico-philosophical universality. Its objective is not what legislators and philosophers from Solon to Kant have dreamt of, namely, to establish itself between the adversaries at the centre of and above the confrontation, to impose an armistice, to found a reconciliating order. It establishes a law marked with dissymmetry functioning as the privilege to maintain or to restore, it assesses a truth that functions like a weapon. The subject that maintains such a discourse deems universal truth and general law as illusions or traps".[15]

Law is a strategic design within the dynamics of force relations. The compilation of illegalities inscribed into law conceptualises tactical movements that attain their concretion when force encounters force as the confrontation continues:

> "One must, then, presume that the prison and, no doubt, punishments in general are not intended to eliminate infractions but, rather, to distinguish them, to distribute them, to use them. They do not really aspire to render those liable to transgress laws docile but to facilitate the transgression of laws into a general tactics of subjection [*assujetissements*]. Penality is, then, a way to manage illegalities, to indicate the limits of tolerance, to give some free rein and to constrain others, to exclude a part and to make use of another, to neutralise these and to profit from those. In short, penality does not only and simply 'restrain' illegalities, it 'differentiates' them, it provides them a general 'economy' ".[16]

Foucault, however, is not willing to theorise power but, in order to retain his consistency, is compelled to either confine his observations to the effects of power, or to present theoretical negations; the nature of power itself resists positive formulations. This leads into a curious paradox. Foucault must often approach power with the restrictive orders of a juridico-political discourse: "power is not . . .", "power cannot . . .", and so on.

[13] *Ibid*., pp. 540–541.
[14] Foucault, *Résumé des cours 1970–1982*, pp. 85–87 and p. 92.
[15] *Ibid*., pp. 89–90.
[16] Foucault, *Surveiller et punir*, p. 277.

This is, of course, the point where Foucault's dispute with the Marxist tradition begins. Because of its heterogenic nature, power cannot be established or fixed into a single position or practice. It can only be identified in the singular points in which it produces effects in the world. However, these points of identification are not totally random but constitute a certain regular logic. The regularity integrating singular points enables the analytic to utter and to see, to recognise knowledge. The varieties of knowledge such as law are born as the unique effects of power in the world are integrated within a rule. The use of power is strategic action and, therefore, the knowledge involved in its exercise is as impossible to appropriate as power. This non-appropriable power is not a constant attribute that could be appointed to a specific social group. The effects of strategic action are produced in tactics, techniques and operations. On the other hand, an entity indicated and labelled as "law" can only be identified in the specified points through which power, complying with a certain logic, passes. Law and power are, then, not equatable in, for instance, the accumulation of prescribed privileges and duties. The operation of power is not identifiable in the formal structure of law as the allocation of rights and obligations but, on the contrary, power can only be approached in its singular manifestations, in the unique ways in which it produces effects in the world.

Neither is power internalised into law in a way that would permit to hierarchise the latter into an instrument of subjugation within a quantitative logic. Foucault's power analytics is not based on an oppositional scheme that divides society into the dominating and the dominated. A key characteristic of power is that the totality of force relations accounts for all levels of social agents. Juridical discourse, for example, is not the privilege of the sovereign but penetrates the whole of society enabling micro-level agents to juridisise the regulation of their everyday conflicts. Foucault's well-known example is a procedure of appeal dating back to eighteenth century France, the *lettre de cachet*, with which the subject could directly approach the king or his representative in trying to find an authoritative resolution to an individual disagreement.[17] Within the procedure, the micro-level, mundane conflicts (parent/child, husband/wife, farmer/labourer, and so on) are both formulated and resolved in accordance with a juridical logic that allegedly still relates to the sovereign power.[18]

Because power and law cannot be equated and simultaneously identified in a state-like structure, the juridical tradition has had problems in finding a relevant object of study relating to Foucault's theories. One must consider the possibility that there is no conceivable, juridically relevant entity involved here. Law

[17] Farge and Foucault, *Le désordre des familles*, pp. 350–356. See also Foucault, "La vérité et les formes juridiques", n. 12 above, pp. 600–603.

[18] Foucault connects this institution with the birth of the police in France. One effect of formulating the conflicts of the mundane world in the *lettres* is, apparently, an "enlightened" civilisation of the masses. On the semantic affinity between the words "police" and "polish"—etymologically *polis* and *polire* respectively—see Starobinski, *Le remède dans le mal*, pp. 26–33. Cf. Donzelot, *La police des familles*, pp. 49–58.

seems to represent but one practice among others that is in no way privileged in relation to the overall moves of Foucault's power analytics. One of the few scholars working within the general framework of the jurisprudential tradition to confront this problem is François Ewald. He considers his research on the history of French social welfare legislation as a philosophy of law, and his apparent aim is to write a Foucaultian philosophy of law.[19] How does Ewald, then, identify law?

The few direct references to Foucault involve Ewald's manner of conceptualising the industrialised world. In addition to its material consequences, industrialisation has also brought about a new social domain of truth within which man identifies himself, orders the effects of his life, and defines the reciprocal obligations directing his social life. The history of social welfare legislation is, then, intimately bound with what Foucault calls "bio-power", but Ewald emphasises the strategic dimension of law by focusing his study on the "juridical instrumentation" of social security.[20]

In his theoretical introduction, Ewald outlines the premises for an "analytics of juridical thinking" founded on three interconnecting themes.[21] The traditional approaches of the sciences of law are deemed essentialist in two different meanings. The first variant reduces law into a systematic whole that, in its very nature, differs from other normative systems, while the other recognises all correctly posited norms as law. Ewald maintains that both variants deny history, and he proposes to reconciliate law with history by introducing the term *juridical experience*. The juridical experience refers to the various manners in which different practices can be recognised as law. Within the juridical experience, practices need not be understood only as available equipment or instruments, but also as ways in which an individual or a collective subject founds itself in relation to the other. The juridical experience can, then, be examined with the same criteria as other forms of subjection.

In Ewald's analytics, the juridical experience is connected to judgement. The *rule of judgement* describes an interpretative shift in social welfare law. In the legislative material regulating labour relations at the end of the nineteenth century, the responsibility of the employer in relation to labour hazards is defined traditionally by way of liability and negligence. But in interpretations of the same material, a new form of responsibility takes shape. Both academic and court interpretations are founded on the notions of acceptable risk and effect. For Ewald, the rule represents a specific regularity in court decisions introducing the norm deduced from law. The rule of judgement operates on three levels: with regard to positive legal propositions as a rule of interpretation, as a juridical logic indexed to a specific political rationality, and, lastly, within certain

[19] Ewald does not state this openly, but the assumption can be supported by the fact that his book is dedicated to Foucault. In addition, Ewald was Foucault's assistant during the *Collège* years, and he is co-editor of Foucault's posthumous publications.

[20] Ewald, *L'État providence*, pp. 26–27.

[21] *Ibid.*, pp. 29–43.

epistemological and political circumstances, as the limit of law, as the rule that indicates the juridical nature of a normative system.

From these themes, Ewald deduces the third, the central theoretical prerequisite for a philosophy of law that examines law as a practice. A Foucaultian philosophy of law is necessarily critical and, therefore, its aim cannot be the theoretical justification of adjudication on a dogmatic level. But neither does it aim at a direct evaluation of social justice on a political level. As critique, Ewald's philosophy of law cannot give answers to questions on the objectivity of a judgement or the social justice of a practice but, on the contrary, it aspires to keep the questions continuously posed and open to the diversity of the juridical experience. However, the "epistemological conjunctures" of our times require that even a critical philosophy of law must necessarily be positive. According to Ewald's *critical positivism*, the precondition of positive law is the only way to maintain the unity of the object of study in an era of disparate singularities.

The dilemma of Ewald's philosophy of law is his reaction to the disintegration of an entity, to the dispersion of a juridical object of study into the non-juridical. By reassembling the disintegrating object back together in accordance with the demands of legal positivism, Ewald forces law and history into a reconciliation that reinstates the non-historical element that he was out to eradicate. Ewald understands essentialism as the neglect of history, but he comes to terms with his own epoch only by disregarding the traits that mark its specifity. The "epistemological conjunctures of the era" and the alleged "dispersion" are both elements within an historical formation, objects of research for any Foucaultian power analytics. By objectifying the position of the philosopher beyond history, Ewald reduces his analytics of juridical thinking into a specifically non-Foucaultian philosophy.

III

The openness of Ewald's juridical experience leaves law in a curious no-man's-land between the discursive and the non-discursive. But before attempting to situate law in one or the other, the interrelation between the two must be accounted for. This is one of the main issues in Deleuze's interpretation of Foucault, and, in this context, he takes up the different ways in which truth is produced in knowledge.[22] In *Surveiller et punir*, the prison as a social practice cannot be deduced from penal law regardless of the *a priori* nature of discursive practices. On the other hand, as a discursive practice, penal law produces a language of delinquency independent of the prison. This leaves the relation between the two unaccounted for and, taking into consideration the gracious nature of Deleuze's reading of Foucault, even the possibility of analysing them within a single historical formation problematic.

[22] Deleuze, *Foucault*, pp. 70–75. Cf. Dreyfus and Rabinow, *Michel Foucault*, pp. 75–78.

Deleuze approaches and structures the problem with the help of *procedures* that produce truth.[23]

Deleuze's interpretation, emphasising the consistency of the archaeological project, requires that there are two different procedural games of truth. Social or non-discursive practices operate through processes (*processus*) that address knowledge by posing questions about the visibility of objects and things, their ordering in the imminence of discursive formations, and the appearance of truth and the position of the seer. On the other hand, discursive practices address the corpus of the discursive formation through methods (*procédé*): what are the utterances uniting the words and the propositions of the corpus? Who may position themselves as subjects of the utterances? Deleuze concludes that, for Foucault, knowledge can make truth appear only through problematisations within the procedures of discursive and non-discursive practices.

The reciprocal relation of producing truthful effects is, however, still open as the different procedures cannot be uniform. For instance, the way in which the penal legislation and jurisprudence of the nineteenth century defined the responsibility of the accused for his actions—responsibility based on act and guilt—does not concur with the way in which the adjudicative authorities condemned the accused to punishments. Responsibility was, rather, determined through the social damage and repugnance of the crime and the potential danger of the offender inferred thereof.[24] Truth is, then, not produced by uniformity because the relation between discursive and non-discursive practices is disjunctive. According to Deleuze, the only uniting factor is the limit separating the discursive from the non-discursive. The practices have no common form, but on the border they confront each other as enemies on a battlefield.

As a discursive practice, penal law comprises both language as a condition and the utterances it makes possible, just as the prison, in its non-discursive nature, encompasses light and what it enables to be seen. Truth is produced in the disjunctive relation of the respective procedures, that is, the processes and the methods. In the engagement of procedures, the visible penetrates into an area between language and utterances enabling language to produce new utterances to be spoken. As a social practice interpreting laws in a certain manner, adjudicative decision-making drifts into the corpus of law producing, at the same time, new utterances of a second order on, for instance, the foundations of juridical responsibility. But in a very similar manner, utterances drift between light and the visible producing new things to be seen, new adjudicative practices. As a discursive practice on responsibility in civil law makes its way into the practice of the criminal courts, a new truth arises for jurisdiction: the notion of

[23] Deleuze's reading remains problematic in that elsewhere Foucault identifies these procedures with matrices.

[24] Foucault, "L'évolution de la notion d'"individu dangereux' dans la psychiatrie légale du XIXe siècle", in Foucault, *Dits et écrits III*, pp. 459–461. Cf. Ewald, *L'État providence*, pp. 351–358; Ewald, *Histoire de l'État providence*, pp. 15–18.

the offender's "virtualities", the possibility of imminent crimes based on the notion of dangerousness.[25]

Surveiller et punir has often been understood as the borderline that marks Foucault's rejection of the archaeological project and a reformulated interest in the social practices that found the discursive domain.[26] The relation between the discursive and the non-discursive is, however, far from clear. For a philosophy of law, at least two sets of questions can be formulated. How is the position of law to be understood in the division of practices into discursive and non-discursive? Can law be conclusively situated within the discursive as Deleuze seems to do with penal law? Is the traditional object of juridical research, due to its essentialist nature, incompatible with a Foucaultian power analytics? Or should we, perhaps, rather talk about the juridical, a modus of power-knowledge indexed to a distinct logic, entailing both discursive and non-discursive elements?

The other set of questions refers to the "founding" relation of social, non-discursive practices in relation to discursive practices. How can one account for Foucault's obstinacy in explaining this relation with juridical and quasi-juridical terminology? How should one integrate theoretically the regulative logic of, for example, the rules of formation[27] to Foucault's later position on refuting the repressive hypothesis according to which a juridical logic must be abandoned altogether:

> "This image we must break free of, namely, of the theoretical privilege of law and sovereignty, if we wish to analyse the concrete and historical development of the methods of power. A power analytics must be constructed that no longer follows law as a model and a code".[28]

The question, then, concerns the juridical nature of the *internal* logic of Foucault's theory. The central position of power in Foucault's later work cannot account for this logic. But in the introduction of *Surveiller et punir*, Foucault clarifies one aim of the research by referring to matrices:

> "Instead of treating the histories of penal law and the human sciences as two separate series whose overlapping would have had, depending on one's perspective, either a damaging or a useful effect on one or the other—or perhaps on both—we should look into the possibility of a common matrix or that they both derive from a 'juridico-epistemological' process of formation".[29]

In other words, discursive practices such as penal law and the human sciences share a matrix that, in turn, is inferred from social practices such as the prison. Later Foucault does take up the matrix of examination (*examen*), a ritual connected to the formation of knowledge that enables the singularisation and the

[25] Foucault, "La vérité et les formes juridiques", n. 12 above, p. 593.
[26] E.g. Blanchot, *Michel Foucault tel que je l'imagine*, p. 34.
[27] Foucault, *L'archéologie du savoir*, p. 53.
[28] Foucault, *La volonté de savoir*, pp. 118–119.
[29] Foucault, *Surveiller et punir*, p. 28.

objectification required by disciplinary power.[30] The essential components of the examination are the moving of the domain of visibility from its source to its objects, the development of detailed and observable characteristics suitable for documentation, and, lastly, with the help of the developed symptomatology, the possibility of singularising the visible object of power:

> "the examination is at the centre of the procedures that constitute the subject as effect and object of both power and knowledge".[31]

In *La volonté de savoir*, Foucault differentiates the objective effect of the examination from the subjective effect of the confession (*aveu*). In the confession, the speaking subject and the subject of speech become one in a juridico-religious ritual in which:

> "truth is authenticated by the obstacles and resistances it has had to overcome in order to be formulated".[32]

The matrix is not a social practice as such but a structural reduction thereof—of juridical practices, medical practices, religious practices, and so on.[33] Through the procedures, the matrix uniting different social practices effects the discursive field. But although the relation between the discursive and the non-discursive is disjunctive, the effect is formative. In *Surveiller et punir*, Foucault mentions briefly two other juridico-political matrices that are connected to the formation of knowledge:

> "It is, perhaps, true that, in Greece, the mathematical sciences were born from the techniques of the measure [*mesure*], but towards the end of the Middle Ages, the practices of the investigation [*enquête*] at least partly contributed to the birth of the natural sciences".[34]

In other, less well known texts, Foucault takes up the matrices in more detail. This is one of the most important law-related aspects of Foucault's work from the 1970s. One of the aims of his morphological project is to write, with the help of the matrices, a history of power. The matrices uniting social practices account for the formative effect of the non-discursive *vis-à-vis* the discursive. The epochal periodisation of Foucault's history can be structured as a succession of matrices derived from, for the most part, juridical practices: the time preceding Greek democracy and the trial (*épreuve*), the *polis* and the measure, the Middle Ages and the investigation, and, finally, the examination and the confession of modernity discussed in detail in *Surveiller et punir* and *La volonté de savoir* respectively. The individual practices, in turn, are responsible for the production of truth in power-knowledge relations.

[30] *Ibid.*, pp. 186–194.
[31] *Ibid.*, p. 194.
[32] Foucault, *La volonté de savoir*, p. 83.
[33] On the confession, see, e.g., Foucault, "Le jeu de Michel Foucault", in Foucault, *Dits et écrits III*, pp. 316–318.
[34] Foucault, *Surveiller et punir*, p. 227. Cf. Foucault, *La volonté de savoir*, pp. 78–80.

IV

Details on the different matrices mentioned above and their indispensable affinity with juridical practices come up in a lecture series entitled "La vérité et les formes juridiques" from 1973.[35] Initially, Foucault refers to the matrix of the trial in *The Iliad*. In the song mentioned, Antilochos and Menelaos are engaged in a dispute concerning a horse race that has been organised in honour of Patroklos's death. For Foucault, the important figure in the song is, however, the *histōr* supervising the races:

> "and beside it he stationed a judge, Phoinix the godlike, the follower of his father, to mark and remember the running and bring back a true story".[36]

Menelaos argues that Antilochos has won the race by breaking the rules, but he does not refer to the *histōr*. Instead, he requires Antilochos to take an oath:

> "Antilochos, beloved of Zeus, come here. This is justice. Stand in front of your horses and chariot, and in your hand take up the narrow whip with which you drove them before, then lay your hand on the horses and swear by him who encircles the earth and shakes it you used no guile to baffle my chariot".[37]

Because Antilochos refuses to take the oath required, Menelaos wins the dispute and, consequently, the race as well.[38] The dispute is, then, not settled by referring to the testimony of the observer and to the irregularities that have taken place. The confronted participant of the dispute is challenged to take an oath before the gods.

As a juridical practice, Foucault identifies the trial in early medieval Germanic law. Foucault names, first, the social forms of the trial in which the contended party attempts to establish his significant position in the community with the help of what we today know as character witnesses. In addition, Foucault distinguishes the verbal forms of the trial requiring the contested party to pronounce accurately a legal formula from magico-religious forms as exemplified

[35] Foucault delivered the lecture at the Pontifical Catholic University of Rio de Janeiro in 1973. It was published in Portuguese the following year. The original French text was never published as such, and it seems that the Brazilian edition has now been retranslated into French. In addition, a Spanish edition, translated from Portuguese, has been available. The accuracy of the various editions remains uncertain. The Spanish translator notes that his Brazilian colleagues have respected their source material to such an extent that the text remains rigid and repetitive, full of colloquial and redundant expressions. See Foucault, *La verdad y las formas jurídicas*, p. 11. Foucault's lecture was also an immediate response to Deleuze's (and Guattari's) *L'anti-Œdipe* published a year earlier in 1972. It was meant to be the beginning of a dialogue that sadly ended in the silent dispute between former friends only a few years later. In addition to a few scattered book-reviews, Deleuze was able to reply only in some private notes from 1977 that have also now been published. Deleuze, "Désir et plaisir".

[36] Homer, *Il.* XXIII 359–361 (this translation is Lattimore's).

[37] Homer, *Il.* XXIII 581–585. In the original, "justice" is *themis* and, therefore, should rather be understood as binding custom.

[38] Foucault, "La vérité et les formes juridiques", n. 12 above, pp. 555–556. See also Foucault, *Résumé des cours 1970–1982*, p. 15.

in the oath of *The Iliad*. The best known trials are, however, corporeal: physical tribulations or ordeals that the contested party must survive in order to attest that he is right.[39]

Foucault, however, emphasises that, as a practice, the trial does not relate to the production of truth but is, rather, the ritualised extension of the dispute in which a procedural regularity is essential. In the trial, force is transformed into the right within a formalised duel that attempts to end the confrontation into a temporary armistice.[40] The third party that occupies the position of the judge does not call for testimony or proof but only supervises the regularity of the process:

> "the function [of the trial] is not to express or to manifest the truth or to make it appear. The trial is not an operator of truth or an apophantic operator, it is an operator of law".[41]

Just as the resolution to the dispute in *The Iliad*, the trial of the early Middle Ages is a practice in which the stronger opponent of the dispute is defined at the same time as the conflict itself is ritualised. This is why Foucault insists that the trial has nothing to do with the production of truth; it does not correspond with any particular form of knowledge. Other knowledge-related practices from the latter half of the Middle Ages still obey the same logic of the trial. Alchemy, for instance, is not a search for knowledge in the sense of the experimental sciences but a confrontation between the alchemist and nature protecting its secrets. In this confrontation, the alchemist operates both as a participant and as a supervisor of the process. In addition, in the university habilitation of medieval Europe, the *disputatio*, knowledge is not authenticated with experimental evidence but is set into a game where the sources of knowledge operate as an authorisation of the position of the orator.[42]

In his reports to the *Collège*, Foucault also mentions an archaic juridical practice of Greek origin that was used as:

> "a just measure not only in economic exchanges but also within the social relations of the city, with the help of the institution of money".[43]

The juridical practice that finds its shape in the measure, the second matrix, refers to a truth that is produced as visible, verifiable and assessable. The laws of truth correspond to the laws of the order of the world. The measure both founds and sustains order in human conflicts and, at the same time, furnishes the matrix for the mathematical sciences. As order, the measure is both the means and the effect in relation to its function.[44] The measure seems to be a preliminary stage as all later matrices require truth to be produced as visible in social

[39] Foucault, "La vérité et les formes juridiques", n. 12 above, pp. 574–575.
[40] *Ibid.*, pp. 572–573 and 576–577.
[41] *Ibid.*, p. 577.
[42] *Ibid.*, pp. 586–588.
[43] Foucault, *Résumé des cours 1970–1982*, p. 15.
[44] *Ibid.*, pp. 19–21.

practices. The measure enables the correspondence between entities of a different ontological nature, it furnishes the foundation of an ontology of the visible that can be correlated with the "correct" order of the world.

After the brief and scattered remarks on the trial and the measure, Foucault passes on to the investigation, a medieval juridico-political matrix that he designates as decisive for the historical development of Occidental society. As the name of the matrix already indicates, its structural framework is the practice of administrative and clerical inquisition. In the investigation, the past is verified as the truth by reconstructing the chain of events with the help of testimonial evidence. The matrix is also intimately bound to the centralisation (*étatisation*) of juridical power in the Middle Ages.[45] The investigation is:

> "a means to certify or to reconstruct the facts, the events, the acts, the attributes, the rights; but it is also the matrix of empirical knowledge and of the natural sciences".[46]

According to Foucault, the first indication of the investigation is, however, Sophocles's *Oedipus Rex*, and Foucault proceeds to elaborate the structure of the investigation by way of a close reading of the tragedy. Foucault denies the Freudian interpretation, deep-rooted in Occidental mythology, that Oedipus's story represents the universal structures of desire. For Foucault, the tragedy deals with power and the potentiality of losing it, the way in which truth can constitute a threat to sovereign power.[47] Although the tragedy still has traces of the matrix of the trial[48], the uncovering of the truth follows a law of halves (*loi des moitiées*) characteristic of the investigation. The parts of the story come together composing, in the end, a whole which appears as the truth.[49] Foucault uses the metaphor of the symbol to describe the way in which the truth is composed and structured in the investigation: the *sumbolon* or the broken vase the connecting halves of which are later reassembled in order to, for instance, confirm the authenticity of a messenger.[50]

Foucault singles out the two halves of the tragedy and the smaller parts of which the halves are, in turn, composed of.[51] The first half describes the divine message that is delivered by Creon: the land is cursed by a plague because a crime, the murder of Laïus, has gone unpunished,[52] and as king, Oedipus commits himself to do justice by punishing the criminal.[53] In the second half, the identity of the murderer of Laïus and the consequences that this knowledge

[45] Foucault, *Résumé des cours 1970–1982*, pp. 21–23; Foucault, *Surveiller et punir*, pp. 226–229; Foucault, "La vérité et les formes juridiques", n. 12 above, pp. 580–584.

[46] Foucault, *Résumé des cours 1970–1982*, p. 20.

[47] Cf. Deleuze and Guattari, *L'anti-Œdipe*, especially pp. 126–134. Foucault, however, emphasises that his interpretation is not Deleuzian even though the premises are the same. Foucault, "La vérité et les formes juridiques", n. 12 above, pp. 623–624.

[48] e.g. Creon's pledge of loyalty to Oedipus: Sophocles, *OT* 644–646.

[49] Foucault, "La vérité et les formes juridiques", n. 12 above, p. 557.

[50] *Ibid.*, pp. 559–560.

[51] *Ibid.*, pp. 557–559.

[52] Sophocles, *OT* 100–117.

[53] Sophocles, *OT* 229–231.

must lead to are established. Teiresias, the blind envoy of the gods, is the bearer of the oracle in the second half,[54] and the fulfilment of the prophecy is affirmed by the shepherd's story on the true identity of Oedipus's father.[55] In between these two halves, we find a lengthy discussion between Oedipus and Jocasta in which the king already foresees his doom.[56]

In the tragedy, truth configures into three levels: the gods, the sovereign king and, finally, the level of the slaves who provide the testimonial evidence that establishes the truth.[57] At first it would seem that truth is produced when the prophecy is coupled with the story of the shepherd, when the omnipotent and prophetic gaze of the gods connects with the retrospective verification of the prophecy that finally destroys the king.[58] What is, then, the knowledge of the king? According to the traditional interpretation of the tragedy, Oedipus represents the unconscious, that which is not known, but Foucault maintains that:

> "in the mechanism of the *sumbolon*, in the game of reciprocities between the shepherds and the gods, Oedipus is not he who did not know but, on the contrary, he who knew too much. Who united his knowledge and his power in a condemnable way and whom the story of *Oedipus* was to conclusively exile from history".[59]

It is more or less apparent that, in his reading of *Oedipus Rex*, Foucault is not talking about what came to be known as disciplinary power but about an anterior mode of power-knowledge, something that could, perhaps, be called juridical. This is the power of the sovereign king that still haunts the understanding of our own epoch, the power that, as Foucault frequently emphasises, leads any analysis of modern society astray. But in an almost nostalgic tone, Foucault designates the productive and positive attributes of such power. Oedipus's wavering destiny resembles that of the *hērōs* who must, in his adventures, time and time again, confront the unknown. The unknown introduces an uncertainty that may force the king and the hero to venture their privileged positions at any given time. On this positive level, Oedipus is also characterised by a certain affinity with Solon in that the king must attend to the well-being of his realm just as the legislator is expected to prescribe just laws for the city.

What, then, has made the king a tyrant? Why is Oedipus the monster that was to be evicted from the history of man? The tyrant rules over his city presuming, at the same time, that he is one with his people. This is, however, not the case. The power of Oedipus is not confined by the laws of the city. The will of the tyrant is itself the law that does not obey the restrictions of the right (*dikē*). In addition, the tyrant's power is characterised by a specific mode of knowledge. Like Solon, Oedipus is the sage (*sofos*), but in order to solve the riddle of the Sphinx, he must also posses practical knowledge (*technē*) with which individual

[54] Sophocles, *OT* 350–353.
[55] Sophocles, *OT* 1182–1185.
[56] Sophocles, *OT* 609–616 and 792–794.
[57] Foucault, "La vérité et les formes juridiques", n. 12 above, p. 560.
[58] *Ibid.*, pp. 560–561.
[59] *Ibid.*, p. 562.

problems are resolved and obstacles are overcome. Finding solutions (*euriskein*) is seeing, taking action while opening one's eyes and disregarding the interests of the surrounding world. It is experimental knowledge, the lonely knowledge of the despot with which the tyrant can rule his city like a captain commands his ship. By opening his eyes in order to see what lies ahead, the tyrant must also confront the unknown, his destiny (*tuchê*), and, thus, surrender his power to the dangers of the future.[60]

Oedipus exercises his despotic and lonely power by refusing to heed the oracle, and by dismissing the will of the people, and wanting to see everything for himself, he merges the prophecy of the gods together with the testimonial memory of the people. This is why the tyrant is a monster who knows too much. In this negative description about the relationship between power and knowledge, Foucault recognises the slight of Platonic philosophy over the sophist's knowledge.[61]

For Foucault, the ideal of Greek democracy that finds its configuration in the tragedy of Oedipus manifests the final destruction of a long Assyrian tradition that conceived of power and knowledge as one. Ever since Oedipus, power has been understood as blind and ignorant while the task of philosophers has been to search for, on the one hand, the eternal truths of the gods and, on the other, the testimony of the people in whose memory the traces of truth are still sustained. This is the antinomy of power and knowledge: power is blind while knowledge either faces the light of the gods ahead or turns retrospectively back to the history of the people. The aim of Foucault's Nietzschean power analytics is to destroy this myth.[62] The only explanation for Foucault's nostalgic longing for the Assyrian kings still present as traces in the story of Oedipus is that, in relation to the omnipercipience of disciplinary power, the tyrant can still be dethroned. The juridical power he represents is precarious to the point that an interventive critique is still conceivable.

V

What would, then, a Foucaultian philosophy of law involve? What would its themes and perspectives be? It could, of course, limit itself to the traditions of the legal sciences and restrict its analyses to law understood as a distinguishable and unique entity. A Foucaultian power analytics would, consequently, offer but a method to study a stipulated object of research. This seems to be the point of departure of, for instance, Ewald's critical positivism. It is, however, a constricted perspective in that, for Foucault, the structural elements interconnect-

[60] Foucault, "La vérité et les formes juridiques", n. 12 above, pp. 564–567. On Oedipus and the "desire of knowledge", see also Lacoue-Labarthe, "Œdipe comme figure", in Lacoue-Labarthe, *L'imitation des modernes*, pp. 220–223.

[61] Foucault, "La vérité et les formes juridiques", n. 12 above, pp. 567–568.

[62] *Ibid.*, pp. 568–570.

ing disparate practices is much more essential than any single practice. Therefore the prison, penal law, pedagogy and medicine are analysed concurrently and, consequently, are structurally reducible into matrices.

As the genealogical perspective enables the observation of dissimilar practices together and, therefore, both the juridical and the non-juridical are observed concurrently, the integral issue becomes the common factors that provide the foundation of the mode of power-knowledge typical of the *epistēmē*. *Surveiller et punir* and *La volonté de savoir* both depict disciplinary power and the juridico-political matrices involved: the examination and the confession. If we are able to delineate an anterior mode of power-knowledge in relation to the investigation, an epochal *juridical power*, perhaps we would also be able to envisage something in relation to the measure, perhaps an *arbitrative power* that is founded on the compatibility of the orders of knowledge and the world. The trial, however, represents Foucault's initial point of departure: power and knowledge as inseparable. Within the morphology Foucault was outlining in the early 1970s, an analysis of matrices would, then, provide a theoretically consistent epochal account of power, a "history of systems of thought". Foucault never finished any such project, and it is likely that he abandoned it long before the publication of his major works on power from the middle of the decade.

Even so, the enigmatic question concerning the formative logic interconnecting social practices to discursive practices remains. The enigma is this: in addition to emphasising the significance of juridical practices themselves in analysing the social domain, Foucault insistently names the matrices with either juridical or quasi-juridical terms. Can we assume that the formative logic, if not identical with the juridical, at least patterns a juridical mode of authority? Even if the individual corpus of penal law is understood as discursive, Foucault's conception of law in general seems to be more intermediate. It is not a mega-practice encompassing both discursive and non-discursive elements but rather a relay that mediates between the visible and the utterable, between "words and things".

As matrices, law conveys the visible into the domain of language in a way that is both formative and bellicose. Through the procedural methods working within the matrical framework, social practices instruct and direct (*maîtriser*) the discursive domain of knowledge just as the master attends to the training and schooling (*formation*) of his apprentice. But at the same time, it must necessarily also involve the strategic element of war because the formative relation between the discursive and the non-discursive is disjunctive. In delivering the social to the discursive, law as disjunction accounts for the paradox of simultaneous order and conflict. The structural regularity of diverse social practices reveals the epochal matrices that Foucault understands as law, and law, in turn, designates the way in which the matrical framework of the visible domain of an *epistēmē* both forms the discursive domain and enables its dissemination. Law is, then, not a practice, be it discursive or non-discursive, but the "juridico-epistemological" matrix of a given epoch through which the social world penetrates into language. Through its formative or ordering aspect, law enables the recognition of the social in language, but, at the same time, its disjunctive or conflictive aspect accounts for the dissemination of a discursive corpus into new utterances of a second order. As the matrix distinctive of its *epistēmē*, law first relays the human world into language and then opens the seemingly closed system to speech. This is, undoubtedly, a fundamental question for any Foucaultian analytics of law worth the characterisation "philosophical".

Lastly, we must also turn to the philosophical task that Foucault gave himself. A Foucaultian philosophy of law would be obliged to consider the will to knowledge and its relation to the notion of the modern subject autonomously ruling its world, a notion that Foucault consistently criticised.[63] For the will to knowledge to remain within the volitive, something must function as an impediment as man aspires to appropriate his world. Something must inhibit man from achieving fulfilment as he attempts to make the world his own lest the founding volitive structure is annulled. What is the restrictive barrier that constitutes man as willing?

At this point, the philosophy of law can recognise a familiar theme that has haunted its enterprise from Hegel to current psychoanalytically inspired theories. Foucault's attempt to conceptualise the will to knowledge touches upon the theme of desire and law regardless of the fact that Foucault explicitly rejects the idea of law as the constitutive element of desire. Man cannot reign autonomously in his world because law engages him into the conflictive universe of contradicting desires. But neither can he plunge into the rage of his instinctive life because law imposes orderly meaning into the world. Like the prohibition of incest, law both constitutes the originary object of desire and maintains the indispensable distance in relation to it.

[63] It is, perhaps, worth noting that the title of Foucault's first report to the *Collège* in 1970 was "La volonté de savoir", the same title that was to end the project of power-analytics.

7

Ethics Without Passion

> "This internal war of reason against the passions has made a division of those who would have peace into two sects. The first would renounce their passions and become gods; the other would renounce reason and become brute beasts".
>
> Blaise Pascal

I

Earlier I have tried to demonstrate how the relationship between law and critique has always been more or less problematic in the study of juridical phenomena. Partly this is due to an explicitly modern, non-philosophical understanding of critique. An etymological analysis of the Greek adjective *kritikē* will ultimately lead to two words: to *krinein* and to *technē*. If we understood critique literally, it would, consequently, denote an "art of discerning". In one sense, then, the scientific enterprise must necessarily be critical. But within the science of law, the word "critique" has almost uniquely come to mean an "art of governing", *politikē*. Critical legal scholarship is accordingly understood as a political science, a rather dubious alliance uniting the allegedly objective judgement of scientific reason with the subjective prejudices of political commitment.

The historical development of the science of law is, indeed, often portrayed as a succession of political positions in which the legal scholar defines himself in relation to a normative order and its scientific associates. Beginning from the last half of the nineteenth century, the jurisprudential preferences of European juridical thinking have been challenged, not only by somewhat nostalgic allusions to the natural law doctrine of pre-modern times, but also by the more political discourse of a sociologically inspired orientation. This social jurisprudence, emphasising that the main objective of legal scholarship is the administration of a given society and the prevention of unwanted social phenomena—that is, the very functions of the juridical order itself—has since become the doctrinal basis of contemporary legal scholarship.

During the first half of the twentieth century, the rather crudely defined interests of this new scientific era evolved into what can more generally be called modern law. Deviance in relation to a social order is no longer understood as a moral evil or as blameworthy action but, rather, as a malady that, with the help of modern science, was to be treated and done away with. The overexposure of law to the epistemological premises of the natural sciences and the resulting promises of final solutions has, in turn, later been confronted by both the more fundamental criticism of critical legal scholarship as well as the "alternative legal dogmatics" of the welfare state with its dialogue of social equality and legal safeguards.[1] Despite the substantial dissimilarity of the different critical approaches, a pattern of succession emerges: the critic moves from one political position to another, but the basic theoretical premise of the science of law remains constant. It obliges the legal scholar to regard his science as part of a juridical technology, as a preventive.

The technological premise of the legal scholar is partly due to the ambiguous use of juridical language. In English, the word "law" has two specific meanings that are frequently merged together without making an appropriate distinction. On the one hand, law denotes positive law or the corpus of juridical norms that regulate social phenomena. In this meaning, law is more or less equivalent with juridical order. But on the other hand, law is also a scientific enterprise that studies and analyses this corpus; law is, in other words, also the science of law. If the positive law that is observed and studied and the scientific enterprise that observes and studies are indistinguishable, the legal scholar must also find himself either in the position of the practising lawyer or, alternatively, lost, without a place of his own in the world of law he studies. And even in the latter case, one option he is left with is identification with other characters of the juridical play, other places and positions of which none is strictly speaking scholarly.

In this role game of places and positions, the critical judgement of the scholar is most frequently identified with the passing of judgment in individual cases. When the juridical is equated with the judicial, the scholar comes to occupy the place of the judge, and, in fact, a popular vein in jurisprudence is founded on the analogy between court room reasoning and the reason of the science of law. The scholar, it is said, derives the correct content of positive law—a text—by employing an allegedly scientific rationality not unlike the reasoned judgment given by a court room judge. Even if the scholar is not required to present binding conclusions in individual cases, he is, nevertheless, more or less aware of a *common juridical ethics* that binds both judge and scholar. The core of this juridical ethics concerns the question of admissible sources of law and the limits of interpretation: how far can an acceptable interpretation expand? The ethical correctness of an interpretation of law—be it juridical or judicial—must, in the end, be evaluated with the help of a conceptual tool, namely a distinction between legislation and adjudication, between the creation of positive law and

[1] The latter, a "critical black letter law", can be traced back to the Italian movement of "*l'uso alternativo del diritto*" which was especially strong in the 1960s and 1970s. It was—and is—the central theoretical inspiration of the "alternative legal dogmatics" that has been practised in the Nordic countries. See, e.g., Cerroni, "Per la critica della dommatica giuridica". It would, then, also have similarities with Ewald's particular brand of "critical positivism".

its interpretation. This distinction designates the ethical limits within which both judge and jurisprudent must reason.[2]

In this chapter, then, my aim is to look more closely at the possibility of confining a juridical decision to the interpretation of a given text. First, is it possible to distinguish clearly between creation and interpretation? Can an interpreter such as a scholar or an adjudicator limit himself ethically to the parameters of a source of law? My reply will be negative: no such clear-cut distinction between creation and interpretation or between legislation and adjudication is possible. I will try to demonstrate this by examining the Heraclean constitution that Ronald Dworkin confers upon his interpreter of law. And if the distinction between creation and interpretation remains ambivalent, the ethics that confines the activities of the interpreting adjudicator—and juridical scholar—must somehow resemble the ethics of a legislator. This is, then, my second question: what are the ethics of the legislator? Or is the sovereign law-giver by definition superior in relation to all juridically relevant ethical norms, even in relation to the laws and statutes it has handed down itself? Can the legislator be held accountable only with the help of a theory of *ius naturalis*? The answer is intimately bound to the question concerning the position of the legislator, in general: does the law-giver occupy a *juridical* position to begin with, or is the creation of law merely a political agency?

II

Dworkin's "liberal" and anti-positivistic theory of law is, perhaps, the most widely known account of how the jurisprudent is transformed into the judge—or, perhaps, vice versa. Its claims are in strong opposition with the foundational premises of traditional positivism, and one of its most controversial contributions to jurisprudence is Dworkin's notion of the super-judge, that is, an adjudicator of impeccable moral and ethical character who is also an enlightened master of *iurisprudentia*, of "juridical wisdom". Dworkin's judge-turned-jurisprudent does not accept the binding ethical limits of interpretation set by the tradition of juridical scholarship at face value. The proponents of a more restricted notion of interpretation claim that this new adjudicator intentionally transgresses the limits of interpretation. In other words, the judge assumes the role of a juridical creator legislating his own statutes in the name of interpretation.

Dworkin, of course, must deny this, and in his counter-arguments, he can either assume that the legislative creation of the judge-turned-jurisprudent is ethically acceptable or, which seems more likely, establish that the judge-turned-jurisprudent's ruling is, in the end, mere interpretation after all. As

[2] It is clear that interpretation always involves an element of creation. In hermeneutics, this creation is evident in the constant "expansion" of the hermeneutic circle. Here I am, however, not dealing with the distinction as such but, rather, with the structural premises of a juridical ethics.

Dworkin's theory is, at least implicitly, more or less dependent on the hermeneutics of Hans-Georg Gadamer, it is more plausible that the counter-arguments that he presents to his critics derive their persuasive impact from the latter possibility: the judge-turned-jurisprudent does not, in fact, cross the delicate line between legislative creation and judicial interpretation. By narrowing interpretation within limits that are too confined, the positivistic tradition has merely misunderstood the concept of interpretation. Dworkin defends his views in the third part of his well known essay "Law as Interpretation".[3]

Whatever the substance of the arguments and counter-arguments of the debate may be, they must necessarily rely on a conceptual distinction between legislation and adjudication, between creation and interpretation. Dworkin contends that:

> "there is a difference between interpreting while creating and creating while interpreting, and therefore a recognisable difference between the artist and the critic".[4]

The adjudicator is, then, the critic, not the artist. But the title of the essay, "Law as Interpretation", releases the same demons of significative ambiguity that we encountered in the use of the word "law" in general. Dworkin gives the word "law" several different senses, but as the essay deals with the similarity of the activities of a judge and a scholar, we are, no doubt, talking about law in an active sense of the word. Law is, then, a practice, a social agency defining common parameters for both adjudication and juridical scholarship:

> "legal practice is an exercise in interpretation not only when lawyers interpret particular documents or statutes but generally".[5]

But even then, law understood as a scientific enterprise may have a more active and a more passive meaning: it is a scientific *activity* embodied in specific traditions and methods, but it is also the *outcome* of such an activity, it is *iurisprudentia*, "juridical wisdom". On the other hand, the term "interpretation" also suggests an active and a passive connotation. It can mean the act of interpretation, *interpreting*, or the *outcome* of this activity as in "Dworkin's interpretation of this-or-that". The two terms are bound together with an indeterminate copulative adverb, "as", suggesting that the author has several traits concerning law in mind. Law is, for example, "like literature", which is not the same as stating that law *is* literature. And in a similar indeterminate way, one cannot conclude that law *is* essentially interpretation, but only that, "as" interpretation, the author has adopted this perspective to law *here and now*, by way of choice.

The manifold ambiguity of Dworkin's conception of "law as interpretation" gives us several possible ways in which to come to terms with what he can mean by jurisprudence. The obvious chain of possible connotations is, of course, that

[3] Dworkin, "Law as Interpretation", in Dworkin, *A Matter of Principle*, pp. 167–177.
[4] *Ibid*., p. 146.
[5] *Ibid*.

the science, "law", is an interpretative activity, "interpreting", giving us a certain outcome, an "interpretation", which, in its turn, is again "law" in the more passive sense, that is, jurisprudence. But the text does not give itself away so easily. Even for Dworkin, law is also a normative corpus, a body of norms or "rules and principles"[6] which can also be understood as an interpretation, as an outcome in itself. If a norm of law is, in itself, an interpretation to begin with, it must necessarily be an interpretation *of something*. There must necessarily be something *prior to* the norm of positive law, a hidden element that is to be read into the open by way of interpretative activity. It is no coincidence that Dworkin's personal history is a collection of anecdotes about deep sea fishing and hunting; Dworkin's jurisprudence also presents itself with the vocabulary of search and exploration, of a quest for a hidden element.

Dworkin's jurisprudence is, then, interpretation on (at least) two different levels. First, the juridical norm or the text to be interpreted is, in itself, already an interpretation of something; it is, perhaps, a legislative interpretation of, to use Dworkin's own terminology, "an underlying principle". The underlying principle that has been legislated into a norm of positive law is also a projection of the outcome of interpretation on the adjudicative level. It is an allusion to what has not yet been found but what will most certainly follow. The presumption of an underlying principle is, of course, also a cause for controversy with the dogmatists of positivism: is this natural law revisited?

Secondly, the activity of the judge-turned-jurisprudent is interpreting a chosen norm, an activity the aim of which is to come to a desired result. This result, this "wise" interpretation, is the restoration of the underlying principle that, in its turn, is to serve as a normative element in future adjudication. Thus, we find a circle taking shape.

The circular movement of Dworkin's jurisprudence is, naturally, more than a faint allusion to Gadamer and the hermeneutic circle. Dworkin's own spin commences with the presumption about and the projection of the underlying principle the linguistic expression of which is law, a juridical norm, a juridical text. The interpretative activity of the judge-turned-jurisprudent turns the wheel while extracting an interpretation from the juridical text. The aim of this interpretation is to restore the underlying principle to its proper place at the centre of the juridical arena. But the interpretative activity cannot cease with this restoration. The underlying principle was originally submitted to legislative interpretation for a motive. If the principle itself is sufficient, there would be no need for interpretation and, accordingly, for legislation. Thus, the restored principle must also find a form suitable for future adjudication, a textual expression.

Dworkin's pseudo-hermeneutics is a ferris wheel rotating in two alternate worlds of a Platonic universe: the textual world of a juridical norm, and the significative world of underlying principles. The text to be interpreted—the

[6] For example, the "law" that "provides" certain consequences. *Ibid.*, p. 126. Later Dworkin fuses these conceptions into an "attitude": Dworkin, *Law's Empire*, p. 413.

juridical norm—must first emerge from its textual world into existence, into the ideational world of true meaning and signification where it will find its sense as principle. But the rotating movement must be continuous. Having once come into existence in the world of meaning, the principle must once again submerge into the textual world of a juridical norm. From the perfection of an ideational principle to the textual ambiguity of a juridical norm, interpreted into the idea of the principle, and, once again, transmuted into a juridical text: the hermeneutic circle of juridical interpretation is complete.

But there must be something that turns the ferris wheel, a generator that sets the hermeneutic circle into its spinning motion. If law is interpretative activity, there must necessarily be a motive for interpretation, a flaw in the original text that requires the purifying craft of the judge-turned-jurisprudent. The *dunamis*, the generative power of Dworkin's theory of law, is the profound inadequacy of langauge—the text of law—in expressing the ideational perfection of the underlying principle.[7] This inadequacy is a basic element in Dworkin's understanding of textual entities. On the other hand, the principle is, in its majestic perfection, always non-appropriable as such, unfit for human utilisation. It must first be degraded and returned to the textual world of a normative corpus.

This rotating movement between norm and principle, between text and meaning, is also embodied in Dworkin's own rhetorics about the "hardness" of ambiguous juridical texts and the "rightness" of interpretative outcomes, of ideational principles. The "hard" and the "right" constitute the Platonic universe of text and meaning in which Dworkin spins his jurisprudential ferris wheel.

The interpreter of Dworkin's theory, that is, the judge-turned-jurisprudent, is as two-dimensional as the textual apparatus that he rotates. The fundamental dualism of the interpreter is evident in Dworkin's way of presenting him as an ascending character in the roles of adjudicative interpretation: he is a new figure, a more potent figure. But most of all, the dualism is illustrated by Dworkin's own choice of metaphoric proper names describing two different traits of the juridical interpreter: Hermes[8], the feeble herald who, lacking "ability and insight", merely delivers messages others have written, and Hercules,[9] the almighty being, "a lawyer of superhuman skill, learning, patience and acumen". Hermes is, of course, the patriarch of traditional juridical thinking, the powerless patron of the interpretative sciences whose basic weakness is his persistent belief in legislative intention or, to be more exact, his unfounded presumption that legislative intention can be extracted from juridical texts through strict interpretation.

The choice of proper names can be no coincidence. Despite his hearty allusions to Gadamer's hermeneutics, Dworkin wishes to criticise his main source

[7] Dworkin, *Law's Empire*, pp. 350–353.
[8] *Ibid.*, pp. 317–337.
[9] Dworkin, *Taking Rights Seriously*, pp. 105 and 119.

of Continental philosophy. Hercules, on the other hand, is convinced that legislative intention—it is still to be taken heed of—lies elsewhere. And if we are totally sincere, Hercules's primary problem is not the method of arriving at a "correct" interpretation or the juridical ethics of interpretation, but, rather, the formulation of an acceptable justification for a politically sound decision:

> "He must *construct* a scheme of abstract and concrete principles that provides a coherent justification for all common law precedents and, so far as these are to be justified on principle, constitutional and statutory provisions as well".[10]

Justification, *iustificare*, "to actively render just", to "correct", to "right" a wrong—we are confronted with Dworkin's obsession with "taking rights seriously"—to retribute a previous injustice; this active "justification" is also the evidence of Hercules's strength, the superhuman quality he is expected to use in the ordeal of textual interpretation. There can be no doubt that such an activity requires more than what Hermes has to offer, more than the pious submission to juridical texts. In justifying his decisions, Hercules must necessarily also create new juridical material that can only be of a textual nature. Hercules's problem is similar to the legislator's original dilemma: one cannot utilise an ideational principle as justification, it must first be transformed into a text.

On the other hand, the original text that the judge-turned-jurisprudent was to interpret remains passive. In a rather vague way, it does "set limits"[11] to what Hercules may do, but as any other juridical text, it is unable to define these limits without the assistance of a hardy interpreter. Therefore, not only does Hercules "interpret" the true meaning of a text by actively creating a justification for his own (political) decision, but he also defines the limits within which he may himself manoeuvre, the ethical bounds that restrict his adjudication and designate the dividing line between judicial interpretation and legislative creation. The fundamental inadequacy of the juridical text is not only the source of power for interpretative activity, but it turns out to be the evidence of the text's own weakness when confronting the interpreter, as well.

Therefore, the interpretation of a text in Dworkin's jurisprudence can never be a *reading* in the strict sense of the word. It must necessarily be, as the metaphor of the "chain novel" suggests, a *writing*, an *act of legislation* for which a non-textual signification, an ideational principle, has been predetermined. Hercules's starting point is a fundamental juridical principle, an idea of justice for which he must supply a text. With the original text as a mere pretext—in the literal sense of the word—he then proceeds to create, to write a suitable text himself. He realises that behind the inadequate and vague juridical text that he should interpret, there lies a supreme law. So instead of confining himself to the tedious and unrewarding task of everyday jurisdiction, Hercules is "out to catch the big one". As creator, Hercules's firm intention is to legislate, to present an acceptable justification and a new writing.

[10] *Ibid.*, pp. 116–117 (my emphasis).
[11] *Ibid.*, p. 110.

And in the double role of the judge-turned-jurisprudent, it is especially the jurisprudential element that is responsible for the creative writing. The jurisprudent occupying the place of the judge is necessarily also a law-giver.

III

Dworkin's conception of interpretation is largely based on an analogy between law and literary interpretation. How is law, then, "like literature" as Dworkin suggests? The suggestive title is, in itself, a jurisprudential claim to begin with, an element within Dworkin's science of law, and as such the claim should itself be treated as some kind of literary language. If we, in our own jurisprudential inquiries, are to read the semantic content of Dworkin's claim as if it were literature, it should not, of course, be taken at face value, *à la lettre*. "Law like literature" is Dworkin's allegory about the complexity of juridical and judicial interpretation, about the proportionately small number of "easy cases" and simple texts.[12]

But in contrast to this, Dworkin's conception of literature is rather specific and narrow. He draws his analogy from the prose of classic fiction: *Hamlet*—Dworkin does not read the tragedy as poetic language but, rather, as a narrative with a plot—and *The French Lieutenant's Woman* in "Law as Interpretation", and *Moby-Dick* and *The Merchant of Venice*—again reduced to a plot—in *Law's Empire*. If law is like literature, we must undoubtedly be able to read Dworkin as literature or as figurative language, as well. Nevertheless, I shall read Dworkin's subtitle *à la lettre* despite the obvious error that I am making in doing so.

If Dworkin's jurisprudence is, indeed, a literary exercise on the dividing line between legislation and adjudication, between judicial interpretation and legislative creation, it would seem appropriate to examine it as a novel about law and legislation. In classical fiction, that is, in Dworkin's own choice of literary genre, the "Robinsonad" furnishes us with an archetypical form of legislative prose. Daniel Defoe's *Robinson Crusoe* is, of course, the prime example. It has been noted that an urge to govern his island through legislation arises in Crusoe at the arrival of Friday, at the appearance of an other.

Although plausible, the statement is not altogether accurate. Having recovered from the initial shock caused by the first encounter with the "brutish and inhuman" behaviour of "Indian" savages, Crusoe quite composedly refrains from judgement of a juridical nature:

> "What Authority, or Call I had, to pretend to be Judge and Executioner upon these Men as Criminals, whom Heaven had thought fit for so many Ages to suffer unpunish'd, to go on, and to be as it were, the Executioners of his Judgements one upon another . . . How do I know what God himself judges in this particular Case? . . .

[12] Dworkin, *Law's Empire*, pp. 353–354.

> [These People] do not know it to be an Offence, and then commit it in Deviance of Divine Justice, as we do in almost all the Sins we commit".[13]

Judgement requires blameworthiness, and blameworthiness requires intentional transgression; Crusoe identifies innocence of volition with innocence of comprehension. But later, realising that his island is no longer deserted but inhabited by a motley crew of survivors including the bond servant Friday, his father, and the Spaniard, Crusoe is less bashful about proclaiming his legislative status:

> "My People were perfectly subjected: I was absolute Lord and Law-giver".[14]

In accordance with his puritan ideals, Crusoe governs his island rather through organised labour and religious meditation than through the legislation and the execution of juridical statutes. He also addresses Friday rather in the same manner as a formative governor lecturing a pupil than as a political governor addressing a serf. But there is a Robinsonad with more explicit juridical references to which one can compare some thematic features of Dworkin's jurisprudence, namely Michel Tournier's novel *Vendredi*.[15] Like Dworkin's pseudo-hermeneutic jurisprudence, Tournier's novel is structured around a circular movement, a succession of rites of passage that are illustrated through Robinson's affinity with the elements.[16] Tournier's Robinson ascends into a super human being of Heraclean magnitude by surviving four ordeals.

Robinson's ascension commences with the original disaster: the shipwreck, the deserted island, the need, the hunger, all portrayed through the element of water. This is the fundamental starting point of all Robinsonads: man's capacity to endure suffering face to face with a hostile nature, the solitary and naked human figure rid of his cultural status. The dynamic character of this aquatic period resembles the initial inadequacy of language to explicate ideational principles in Dworkin's scheme of juridical interpretation. Robinson's dearth is a necessary source of power for his ascension, but already this inadequacy presumes an underlying perfection towards which the trials of the island—appropriately named "Speranza", hope—send him. This perfection is embodied in a projection of natural man.

But the objective of Robinson's ordeal is very different from Crusoe's. Gilles Deleuze explains this difference by showing how Crusoe's final victory, that is, his triumph over human suffering, is essentially the conclusion to a narrative of means, a successful re-creation of the shipwreck's humanity and a restoration of his cultural and spiritual puritanism in a hostile environment. The story of

[13] Defoe, *Robinson Crusoe*, pp. 170–171.

[14] *Ibid.*, p. 241.

[15] A shorter and more subtle version of this novel was published a few years later. Cf. Tournier, *Vendredi ou la vie sauvage*. The protagonist of Tournier's novel will be referred to as Robinson to distinguish it from Defoe's Crusoe.

[16] Robinson's ritual ascension by way of the elements has been documented in, e.g., Bouloumié, " '*Vendredi ou les limbes du Pacifique*' *de Michel Tournier*", pp. 124–134.

Robinson, on the other hand, is not as concerned with restoration or re-creation as it is with evolution and creation: it is a narrative of ends:

> "these ends represent a fantastic deviation from our world, under the influence of a deviant sexuality, rather than an economic reproduction of our world, under the impact of a continuous effort".[17]

This difference can be well illustrated by the dissimilar ways in which the two Robinsonads tell their story. The narrative of Crusoe is presented as a posterior account of the adventure retold by Crusoe himself as narrator. This textual re-creation is written entirely in the first person. After an account of Crusoe's background and fate, the narrator-Crusoe cites directly from his own "journal", a sub-text that is supposedly written by Crusoe himself during his stay on the island.[18] For the most part, Crusoe's journal is, indeed, a detailed day-to-day description of how he organises his working day, what his daily chores and immediate plans are, and so on:

> "*April 28*,*29*. These two whole Days I took up in grinding my Tools, my Machine for turning my Grindstone performing very well".[19]

The story of Robinson is composed of two different textual forms, as well: an objectified account written in the past tense, delivered by an anonymous and impersonal narrator addressing Robinson in the third person, and a "logbook" that Robinson himself keeps on the island. The difference between the subject matters of Robinson's logbook and Crusoe's journal is significant. Robinson reflects on his own writing:

> "Is this not what is called 'philosophy', this that I have just written? What strange transformation is taking place within me that I, the most positive and least speculative of men, should be not only putting such questions to myself but, as it would seem, answering them!"[20]

In addition to the logbook, Robinson's story also makes direct reference to the laws that he legislates on the island. These laws, the constitutional Charter and the Penal Code of the island of Speranza, both given on the 1000th day of Robinson's personal calendar, are partially cited. Both laws are a curious mixture of logbook and narration. The articles themselves are offered within the overall frame of the novel as quotations from Robinson's own writings, but instead of using the first person as in the logbook, Robinson writes about himself as if from an exterior point of reference. Article the First of the Charter nominates Robinson governor of the island using a passive tense, "is appointed" (*est nommé*), suggesting that the nomination has come about by way of agreement between several parties. In his own legislation, Robinson also chooses to

[17] Deleuze, "Michel Tournier et le monde sans autrui", in Deleuze, *Logique du sens*, pp. 352–353.
[18] The citation from Crusoe's journal begins abruptly only to curiously fade away some 25 pages later into the posterior account given by the rescued shipwreck. Cf. Defoe, *Robinson Crusoe*, p. 70.
[19] *Ibid.*, p. 83.
[20] Tournier, *Vendredi ou les limbes du Pacifique*, p. 89.

address himself in the third person thus implying to a hypothetic reader that the text has been written by another, by a sovereign power in the name of which Robinson governs the island:

> "As holder of this Office *he* has full Powers of Legislation and Execution throughout the Territory of the Island and its territorial waters, in accordance with the dictates of *his* Inner light".[21]

The personal ambiguity of Robinson's laws illustrates the paradox of all constitutional texts, juridical or other: in "constituting" or founding an institution, the constitutional text must necessarily be a self-nomination. The constitutional text is always written without the authority to nominate and, therefore, the text requires a foundation, a fictive supreme authority granting the text the necessary juridical power, and this can only be achieved with references to an origin.[22]

The fictive character of a sovereign authority granting power to a governor is emphasised even more with the numerous notes with which Robinson interprets—in the first person—his own laws. The legislative governing of the island constitutes the second rite of passage, the telluric period in Robinson's ascension, and it is Robinson's own equivalent of the activity of juridical interpretation. Once he has come to terms with the initial inadequacy of being shipwrecked alone on a desert island, Robinson starts to render his life perfect, partly by reproducing the basic elements of his former world through interpretation, but also by creation, by structuring a new world from the little means he has available. As in the case of Dworkin's jurisprudence, Robinson's sense of inadequacy and the dynamic drive of his activities must necessarily be based on some pre-understanding of perfection, on a projection—conscious or unconscious—about the final stage of his ascension.

This projection begins to take shape in the shipwreck's account of his separation from humanity. Crusoe attempts to restore his humanity and restructure his cultural status as a human being mainly by way of hard labour, but the idle moments he either grants himself due to exhaustion or is forced to pass because of weather conditions remind him of his pitiful fate at the mercy of a cruel nature. Crusoe finds himself sinking into a savage state, but he manages to overcome the temptation of indolence by gradually dedicating these moments to the study of the scriptures.[23] Robinson, on the other hand, realises the philosophical potential of his dehumanisation much more explicitly.[24] For Robinson, dehumanisation is a liberating experience which does not necessarily lead to

[21] *Ibid.*, p. 71 (my emphases).

[22] On the functions of the name as founding reference, see Legendre, *Le désir politique de Dieu*, p. 20.

[23] There is a lovely passage in which Crusoe reasons on why he should thank God for his "forsaken solitary condition": Defoe, *Robinson Crusoe*, pp. 112–114.

[24] This is perhaps best portrayed in Robinson's logbook text on the subject of the other's nonexistence and its effect on Robinson's own consciousness: Tournier, *Vendredi ou les limbes du Pacifique*, pp. 52–55.

degradation. Uprooted from the cultural soil of humanity, Robinson is free to rise or fall, to descend into the bestial or to ascend into the divine.

This aeolic period during which Robinson realises his affinity with Friday the savage marks his ascension from the cultural foundation of humanity into a super human being. But this Heraclean figure has yet another rite of passage to survive. The ship, "Whitebird", arrives to deliver the shipwreck and his companion to safety, but by refusing the rescue Robinson finds his final destiny in the sun, in the element of fire:

> "Standing fully erect again, he confronted the solar ecstasy with a joy that was almost painful. The bright splendour which surrounded him washed him clean of the mortal stains of the past day and the night. A blade of fire penetrated his flesh, causing his whole being to tremble".[25]

This purification with fire is the missing episode of Dworkin's account of the Heraclean legend. In Tournier's Robinsonad, the solar period represents Heracles's ordeal on Mount Oile. A jealous wife, Deianeira, has given the *hēros* a garment poisoned with the blood of Nessos, the Centaur Heracles has slain. To avoid the agony of dying, Heracles climbs the mountain with the intention of burning himself at the stake. But as the sacrificial fire is ignited, a thundercloud descends and lifts Heracles to the heavens. On Mount Olympus, Heracles, once a human being of spectacular skills, is finally given his rightful place among the Pantheon of gods.

While Tournier's Robinson joyfully accepts his solar ecstasy as the sign of ascension to divinity, Dworkin feels obliged to deny Hercules the final destiny that a creator must necessarily take on. Hercules must be denied the status of the law-giver because his position as the interpreter of law involves a particular juridical ethics, a voluntary submission to the dictates of the legislator. But the element of creation problematises the nature of the formidable adjudicator's Heraclean ethics.

IV

The difficulty of excluding legislative creation from interpretative activity is not, of course, only a conceptual dilemma concerning juridical scholarship of a jurisprudential kind. Most sociologically oriented scholars within law take actively part in, for instance, the drafting of parliamentary legislation in ministerial projects and government-sponsored research programmes. But what are the ethical consequences of the scholar's explicit or implicit identification with the legislator?

A widely accepted approach within contemporary research justifies this position by referring to the legitimate nature of participation in the democra-

[25] Tournier, *Vendredi ou les limbes du Pacifique*, p. 254.

tic process. This approach has, however, also been criticised, and the reasons behind this critique can be illustrated by taking a closer look at the legislator's own relationship to ethical structures. In a popular version of this critique, the core of the problem is the ethical limits within which juridical creation must operate: how far does the sovereignty and the autonomy of the law-giver reach? It is presumed that the transgression of certain vaguely formulated limits may constitute an ethical violation, an unacceptable use of legislative power.

In the juridical thinking of the classical *Rechtsstaat*, morals or ethics were the *raison d'être* of the jurisprudential enterprise. The juridical scholar's point of departure was that the democratically elected sovereign power had both factually and logically an absolute right to legislate, but the limits within which the legislator was to operate were to be formulated by an ethically motivated science of law. This was the main ethical idea behind the philosophy of law of, for example, neo-Kantians such as Rudolph Stammler and Gustav Radbruch that I have dealt with before. The objective of their philosophies of law was to define an acceptable foundation for the use of law in society: when is positive law "right" or "correct"?

But the theoretical jurisprudence of the welfare state understands its goal in an entirely different way. The fundamental question concerning modern law is whether or not law is *technically appropriate* in creating a just society, whether law is an efficient means to a predefined end. The "juridical wisdom" of modern law is a technology, a *juristique* as Henri Lévy-Bruhl's unfortunate choice of neologism seems to indicate.[26]

Critical legal scholarship has criticised such a conception of law, referring often to the exclusion of ethical discourse in an instrumental understanding of law, but, in the end, its own conception of ethics is rather similar. Critical legal scholarship is often forced to make nostalgic references to the critical function of ethics that once allegedly dominated the jurisprudential debate, to the ability and the objective of the science of law in maintaining the use of normative power within ethically acceptable limits. In this sense, critical legal scholarship is as functional as the law it criticises: it seeks to operate in the name of a ceased function, as its substitute and nominee. Its aim is to secure the operation of a critical function, to limit the use of legislative power, to submit (juridical) norms to yet other (ethical) norms. Such a formulation of the ethical question is, if not instrumental, at least technical.[27]

I would propose to present the ethical question of jurisprudence in another way by asking: where does a legislative science of law find its *hubris*, its self-assurance and confidence in its own powers to appropriate and to manipulate the world? In his "science of legislation", Jean-Jacques Rousseau gives one possible answer. Rousseau claims that the people, "a blind multitude" that does not

[26] See, e.g., Lévy-Bruhl, *Aspects sociologiques du droit*, p. 41.

[27] A good example of nostalgic and "technical" critique is Renaut's "return to Fichte". See Renaut, *Le système du droit*, pp. 5–19.

often know what it wants because it seldom knows what is good for it, cannot successfully fulfil a complicated task such as legislating its own laws. Therefore, a law-giver or a legislator is needed:

> "In order to discover the rules of society best suited for nations, a superior intelligence that beholds all the *passions* of men without experiencing any of them would be needed . . . It would take *gods* to give men laws".[28]

In fact, the whole chapter on the law-giver is a discourse on gods, on the super-human quality of the legislator that also marked the final stage of the legend of Heracles and the solar purity of Tournier's Robinson. What separates man from the divine wisdom of the law-giver is the former's experience of passion, of *passio* or *pathos*. It is, of course, no passion of love. It is the passion of Christ, the ability to suffer that distinguishes the Son from the Father, that makes the Son of God partly human. And without this *pathos*, unable to experience suffering, the divine law-giver is also without an *ēthos*, without a place or a communal bind that would make it one with the people. Consequently, the law-giver is without an ethics.

As a divine creator, the law-giver must necessarily be able to legislate without ethical limits, for otherwise it would be degraded into something human, "all too human", a being too blind to realise its own desires and needs. Dworkin's Hercules and Tournier's Robinson are both narratives on the unethical quality of legislation. Both start out as suffering creatures, but in the end only the latter may realise his Heraclean destiny by ascending into a passionless and autocratic creator. As a divine law-giver, Robinson is unlimited by ethical restrictions and must necessarily find himself in the position of the absolute sovereign. On the other hand, Dworkin's Hercules is obliged to restate its mundane origins regardless of what the ultimate fate of the *hēros* may be.

Hercules and Robinson are also alike in that, in the beginning, both were misplaced, just as the jurisprudent, who lacks a place of his own in the world of law that he studies. His science, then, is not originally determined by the ethical positions of either judges or law-givers. Homeless, he can only search for a place of his own, a position from which a juridical ethics and a philosophy of law may become possible.

What are the minimum requirements of the jurisprudent's search? In a reply to a commentator, Philippe Nonet has written about the nature of the questions that philosophy asks:

> "From the work of great thinkers as from works of art, we learn only as much as the questions with which we approach them permit. Certain questions are bound to distract us from the essential. First and foremost among them are questions of the practical kind, which, be they "moral", "legal", or "political", always keep our eyes riveted on worldly, daily concerns. Thinking proper does not begin until the seventh day,

[28] Rousseau, "Du contrat social", in Rousseau, *Œuvres politiques*, p. 276 (my emphases). Cf. Bennington, *Dudding*, pp. 69–80.

when, having let all such matters come to rest, we turn at last to the light in which they appeared, and wonder at the sense of their being".[29]

As an answer to the luminous question of the seventh day, Nonet already anticipates a "juridical wisdom". It is, perhaps, once again the *orexis tou eidenai*, the "desire to see" of the philosophy of law. But can the philosopher of law see like the gods, like the divine law-giver that passionlessly posits the world?

[29] Nonet, "Reply", 723.

8

Tropisms

> "These movements, of which we are hardly cognisant, slip through us on the frontiers of consciousness in the form of undefinable, extremely rapid sensations. They hide behind our gestures, beneath the words we speak and the feelings we manifest . . . I gave them this name because of their spontaneous, irresistible, instinctive nature, similar to that of the movements made by certain living organisms under the influence of outside stimuli . . . [tropisms] are produced in us by the presence of others . . ."
>
> Nathalie Sarraute

I

In the previous chapter, I already suggested that the core of what is commonly understood as "ethics" in law is revealed in the subject's relationship to the other, in the way in which Defoe's Crusoe and Tournier's Robinson apprehended their respective Fridays as part of their lives. We are, then, dealing with the way in which an alien element is understood and incorporated into the world. One permanent sign with which the alien is assigned a particular position in this world is race.

As a political and social phenomenon, racist violence has recently become commonly associated with the disquieting re-emergence of populist nationalism and neo-fascism in Europe. Young adherents of various nationalistic parties, frequently identified as "skinheads", have been responsible for violent attacks against ethnic minorities. In France and in Austria, similar hostility of racist nature as well as the persecution of the Jewish population have been more or less openly supported by leaders of the local extreme-right parties.

Racism has, naturally, always been a central issue of the "law and society" variant of critical legal scholarship. It is a social problem, and, in a modern welfare state, law is first and foremost conceived of as a means to an end, as a just remedy to an annoying disease. But despite its often violent nature and its alarming political implications, the core of the problem does not seem to be the spectacular nature of contemporary racism. Quite the contrary, racism has become banal, worldly, matter of fact, a normal phenomenon. The myriad of racist images has, indeed, "seduced" the referent, made racism itself disappear.

But an element of normalisation is quite evident in the juridical domain proper, as well. Racism is not the "evil" it once was. The logic of welfare state legislation has relativised racism into a social problem among others. François Ewald has depicted the characteristics of welfare state legislation in his conception of social law. Social law resolves disputes through juridical settlements, not by differentiating between the right and the wrong.[1] The government of racism through social law would suggest, first, that the conflicting parties are already in a mutually obliging contractual relationship. A juridical evaluation of racism in the welfare state would mean that racism is a "breach of contract", violating the terms of an agreement of peaceful coexistence. The coexistence of races is, therefore, based on a contract presupposed to be mutually profitable.

Secondly, government through social law objectifies racism into a conflictual social order that promotes the well-being of society as a whole. In this context, Ewald specifically mentions Augustin Thierry's doctrine of race war as a *primus motor* of historical progress. In this conflictual order, all parties possess rights, and conflicting rights are balanced through proper government. Racism is, accordingly, a necessary ingredient of social progress.

Thirdly, the juridical settlement conceived by social law requires solidarity and concessions from both parties of the conflict. This calls for compromises *vis-à-vis* "absolute rights" as well as mutual tolerance. In the resolution of racial conflicts, both parties involved are sympathised. Legitimate grounds can be found for the actions of both, and this tolerance is understood as the credo of the welfare state and its social law:

> "one must not only tolerate the difference, the otherness, the equal value of the other, but even, to its benefit, the limit of its right. Social law is symbolic of a mass society in which, because space is running short, each must learn to put up with the other and its unavoidable encroachments".[2]

Europe has unfortunately learned to live with her racism or, to be more exact, she has never learned to live without it. This normality of racism presents the law with a problem: how does one regulate racism? How can the normative penetrate into the normal?

Coinciding with the normalised racism described above, a new variant of racial tolerance, less overtly political than the critique of racism of the decades before, has taken shape. This new variant is founded on the ideal of the "global village", and its discursive elements are present in, for example, the ecological emphases of the "green" ideology and in the wide interest concerning different manifestations of world culture. Perhaps campaigning for rain forests or praising world culture cannot be accounted for as explicit critique of racism, but the essential notion of racial esteem is, no doubt, present.

Occidental racial thought has seldom been analysed by way of its enlightened and tolerant half, and yet most attempts to confront racism as a social problem must necessarily be based on some notion of racial esteem. It would seem, then, that the opponents of racism do not know what they are doing or, more accurately, how they are doing it. The ideal of the global village is, of course, only one variant of racial esteem among others. The common denominator uniting

[1] Ewald, *L'État providence*, pp. 457–468.
[2] *Ibid.*, p. 462.

different variants of racial thought is the opposition intolerance/tolerance, the self-ironical etymology *tolerare* connoting, on the one hand, that Occidental racial respect has always been a matter of enduring, of "putting up with differences"[3] and, on the other hand, that Occidental racial debate is often of a rather tempered nature. A racial debate implies a biological meta-logic, a science of the physical and intellectual qualities of the different races. Racism is always a discourse on the superiority of the subject, while the critique of racism denies the validity of racial biology, in general.

Yet racism and its tolerant opposite both require a language, a cultural logic. In other words, the bio-logic of racial discourse, its *logos* of life, is the language it speaks. In one of his few explicitly political texts, Jacques Derrida outlines the *logos* of race:

> "there is no racism without a language. The point is not that acts of racial violence are only words but rather that they have to have a word. Even though it offers the excuse of blood, colour, birth—or, rather, because it uses this naturalist and sometimes creationist discourse—racism always betrays the perversion of a man, the 'talking animal'. It institutes, declares, writes, inscribes, prescribes. A system of marks, it outlines space in order to assign forced residence or to close off borders. It does not discern, it discriminates".[4]

Racial thought—be it intolerance or tolerance—is inscribed into the language of race through a conception of cultural identity. In cultural identity, the Occidental subject brings itself into contact with a foreign culture or its representative. As it is uttering "I am . . .", the subject must necessarily also affirm that "I am not . . .", "I am not the *other*". In the metaphor of race, the strangeness of the other is concentrated. A different race presupposes numerous other differences as well, and since race is a relatively stable characteristic, it keeps the other at a safe distance. The observation of a foreign culture requires the subject to "objectify" the other beyond itself, to perform a distinction between itself and it. Reflecting on the other through and in itself, the subject can acquire a sense of identity, define the limits of a cultural terrain where the subject can be "what it is".[5]

This structure of identity that can be traced from most manifestations of Occidental ethnocentricity is as old as Occidental culture itself. It is, however, a rather weak version of discriminatory thought. Its structure is still fluid, lacking the constancy and unconditional character of brutal racism. In the Greece of Antiquity, the *barbaros* who "sounded different" could still challenge Hellenic supremacy by refining his accent. Ethnocentricity is open; the centre can always

[3] Ewald seems to reserve the attribute of tolerance exclusively for the welfare state. Cf. *ibid*., pp. 488–489.

[4] Derrida, *Psyché*, p. 355.

[5] In a textbook on legal anthropology, Rouland defines anthropology as a discourse on otherness and maintains that structuring the world as a relationship between the viewing subject and an object under observation is primarily an Occidental characteristic: Rouland, *Anthropologie juridique*, pp. 25–40.

be redefined, the alleged boundaries of the periphery redrawn. But intolerance in the form of racism and overt discrimination thrives on a *stigma*, a permanent stain. It requires that the superiority of the subject *vis-à-vis* the other is fixed into a structure with mandatory power, into a law (*nomos*) or a name (*nomen*). This structure reduces abstract identity into individuality by prescribing the subject a privileged position, by transforming it into a person.

In Latin, the etymology of the word *persona* refers to *per sonare*, "with a mask". In Roman society, the *persona* was originally a character in a dramatic presentation, a personage acted out with a theatrical mask. The mask was also of social significance in the various religious rites performed by the families of Roman society. Certain members of society were entitled to take part actively in the rites by using specific masks. The ritualistic characters displayed with the masks included corresponding names, and the entitled users of the masks eventually attained a right to use this name. The ritualistic right to use a name was later handed down to the next generation of the family. Thus, the name developed into a juridical privilege of the family distinguishing it in a permanent fashion from the non-privileged.[6]

As non-humans and inanimate objects of property, slaves were deprived of such names. On the other hand, the privilege to use the sacred name of the *gens* was restricted to only certain patrician families, and it also marked the dividing line between Roman citizens and free individuals of foreign origin. In the Senate, the *pater* of the privileged *gens* was a *persona* with the right to use the corresponding name of his family. However, as a *persona*, he did not only represent himself, but also the continuity of his family, his ancestry and his posterity. The *persona* was a representation rather than a representative, a *simulacrum* of someone else, of the other.

This dual characteristic of the *persona* and the corresponding name, that is, the capacity to possess a subjective right and the representational relationship between the subject and the other, depicts Occidental ethnocentrism in its fixed structure, as well. Racism as intolerance defines the subject as a stable privilege or right and the other as a representation of the subject. But since tolerance is always reflected against intolerance, it must accordingly display the same structural elements. The evaluative outcome is, of course, very different.

I propose to observe the language of racial tolerance by way of its "tropisms" in accordance with a notion that the French author Nathalie Sarraute has coined. In the theory of the *nouveau roman*, a tropism is a minute expression that reveals the way in which the subject defines its position in relation to the other; the subject's rapport with the other is perceivable rather in the delicate manœuvres with which it distances itself from the other than in the manifest communicative intents that it gives as its reasons for doing so.[7] In other words, the benevolent intentions of a tolerant discourse cannot account for the way in

[6] Cf. Mauss, "Une catégorie de l'esprit humain: La notion de personne, celle de 'Moi' ", in Mauss, *Anthropologie et sociologie*, pp. 331–362.

[7] Sarraute, *Tropismes*.

which the subject of Occidental culture defines itself with and through the other. A more subtle reading is required. I will exemplify these tropisms with three variants that can be regarded as discourses of racial tolerance: a scientific tropism, a political tropism, and, finally, a cultural tropism. However, my ultimate aim is to problematise the presumption that tolerant discourses can be used to overcome social problems such as racism. I would rather suggest that such discourses merely reiterate the basic logic of racism.

II

My preliminary variant of racial tolerance is a scientific tropism, that is, an axiology based on the ideal of cultural pluralism.[8] Prior to the emergence of cultural pluralism, the racial signs that established the supremacy of the European race and its cultural achievements were protected by a more or less unconditional principle. Distinctions between the races were made by referring to racial origins as if they constituted a global caste system with its visible marks of hierarchy. The distinctive sign, that is, race and colour, was protected by a cultural patent: all manifestations of sophistication and progress in the other race were deemed unrecognisable and void. Outlawed from cultural recognition, the other race could never challenge the supremacy of the European subject.

It is ethnological and anthropological science and its ideal of cultural pluralism that first breaks this racist spell and establishes a new relativity that can be interpreted as a first indication of racial tolerance. A similar tone of tolerance is still audible in the writings of, for instance, Claude Lévi-Strauss. In a text entitled "Race et histoire" from 1952, Lévi-Strauss affirms that cultural pluralism is the dynamic force of the anthropological knowledge that his work represents. The diversity of cultures is a challenge to the monotony of racist prejudices that are unable to account for human phenomena: the variety and richness of cultures cannot be explained away with a biological interpretation of race.[9]

In Lévi-Strauss's particular brand of scientific tropism, the relationship between the subject and the other race is an analogy: the other race and its cultural achievements must simultaneously both resemble the subject and possess singular and distinctive traits that can be observed to satisfy the scientist's tolerant curiosity. Lévi-Strauss's text recognises the ethnocentric quality of the analogy but cannot avoid the analogy itself.[10] The tolerance that the text displays, "a sentiment of gratitude and humility", is inspired by a single "conviction", a tolerant faith: "that the other cultures differ *from his own* in the most varied manner".[11]

[8] On race-related axiologies, see, e.g., Todorov, *La conquête de l'Amerique*, and Todorov, *Nous et les autres*.

[9] Lévi-Strauss, "Race et histoire," pp. 377–422, in Lévi-Strauss, *Anthropologie structurale deux*, pp. 377–379.

[10] *Ibid.*, pp 395–397.

[11] *Ibid.*, p. 417 (emphasis added).

The analogical relationship between the races is established by the conviction that the other race must always be different *in comparison to* the subject. But convictions and faiths such as tolerance are always tempted by heretic beliefs. Lévi-Strauss's text names its own heretic variant: false evolutionism or cultural Darwinism. As a mode of intolerance, the heretic belief in evolutionism attempts to try out the tolerant faith, to annul the diversity of human cultures with pretences of absolute knowledge.[12] As a devout believer, the subject of science can never know everything. The other race must remain simultaneously familiar and foreign, recognisable and mysterious. It would be an indication of intolerance to annihilate the scientific enterprise and its tolerant curiosity by knowing too much, by proceeding from partial to inclusive analogy. Therefore:

> "The process consists in taking the part for the whole, concluding, because *some* aspects of both . . . civilisations present similarities—with the analogy of *all* their aspects".[13]

The scientific tropism is a textual movement that involves the reading of signs suitable for the analogical evaluation of races, and the success of an acceptable evaluation requires that the racial signs are liberated from the prescientific unconditional principle. The liberty of cultural pluralism does not, however, lead to new interpretations of given or predetermined signs, of the old caste marks. The scientific tropism moves within an open structure with a luxurious surplus of significative elements. In answer to the intellectual demand induced by the subject's tolerant curiosity, scientific activity must be able to read new signs that make a tolerant evaluation between the races possible.

The overwhelming plurality of readable signs is also evident in Lévi-Strauss's text. Races are rarely isolated internally or externally and, accordingly, the text confirms that diversity is not static. It cannot be reduced into a comprehensive inventory of distinctive signs.[14] Quite the contrary, diversity is always much richer than the subject's capacity to comprehend,[15] and the extent of cultural differences can only be grasped in an incomplete manner.[16] The scientific tropism is, therefore, a generative reading of new signifying elements, a production of cultural differences, movement within an open structure of superfluous distinctive signs.

In an analogical relationship, the subject considers the other race as a fascinating imitation of natural characteristics, a facsimile that feigns the laws of nature. Nature is, then, the axiological scale on which the imitation and the original are distinguishable. Lévi-Strauss's text does not explicitly identify nature, but it does name three categories of culture: the temporally proximate and the spatially distant, the temporally distant and the spatially proximate, and

[12] *Ibid.*, p. 385.
[13] *Ibid.*, p. 388.
[14] *Ibid.*, pp. 381–382.
[15] *Ibid.*, p. 380.
[16] *Ibid.*, p. 417.

the temporally and spatially distant.[17] The remaining category that is unnamed, that is, the temporally and spatially proximate, the here-and-now—Lévi-Strauss himself—must accordingly stand for something other than culture, for "nature".

The text condemns racial intolerance both as exclusion and as inclusion, as rejection from humanity and as interjection that eliminates diversities.[18] On the other hand, the scientific tropism can itself express tolerance only by disregarding differences—something which has already been deemed intolerant—and by focusing on cultural values that are approximately the same for all: language, technique, art, knowledge, belief, and social, economic and political organisation.[19] Yet, it is obvious that this tropism, as it is portrayed in the text, can only be formulated through Lévi-Strauss's own "natural" language, technique, knowledge and beliefs. It is a mode of racial existence, and as soon as the subject of science turns its inspecting gaze on the observed diversities, the existence of the other race is necessarily defined by way of the subject and its status as "natural".

As in any variant of racial tolerance, the anti-racist principle regulating racial thought in the scientific tropism follows a specific normative logic: the logic of a rule. This logic is particularly evident in Lévi-Strauss's frequent metaphoric allusions to the scientific tropism as a game. As the inability to read signs of progress in so-called "primitive" societies, intolerance is the result of defining the rules of the scientific game in an inappropriate way. Intolerance is playing at unfavourable odds in a game with "contributions" to be won. The text promotes tolerance as playing collectively in order to improve the odds at wining.[20]

On the other hand, the text defines tolerance as the recognition of the contributions of the other race to the common patrimony.[21] But this does not mean the comprehensive listing or cataloguing of particular contributions into the estate, it is not a legally governed balancing of the accounts. The contribution is, in fact, an interracial exchange of differences (*écart différentiel*).[22] The French word *écart* also signifies an exchange of cards in a game. In the game of the scientific tropism, the rule of tolerance does not stipulate which racial signs require a tolerant reading; the cards of the game must remain random and arbitrary.

The rule of tolerance regulates the scientific tropism without being transcendent in relation to it. The rule is not "above" the game it describes, it is an immanent part of it. Tolerance is built into Lévi-Strauss's text in a way that makes the game, that is, scientific activity and the corresponding tropism, impossible without observing the rule. Contempt of the rule signifies exemption from scientific truth:

[17] Lévi-Strauss, *Race et histoire*, n. 9, p. 387.
[18] *Ibid.*, pp. 383–385.
[19] *Ibid.*, p. 401.
[20] *Ibid.*, pp. 411–413.
[21] *Ibid.*, p. 377.
[22] *Ibid.*, p. 417. The English translation for *écart différentiel* is given as "contrastive features".

"When attempting to characterise the biological races with particular psychological properties, one strays [*s'écarter*] just as much from scientific truth in defining them positively as negatively".[23]

The rule of tolerance does not draw a clear dividing line between the permitted and the forbidden because it is immanent in the game. One can disregard the rule but not violate against it. In other words, transgression in the form of racist intolerance is inconceivable within the scientific tropism because the rule does not pronounce a moral verdict. The text demonstrates this in the apology of racist anthropology and popular prejudices: intolerance is "naive", "ignorant", "simplistic" and "pseudo-scientific" but never explicitly wrong in the moral or ethical senses of the word. The rule of tolerance is not interested in condemnation, it merely wishes to secure the continuity of the game. This game—unlike the text's conception of history—is clearly cumulative.

The scientific tropism that Lévi-Strauss's text represents is, no doubt, a sequence of scientific authors in a cumulative game. But the rule of tolerance itself requires no authorisation. Both the author and the formulation of the rule are insignificant. The text situates the rule into temporal obscurity by designating the intolerance of a distant predecessor as an "intellectual error".[24] An error can only mean that the unobserved rule was already present but remained unobserved. Since the predecessor is the "father of racist theories", the rule must precede the original insemination.[25]

On the other hand, the manifestation of intolerance in major ethnological texts is done away with as naivete and "total ignorance".[26] This exclusion of the ignorant child from the game of the scientific tropism emphasises that the rule of tolerance is not open for imaginative interpretation. If interpretation is ruled out, the formulation must be irrelevant. Being morally neutral, the rule of tolerance cannot prohibit intolerant conduct. It can only appeal for tolerance because disobeying the rule leads to expulsion from the game, that is, from scientific activity.

The rule of tolerance binds the subject and the other race together in a dual relationship where both presuppose each other. The rule does not perform a distinction between the two parties. In addition, the rule requires merely unilateral tolerance. The text, expressing the feeling of gratitude and humility for the contributions of the other race, states that the beneficiary of the contribution cannot be a world civilisation.[27] How should one, then, understand the "common patrimony" mentioned? A patrimony is a paternal heritage, and since the only father mentioned in the text is an intolerant scientist, it would seem that the beneficiary can only be a descendant in the scientific family line, that is, Lévi-Strauss himself. Therefore, tolerance is not displayed by recognising the contributions

[23] *Ibid.*, p. 377.
[24] *Ibid.*, p. 378.
[25] *Ibid.*, p. 377.
[26] *Ibid.*, p. 405.
[27] *Ibid.*, p. 416.

of the other race to a common heritage, but by accepting, albeit with gratitude and humiliation, the donator's "contribution", a tribal tax. The rule of tolerance does not contest the existing privileges of the subject of science and establish cultural equality. Its sole aim is to secure the continuity of the game and its requirements.

Notwithstanding the securing of this continuity, the rule of tolerance does not have further objectives of a political or moral nature. The essential topic of Lévi-Strauss's text is racial tolerance displayed in scientific knowledge, and only at the closing pages does the text mention a "sacred obligation of humanity" to promote tolerance. Curiously enough, it is exactly the same place where the text ceases to speak about the scientific enterprise and its own commitments. At this point, the text quite innocently transforms itself into a delegation of regulative intentions from science to international institutions.[28] The reason for this is the inability of the scientific tropism to confront intolerant behaviour outside its own game.

As the transgression of the rule of tolerance is inconceivable, the racist counterpart of the scientific tropism suggests a form of intolerance regulated by a similar normative logic. This would require adherence to another rule, a rule of intolerance. It is a ceremonial variant of racism and is, perhaps, best illustrated by the activities of the Ku Klux Klan in the USA and the violent youth gangs of contemporary Europe. But the rules of intolerance and tolerance cannot be juxtaposed as they are two different games, they are of a different order. In both tropism and ceremonial racism, breaking the rule merely expels one from the game without moral condemnation.

And, as contradictory as it may seem, the ceremonial is also the normal. Just as in ceremonial racist violence, the logic of a rule dictates the structures of the most common and everyday forms of racist intolerance: offending humour, membership criteria of social organisations, the cultural depreciation of non-European civilisations, the taboos of interracial sexuality, and the like.

III

If Lévi-Strauss's text delegates the objective of confronting racism politically and morally to international institutions, it must also presume another variant of racial tolerance, that is, a political tropism founded on the advocation of juridical equality. In this context, advocation is the subject's political activity *on behalf of* the other race concerning the latter's political rights and freedoms. The International Convention on the Elimination of All Forms of Racial Discrimination states its advocatory intentions:

> "States Parties shall . . . take, in the social, economic, cultural and other fields, special and concrete measures to ensure the adequate development and protection of certain racial groups or individuals belonging to them".[29]

[28] Lévi-Strauss, *Race et histoire*, n. 9, p. 420.

[29] United Nations General Assembly Resolution 2106 A (XX) of 21 December 1965, Article 2.2.

In other words, the Convention stipulates an obligation for State Parties—the subject—to act on behalf of unnamed racial groups who can only be identified by a certain level of under-development. Social, economic and cultural under-development becomes the significative element that distinguishes the subject from the other race. The common denominator of interracial comparison in the political tropism is social, economic and cultural progress, an evolutionary scale. An emphasis on the economic is conspicuous. The text of the Convention defines economic rights by way of work:

> "the right to work, to free choice of employment, to just and favourable conditions of work, to protection against unemployment, to equal pay for equal work, to just and favourable remuneration".[30]

The right to work also presumes an obligation of labour in exchange for the evolution from economic under-development to the status of a full subject. In the political tropism, racial tolerance is displayed by defining this right and obligation as just, that is, as binding to all "without distinction of any kind, in particular as to race, colour or origin". The free choice of employment does not grant the possibility to evade this obligation, it merely states that there are options between numerous employers. By operating with corresponding rights and obligations, the text of the Convention presumes that favourable working conditions secure maximum efficiency for the benefit of all concerned.

In the political tropism, the relationship between the subject and the other race is based on equivalence, not analogy. The subject and the other do not resemble each other as ontological entities but as values. The axiological scale of equivalent values is constituted in the market. The political movement for the abolition of slavery, for example, would accordingly be founded on the idea that the subject and the other race are comparable as to their market value in production. The injustice of slavery is evident in the improper and condemnable market evaluation of the slave's work.

The Convention's jargon about economic development implies, albeit in a very tolerant manner, that the foundation of racially significant injustice is also due to erroneous market evaluations. If the subject is the only party to receive profits, the economic potential of the other race must either be abused or it has not been properly put to use. The subject represents a more or less balanced value in an ideal market situation while the other race, requiring "adequate development and protection", suffers from certain shortcomings.

In an analogical relationship, the other race is enigmatic and alluring because the subject's capacity to know is necessarily limited. But in an equivalent relationship, the subject knows everything. The other race is as valuable as its potential efficiency on the market but, on the other hand, its ability to provoke fundamental questions is worthless. In its lengthy Preamble, the text of the Convention parades the unlimited comprehension and knowledge of the

[30] Convention, Article 5.

advocatory subject. It acts tolerantly "considering" the context, it is "convinced" and "alarmed" of the problem of racism and its reasons, it "reaffirms" the just nature of its own political conviction, it is "resolved" to act, and so on. But as the Convention is open for signature,[31] it is not exactly clear who the advocatory subject is. If work and production form a single scale of evaluation, the subject and the other race are not as distinguishable as before. The analogical relationship does not question the significant difference between the subject and the other race, while the equivalent relationship already establishes a profound resemblance.

As an analogy of the subject, the other race is also singular and unique. But as an equivalent of the subject, it is plural and standard. The text of the Convention defines the standard as a collection of guaranteed rights "without distinction as to race, colour, or national or ethnic origin".[32] The scientific curiosity that explores the specific characteristics of a singular people, that is, that makes distinctions as to race, colour, and national or ethnic origin, is now replaced with the political tropism that relies on demographic generalisations the ultimate aim of which is a "new economic world order".

The normative logic of the anti-racist principle is obviously also quite different in the political tropism: it follows the logic of a law. Unlike the rule, the law of tolerance must explicitly designate the signs that the subject must take heed of in order to deem an action tolerant in the political sense of the word. The Convention is no game; it is an agreement, a fixed fight that intentionally delineates the possibilities of hazard and chance. The text must, accordingly, come to an agreement about the signs that are to be taken into consideration in the political tropism. The Convention must itself, by way of negation, list the variables that are to be respected in racial tolerance:

> "race, colour, descent, or national or ethnic origin which has the purpose or effect of nullifying or impairing the recognition, enjoyment or exercise, on an equal footing, of human rights and fundamental freedoms in the political, economic, social cultural or any other field of public life".[33]

This meticulous specification of signs suggests that the law of tolerance is transcendent in relation to the behaviour it regulates. Unlike the immanent rule, the transcendent law both commands and prohibits. In other words, the law encompasses both lawful and unlawful behaviour, both tolerance and intolerance. As a law, the text of the Convention first establishes a punitive procedure with which States Parties must "undertake to pursue by all appropriate means . . . a policy of eliminating racial discrimination in all its forms",[34] Secondly, the text of the Convention obliges States Parties to promote institutional support for tolerant behaviour.[35] The rule was valid for one game only, but the law of

[31] Convention, Article 17.1.
[32] Convention, Article 5.
[33] Convention, Article 1.1.
[34] Convention, Articles 2.1 and 4.
[35] Convention, Article 7.

tolerance both requires tolerance and condemns intolerance, and in doing so, it also states its intention of regulating racial thought in general.

The transcendence of the law in relation to the political tropism draws the dividing line between the permitted and the forbidden which was the prerequisite for breaking the law, for transgression. In other words, intolerance as transgression is possible provided that the anti-racist principle requiring tolerance is by nature a law. Both tolerance and intolerance are thus acted out on the same terrain governed by a single law.

Unlike the rule of tolerance of the scientific tropism, the law of tolerance that regulates the political tropism presupposes a law-giver whose identity is never insignificant. Most of the Convention's Preamble is dedicated to emphasising that the agreement has been reached under the auspices of the United Nations. If the text itself possessed sufficient mandatory power, this emphasis would be pointless. The law of tolerance, however, requires a contextual author, an exterior authority to furnish the text with coercive force. The law of tolerance must encompass behaviour that is, strictly speaking, outside its own jurisdiction. As an agreement, the Convention is only a promise given by the agreeing parties, but as a law, it must also evaluate the conduct of those who have never committed themselves to it.

In addition, the law of tolerance is open for interpretation. The political tropism is often precisely the presentation and justification of tolerant interpretations of the law, and the text of the Convention reaffirms this possibility by specifically ruling out interpretations of an intolerant nature.[36]

As a law, the ratified Convention bears a certain date of entering into force.[37] This implies that the law of tolerance is valid only from a certain time. The law of tolerance that the text of the Convention represents is, however, explicitly announced as universal.[38] Despite its extensive and minute formulations of procedures of validation, the Convention only briefly touches upon the possibility of invalidation after the ratification of the law.[39] Hence, the temporal dimension of jurisdiction is more or less left open concerning both the past and the future. Because the law of tolerance both commands and prohibits, one cannot, as in a game, escape the spatial dimension of jurisdiction by violating against the law. It would seem that even by resisting to ratify the Convention, a State Party or any non-agreeing outsider is transgressing the law. This generality gives the law of tolerance the universality of a natural law.

The law of tolerance establishes an equality of a legal nature between the subject and the other race. But before doing so, the law must first make a distinction. As the subject and the other race are equivalent in the political tropism, there is, strictly speaking, only one party. The only way to accomplish the distinction between the two parties is to identify the discriminated. Regardless of

[36] Convention, Article 1.3.
[37] Convention, Article 19.
[38] Convention, Preamble.
[39] Convention, Article 21.

its benevolent intentions, the law of tolerance must itself perform a discriminatory act. The text of the Convention must do what it prohibits, that is, make a distinction between "human beings" "as to race, colour, or national or ethnic origin". After the distinction is made, the law of tolerance binds the subject and the other race in a solidary fashion: tolerance requires reciprocity. The text itself anticipates the rhetorical potential of this reciprocity by regulating the procedures of dispute.[40]

Unlike the rule, the law of tolerance has a far more important objective than the regulation of racial relationships. Tolerance is not even the primary objective of the law. The *telos* of the law of tolerance is a political project, interracial brotherhood:

> "discrimination between human beings on the grounds of race, colour or ethnic origin is an obstacle to friendly and peaceful relations among nations and is capable of disturbing peace and security among peoples . . . the existence of racial barriers is repugnant to the ideals of any human society".[41]

The renowned inefficiency of international conventions in regulating everyday life is based on yet another problem of correlation. Logically speaking, the intolerant counterpart of the political tropism is a political variant of racism such as formally enacted laws of racial discrimination, and conventions and agreements have, no doubt, demonstrated their relative usefulness in regulating these. But if everyday intolerance, the normal and commonplace aspect of racism, is of a ceremonial nature as I have suggested, it is regulated by a rule of intolerance. Once again we encounter the problem of juxtaposing: *a law is irrelevant in relation to behaviour regulated by a rule.* As long as the spell of the racist game lasts, the law of tolerance is powerless. And yet, the racial tolerance that is exhibited in the everyday lives of most women and men must be guided by some normative element.

IV

The rules and laws of both scientific and political tropisms may be inadequate in regulating intolerance, but the extent of racial respect in contemporary society must imply that something or other governs racial thought even in the troubled Western world. This third variant of racial tolerance, the tolerant counterpart of our intolerant starting point, is a cultural tropism, a pseudo-axiology based on the ideal of global humanism. This cultural tropism is perhaps best portrayed in the efforts of the advertising industry to annul the signs of racial difference. A few years back, the trademark *Benetton* illustrated this global humanism in their advertising campaign picturing the races of the world together dressed in uniform clothing. In the cultural tropism of *Benetton*, the

[40] Convention, Article 22.
[41] Convention, Preamble.

other race is not merely a "brother" in the meaning of the Universal Declaration of Human Rights. The subject and the other race are family in a considerably more literal sense: they are homogenous, they originate from the same gene, they are identical twins.

The cultural tropism of global humanism renders the other race into a perfect simulation of the subject. They can be told apart only by a structural difference that is altogether neutral and formal. Therefore, the scale of evaluation is pseudo-axiological and the races invaluable in the literal meaning of the word. The operational and digital logic of structural oppositions eliminates all myths of origin and the remaining inequalities in racial relationships. The black, white, yellow and red races of the *Benetton* campaign are as indistinguishable as the brilliant garments: they are clones of a single model and can be told apart only by a formal cryptogram known solely to the Creator. In its campaign, *Benetton* has never differentiated its merchandise by naming specific models. The races also remain unnamed, and without a name, subjectivity and otherness as a structure of identity is inconceivable. At last, tolerance is comprehensive!

In the scientific tropism, the tolerance of the subject was triggered by curiosity, the fascination for the game, whereas the subject of the political tropism was more like a political animal conditioned to react to the stimulus of abnormal market situations. What, then, motivates the subject of cultural tropism?

The logic of global humanism has been aptly described by Jean Baudrillard.[42] As the all-encompassing humanism of the cultural tropism begins to abolish differences, the subject faces a dilemma: in a homogenous world, there are no differences to tolerate or discriminate. On the other hand, the subject can no longer find the limits necessary for the original distinction or its own subjectivity. As the subject is fading into oblivion, a panic reaction follows. The subject commences to produce new differences in order to save itself and the other race from the terror of a totalised world. The schizophrenic frenzy of global humanism is the compulsion to be simultaneously the same and different.

This is the core of the problem: *otherness and difference are not the same thing*. In the relationship between the subject and the other race, otherness signifies a radical dissimilarity that can never be overcome. Otherness is conspicuous in, for example, the striking uninterest of non-Occidental civilisations regarding the "true" cultural achievements of the West. The other is always incomprehensible, and cultural identity requires that it remain so. Difference, on the other hand, is concurrent similarity and dissimilarity, inclusion and exclusion. Occidental racial tolerance is never founded on otherness, it is always a discourse on difference: the other race is the same and different, recognised and discriminated. As the compulsion to tolerate draws the other race closer and closer, it reaches a point where all differences have been done away with. The tolerance displayed in the global humanism of the cultural tropism manifests this hyper-resemblance in its anti-racist principle. It proclaims the universal

[42] Baudrillard, *Le transparence du Mal*, pp. 129–143.

right to be different in its beautiful slogan: "We are all different". At the same time, it must acknowledge the universality of difference: "In our difference, we are all the same". The universal right to difference is embodied in the metaphoric reference of *Benetton* to state and government: the right to difference is the essential content of the Constitution of the "United Colours of Benetton".

In the global humanism of the cultural tropism, the constitutional right of difference is present in numerous phenomena of contemporary everyday life: Nicaraguan coffee, Vietnamese take-away, Live Aid, Algerian wine, Indian cotton, Afghanistan hashish, Turkish delight, Kama Sutra, Zen, Argentine tango, and so on. The global humanist understands the world as a collection of human accomplishments that the subject must learn to respect as its own. Intolerant universality is finding the latent presence of the subject when it is manifestly absent in the other race, taking difference for deficiency. The tolerance of global humanism, on the other hand, interprets the difference of the other race as something that the subject does not possess. Although the defect has been turned around, the entity the difference represents is, however, an unquestionable phenomenon in a universal world.

In this tolerant universality, the anti-racist principle proclaiming the constitutional right to difference and guiding the subject to acquire and interject the difference of the other race into its own life is a norm. The norm of tolerance, unlike the rule or the law, does not require observation, nor does it command or prohibit. It functions by way of supervision, deterrence, dissuasion and persuasion. The subject displays its tolerance by integrating the difference in a situation that is not obliging.

Ceaselessly and compellingly producing new differences to tolerate and integrate, the global humanism of the cultural tropism totalises the world until it is homogeneous. Born of the same gene, the other race comes dangerously close. Thus, the tolerance of global humanism accelerates the very logic of racist intolerance itself. If the other race is the other, that is, radically different, singular, incomprehensible and unattainable, the subject has nothing to fear. But once the world has been homogenised, the compulsory production of differences necessarily takes on a racist form: "I am not the other!"

The indistinguishability of homogenous clones is, in the end, confronted with the ultimate metaphor of racism. An "alien" may have once been merely illegal, but Baudrillard correctly notes that today it is also a viral monster that spreads into society by reproducing itself like HIV. The viral metaphor has always served as the essence of racist theories such as Sionist conspiracy and, more lately, the rise of the Islamic world. The other race incubates in the healthy organs of humanism, but eventually it will hatch and, in doing so, terminate the life of its dam.

V

This acceleration is the key of Baudrillard's critique of racial tolerance. Even though the critique of racism has confirmed the fallacy of the biological foundation of discrimination, racism has not made way for a tolerant form of interracial relations. Quite the contrary, racism has fragmented into small and isolated forms of everyday incidents that the latest form of tolerance, that is, the global humanism of the cultural tropism, seems only to support. A uniform critique of this fragmented normality is impossible. The critique presented in the name of racial tolerance is always formal in that it only touches the surface.

This is why racism outlives its critique. Critique may have proven the biological fallacy of discrimination, but it has never discredited racial biology. Critique may have touched upon the racist obsession of difference, but it has not indicated the hazardous logic of difference itself. *Racial tolerance is the unfounded fantasy of using the logic of difference for benevolent purposes*, but difference will always lead straight back to racism. This is why the West must rediscover the other, the alterity of the radically different.

Occidental anti-racist critique considers the universal recognition of human rights as a victory of the other race. But it is, of course, an Occidental triumph: the entire world has recognised the universality of Western values. The victory of the rest of the world can be seen in the vulnerability and helplessness of the Western world when confronted by phenomena such as world culture. The mysteries of the world are not secrets because no one hides the answer. On the contrary, through its cultural exchange programmes, the Occident spends enormous amounts of money to import answers for all to inspect, to understand. But it is unable to read the answer. All analyses and reasoning leads to new questions until, in the end, these questions turn into a doubt and a critique of the subject's own culture.

This culture, tormented by its sense of inferiority and illiteracy, constitutes the last primitive people of this world.

9

A Minor Jurisprudence

"How we all absorbed the look of transfiguration on the face of the sufferer, how we bathed our cheeks in the radiance of that justice [*Schein dieser . . . Gerechtigkeit*], achieved at last and fading so quickly!"

Franz Kafka

I

The signing of a name is, among other things, an effort to appropriate a foregoing text, a contract, a written message. The signature attempts to claim authorship and control for what has been written. With his name, a lover attempts to seal a letter to his beloved but encounters only darkness:

"~~Franz~~ wrong, ~~F~~ wrong, ~~Yours~~ wrong
nothing more, silence, deep forest".[1]

The author of the letter finds it hard to claim authorship for what he has written so he puts his name under erasure. He couples the traces of his name to the word *falsch*, "wrong", but with a strong emphasis towards deceit and treachery. The signature and the corresponding name are wrong and deceitful in that they make promises that can never be kept. And yet, under the bar, the name is clearly visible as if it may be assuming authorship: "I, Franz, mean what I write but, then again, I may not",

Franz Kafka has engraved his name into human flesh and, thus, claimed authorship for the story of modernity. The inscription composed by Kafka's writing machine is an obscure signature that has been understood as a token of truth and an oracle of the morrow. The story that the signature claims authorship for is the truth about the experience of modernity, the uncensored tale about human anguish, suffering, and cruelty in a world of philanthropic aims and insufferable consequences. And this experience is spelled out in the author's name; modernity is lived in the name of the Kafkaesque.

Despite the innumerable attempts to delineate the Kafkaesque as an allegory of modernity, the author and his art have remained an enigma.[2] And rightly so:

[1] Kafka, *Briefe an Milena*, p. 131.

[2] The amount of literature on Kafka's art is bewildering. In addition to the standard Kafka scholarship, numerous authors from Adorno and Benjamin to Borges and Kundera could be cited here. I only refer the reader to, e.g., Hartmut Binder's compilation. Such "manuals" are of invaluable help to anyone trying to find their way through the stupendous quantity of Kafka exegesis available: Binder (ed.), *Kafka*.

the Kafkaesque is specifically that which is inconceivable. The author, his art, and his name are reserved for that which escapes the enlightened reason of modern man and his science and, therefore, remains behind a veil of mystery.[3]

Law is one of the main themes of Kafka's literary art, but it is also the object of an enlightened science. Within the Continental tradition of this science, law is understood as a conceptual construct the creation of which is regulated by the reason of modern science. Law is a relational structure formalised from normative phenomena and stratified within a framework of hierarchic rationality: the modern science of law conceives the juridical order as a system. In the critique of the science of law, the basic systematics of hierarchy may be reversed by, for example, subjecting positive law to the ethos of popular justice, but hierarchy in itself is rarely—if ever—questioned.

Within the domain of law, the Kafkaesque often suggests a series of such structural reversals. The name of the author refers to a world in which labyrinthine juridical institutions seem to function according to their own internal rules. In the world of the Kafkaesque, law evades the well-meaning attempts of the man of reason to subject it to the rational dictates of enlightened thinking, but an insistent obscurantism within law leaves him with a sense of helplessness and fear. We have been led to believe that the functioning of law complies with the procedural form of logical sequences. In the world of the Kafkaesque, we are, however, unable to impose this reason on it. The obscurantist quality of law in the world of the Kafkaesque is expressed with a para-theological trope of mimicry in which the symbols of law stand for the purity of the eidetic phenomenon, whereas that which has heretofore been taken for the essence of law has been degraded into a mere shadow of this purity. The symbols of law, the court-room decor, the drapes, the public records, and so on, are not mimetic representations of the essence of law but rather vice versa: the right of law to exist in the world of the Kafkaesque is intimately bound to the way in which it can comply with its own symbols.

In such a world of reversed juridical logic, the Dostoyevskian allegory of crime and punishment is turned upside down. The infallible powers of punishment do not pursue man tormented by a guilty conscience for a crime that he has committed. Punishment exists prior to the crime, and law seeks a guilty party to match with a pre-existing verdict in order to satisfy its desire to punish. In this reversed picture of the juridical world, the para-theological trope of the Kafkaesque provides the narrative with an absurd comical flavour. But comedy in the world of the Kafkaesque is not an antipode for the tragic, it is not a breath of light air that would relieve of the agony of suffering. On the contrary, in the world of the Kafkaesque, comedy incapacitates the tragic foundation of suffering by ridding man of the only comfort left, that is, of the noble experience of the sublime.

But a metamorphosis from man to insect is no more difficult to rationalise than from insect to man; a reversal of juridical logic is as comprehensible to the

[3] Cf. Weinstein, *Vision and Response in Modern Fiction*, pp. 157–167.

modern science of law as that from which it has been reversed. What is, then, law in the world of the Kafkaesque, a law that would escape the juridical logic and the reason of the modern science of law? What are its structural features or, indeed, can it be addressed in the name of structure to begin with? If not, can law be conceived as a system?[4]

In the course of this chapter, I shall attempt to read certain structural features of law from Kafka's short story "In der Strafkolonie" in order to define a particular Nietzschean understanding of law in modernity, that is, in the world of the Kafkaesque. I hope to be able to show that, contrary to the common interpretation, Kafka's account of law is not an image of horror that demands justice through negation. It is much more disquieting than that.

II

In addition to the law of the science of law, Kafka's art embodies another law, namely, a law of literature interwoven into all that the author has written.[5] I shall call this the law of the Kafkaesque. The narrative structure of Kafka's texts often sets the protagonist in a state of innocence from which it is banished into the world of the Kafkaesque during the course of the *récit*. Josef K. and his expectations represent such an innocence *vis-à-vis* the world; K. insolently claims that he is acquainted with the world but must, time after time, acknowledge his own mistake: K. mistakenly thinks he knows the contents of the law, the interrogation room is never where it should be, the position and configuration of the pulpit changes constantly in the dark cathedral, and so on. *Der Prozeß* recounts a story of the losing of such an innocence, the collapse of K.'s seemingly firm and structured world into the state of precarious flux that the Kafkaesque represents.

Kafka's writing begins at the limit of the protagonist's self-assurance, at the line separating wake and dream, the present and the represented, the literal and the figurative. The author encounters a philosophical allegory on the suffering of the world embedded in metaphor and figuration:

> "Always having at hand a dependable compass to guide one in life and to enable one consistently to view it in the correct light without ever losing one's way, nothing is more appropriate than to accustom oneself to view this world as a place of penance

[4] Coinciding with "structure" and "system", one could also speak of a "topology" of law. In his reading of Kafka, Derrida addresses a topology of law, but my aim is much more modest. By topology, I would understand merely a structure of relational components, topology in the sense of Lacanian epistemology, not a "taking place" (*avoir-lieu*) of law. See Derrida, "Préjugés. Devant la loi", in Derrida et al, *La faculté de juger*, pp. 87–139. Another fascinating interpretation of the parable "Vor dem Gesetz" is given by Hélène Cixous in an English translation of her seminars from 1980–81. See Cixous, *Readings*, pp. 14–19. For a Cabbalistic interpretation of the parable and law, see Schmidhäuser, "Das 'Gesetz' in Franz Kafkas Roman 'Der Prozeß' ", in Haft et al (eds), *Strafgerechtigkeit*, pp. 812–817.

[5] Cf. Pierre, *Odradek*.

[*als einen Ort der Buße*], that is, as a penitentiary so to speak [*gleichsam als eine Strafanstalt*], *a penal colony* [English in the original]—an *ergastērion*".[6]

In Kafka's writing on suffering, however, there is no room for metaphor or figuration but only literal truth. There is no *als*, no "as" to mute the coupling of world and penitentiary: for Kafka, the world *is* a penal colony.[7] Kafka's detailed and visual description of the penal colony partakes in the pedantic accuracy of the entomologist observing, cataloguing, and categorising the phenomena of his insect world. This encyclopedic style has certain poietic implications. The minute and pictorial illustration of the world sketches an ever more accurate design that, only a moment ago, only existed as allegory. Before long, the reader faces a literary environment illustrated with such intensity that his reasoned counter-arguments—if there are any—must finally give in. This happens with "In der Strafkolonie" as well.[8] A literary description of the penal colony and its law, at first figurative, unreal, and even chimeric, draws on the power of details to demand access from the represented to the present and, in the end, the reader is more or less obliged to recognise in the nightmare of the short story his own world, in the representation of the literary environment the presence of his literal world.

The reading of Kafka has, however, become regulated by a very different literary law. Our contemporary understanding of modernity has made the Kafkaesque and the debased state of the world itself a point of departure. With no original innocence, the text is preceded only by our awareness that the painful truth is veiled by deceit, that the world is not as it seems, and the reading of literature is an exposing of this truth, a verification of the Kafkaesque assumption. Kafka is often associated with dream or, to be more exact, with the inability to differentiate between reality and phantasm, between wake and nightmare. But in the law of the Kafkaesque, the proper name has already promised us that this nightmare is for real, and in Kafka's literature we encounter the dream portrayed in such detail and with such rigour that, in the end, we would rather doubt our reasoned conception of the waking world than the phantasmal images created by the generative power of literature. The world of the Kafkaesque is not just a product of an author's imagination, nor is it something that could come to be; it *exists* in the historical memory of modernity.

It is in this sense that Kafka is not merely thought of as a visionary author who penetrates through the deceitful surface of reality into the painful truth about modernity, but his texts have also been assigned a prophetic value. Kafka, a Jewish author, not only portrays the horror of the world as it truly is but, with "In der Strafkolonie" written in 1914 and published five years later, also presents a presage that starts to come true during the next twenty years. And so Kafka, a

6 Schopenhauer, *Parerga und Paralipomena II. Erster Teilband*, p. 328 (§ 156).
7 Cf. Sokel, *Franz Kafka—Tragik und Ironie*, pp. 9–30.
8 Politzer, *Franz Kafka, der Künstler*, pp. 156–178.

name with a fateful resonance, a frail face, and a sorrowful gaze, becomes the fixed grounding of a moral and ethical position in relation to the horror of the world.

A paradox is embodied in such a conception of literature and the law written with Kafka's name. The text is read as a preset assortment of signs and structures of the world of the Kafkaesque while the reader merely *re*-cognises something that has already been dictated by the promises of the signature, by the law of the Kafkaesque. Kafka's literature does not generate a world *ex nihilo* but merely verifies attributes of the world that precede the text. These attributes were given in the proper name, but the signature is deceiving; the generative power of literature unrelentingly creates something that the reader of the Kafkaesque, blindly relying on the proper name and the promises of the signature, refuses to see, a supplement that makes the reasoned fixing of the world of the Kafkaesque more or less problematic.

Kafka's thematic obsession with questions of law and justice cannot be overlooked merely by referring to a legal education and profession. The insurance clerk sees something utterly more essential in law, something that depicts the world in general: law *is* the Kafkaesque. Law in the world of the Kafkaesque, as it is written into *Der Prozeß*, is often presented as three principal reversals: the absence of spatial geometry and organisation (*atopical law*), of causality and temporal differentiation (*achronic law*), and of a source of origin and legitimacy (*anarchic law*).[9]

The atopical feature of law is, above all, evident in the disintegration of the hierarchic structures of juridical systems into linear segments of coextensive power. The hierarchy in law is juxtaposed with a formless or supple architecture enabling law to extend its power anywhere. K.'s "search for justice" is, like all similar quests, a search for a hierarchically superior power that would either authorise or prohibit his persistent persecution by the representatives of law—in the end, both are equally acceptable conclusions to K.'s case. Such hierarchies are not decisively absent, but access to a higher level of law is either denied or has become impossible. In the much cited preamble to law recounted by the priest, the "powerful [*mächtig*]" doorkeeper denies the peasant access to law but remarks that the halls of law are garrisoned by numerous other doorkeepers "one more powerful [*mächtiger*] than the other".[10]

Such a reversal is, however, not formless. Leaving K. outside the gate of law imposes on him a horizontal logic of bureaucratic subjugation as opposed to a presumed vertical logic of law. The reversal does not apply merely to the spatial dimension of law, but it is characteristic of the temporal, as well. The element of time is reversed in several ways: a consequence brings on a cause, an end a finalistic means, a guilty verdict demands a crime, a punishment requires a condemned, and so on. The German title, *Der Prozeß*, indicates that the juridical procedure, that is, the empirical evidence of the existence of law, is understood

[9] Garapon, "Kafka ou le non-lieu de la loi".
[10] Kafka, *Der Prozeß*, p. 256.

as a succession of formal sequences of time rather than the "trying" of an accusation or a claimed innocence. The truth of law, as it is understood by K., is analogous to the rigorous observance of the rules of a formal process, and it is the disruption of this temporal formality that provokes K.'s anxiety. The disruption of the formal process does not, however, signify a total absence of time and logic. K. is not in a temporal void lacking structure and form, but he is rather obliged to retreat in a counter-chronological tempo into an unconscious past he is unaware of. Hence the doubts about whether K. has actually committed a crime or not and the resulting nebulous sensations of guilt.

The third reversal, the anarchy of law, signifies the missing personage of a source or a law-giver that would account for the empirically evident validity and justification of law tormenting K.'s life. This law-giver is not, once again, absent altogether, for someone or something governs in the world of the Kafkaesque:

> "It is not a God or a legislator who is cached yet present but, on the contrary, a God who is visible (in the sacred and in rituals) but does not exist any more, like a star that still sheds some light but has ceased to exist thousands of years ago. These images of justice are sinister vestiges of a Law that must have existed but are, presently, without coherence as they are no longer interconnected by any juridical, religious, or moral reason".[11]

Law is here conceived as locution demanding a locutor or a "subject" that speaks a valid law, an authority that "posits" it and, thus, furnishes it with the necessary validity and justification. In the Kafkaesque, such a locutor appears to be reduced to mere functions and images. It would, however, be inexact to view these functions and images merely as mimetic representations, as only symbols of something that has ceased to exist. Law, as it is present in the rituals and the imagery of K.'s trial, is the law of man, human edicts that do not require the legitimation of a divine source, of a super-human law-giver, or of transcendental reason.

III

How is, then, law in the world of the Kafkaesque atopical, without a place? Literally speaking, the penal colony does have a *topos*, a place in the meaning of a geographical site. We are told, for instance, that it is on an island the industrial infra-structure of which includes a commercial harbour with dockyards and dock labourers. The penitentiary is both physically and socially detached from a colonial mother-country representing a legal order and a sovereign power; the colony is insular and isolated. This physical and social isolation has enabled the development of a relatively autonomous judiciary and penal system. We are also informed that the island is in the tropics, and even though the heavy

[11] Garapon, "Kafka ou le non-lieu de la loi", 14–15.

northern uniforms are not fitting for the hot climate, they are "an important reminder of the homeland [*Heimat*]", a vague symbol of colonial authority.[12]

The explorer who has arrived on the island is incorrectly distinguished by the officer explaining the execution to him as a "great Western researcher [*großer Forscher des Abendlandes*]".[13] He is neither a member of the penal colony nor a citizen of the state to which it belongs, and as the explorer only travels for leisure, he insists that his function in the colony is merely that of an observer. He does not initially wish to intervene with the execution of a punishment that he, nevertheless, finds explicitly cruel and unjust.[14]

The geographical setting of the colony and the position of the explorer establish an interior/exterior structure that situates the colony outside the jurisdiction of its homeland, outlawed into lonely existence in a tropical sea. But being outlawed in such a way has hardly been a disadvantageous attribute in this case, for the very isolation of the colony has provided it with its relative autonomy. The creation of an independent penal system with its own laws and own methods of punishment has only been possible because the colony has been cut off from the influence of the colonial homeland and its legal order. But to outlaw is to pronounce judgement requiring the efficacious jurisdiction of a judge, that is, an adjudicator must pronounce the verdict and, in doing so, grant the colony its relative autonomy.

At first it seems that Kafka is trying to depict the divine character of this judge. We can sketch the outlines of a Judaic law that regulates life in the colony. The officer shows the explorer sheets of paper on which the condemned man's sentence is inscribed, drawings of the old Commandant. The officer carries these drawings with him in a leather brief-case as if they were the stone tablets of a chosen people held in a gold plated acacia ark.[15] The officer confirms that the old Commandant's drawings are his "most precious possessions", and the explorer cannot even touch them. In his holy ark, the officer carries the commandments handed down by the old Commandant to his chosen executioner.

These cryptograms are incomprehensible to the explorer, but the officer informs us of the contents of two sheets. Two sentences are revealed: "honour your superiors [*ehre deinen Vorgesetzten*]" and "be just [*sei gerecht*]".[16] We are, therefore, not dealing with sentences as the officer claims but, rather, with laws that regulate life in the colony. Kafka does not, however, even speak about laws but about commands and commandments (*Gebot*) which the condemned have broken, and this underlines the relative autonomy of the colony in relation to the homeland and its legal order.

This engenders an odd contradiction. On the one hand, law is juxtaposed with commands, individual orders and edicts obviously subordinate to the

[12] Kafka, "In der Strafkolonie", in Kafka, *Sämtliche Erzählungen*, p. 100.
[13] *Ibid.*, p. 113.
[14] *Ibid.*, p. 109.
[15] *Ibid.*, p. 107.
[16] *Ibid.*, pp. 104 and 118.

juridical order of the homeland as such commands do not comply with the requirements of universality and systematics essential to the latter. But on the other hand, law is also juxtaposed with the Holy Commandments, the divine pact that the old Commandant has ordained for his colony. The penal system of the colony is, therefore, at once inferior to law in relation to the requirements of universality and systematics but, nevertheless, capable of overruling the juridical order of the homeland with its seemingly divine authority. The old Commandant, the ultimate source of the colony's relative autonomy, appears as a god who has outlawed himself and his colony from the rule of the homeland and its juridical order.

The notion of a "law of laws"[17] above the positivity of individual laws is present in Kafka's text as a more general and dense requirement of "justice" (*Gerechtigkeit*) and other concepts derived from the same root. When, during the old Commandant's reign, the crowd gathered to follow the ceremonial execution of the punishments, all knew that "now justice is being done [*jetzt geschieht Gerechtigkeit*]".[18] And now, as the condemned man becomes aware of his approaching death in the midst of his torturous punishment, his face displays an expression of transfiguration that the officer calls "the radiance of justice [*Schein . . . dieser Gerechtigkeit*]".[19] Needless to say, the explorer finds the execution a mockery of justice: the inhumanity and the injustice (*Ungerechtigkeit*) of the procedure is undeniable.[20] In other words, he finds that the individual command and the prescribed punishment for disobedience do not comply with a higher requirement of justice and cannot, therefore, be expressions of law.

To designate courts, Kafka uses the ambiguous term *Gericht* meaning also judgment and jurisdiction. Towards the end of his description of the execution, the officer notes that "the judgment has been fulfilled [*das Gericht ist zu Ende*]".[21] The officer explains the assets of his conception of law by referring to the disadvantages of the hierarchial structure of the legal order:

> "My guiding principle is this: Guilt is never to be doubted. Other courts [*andere Gerichte*] cannot follow that principle, for they consist of several opinions and have higher courts [*höhere Gerichte*] to scrutinise them".[22]

When law is confined to a single level, legal decision-making assumes the character of bureaucratic subjugation. In such non-hierarchial structures of jurisdiction, the distinction between legislative authority and adjudication becomes blurred. Clayton Koelb indicates the paradoxical relationship between reading and writing displayed in the text. Koelb argues that, in Kafka's rhetoric,

[17] Cf. Politzer, *Franz Kafka, der Künstler*, pp. 251–254.

[18] Kafka, "In der Strafkolonie"', n. 12 above, p. 111.

[19] *Ibid.*, p. 112. On Kafka's use of light as a juridico-religious metaphor, see Beutner, *Die Bildsprache Franz Kafkas*, pp. 118–125.

[20] Kafka, "In der Strafkolonie", n. 12 above, p. 109.

[21] *Ibid.*, p. 108.

[22] *Ibid.*, p. 104.

the writing of the sentence on the condemned man's body is just as much a reading understood as the passive reception of a powerful text:

> "Writing is the creation of a template that directs an act of inscription, and reading is the suffering of that inscription upon the reader's psyche. Obviously, what is needed is a mechanism to mediate, to bring the writer's template text into contact with the reader's psychic matrix. Kafka's machine has just this function".[23]

Rewritten into juridical terms, Koelb emphasises that, in his suffering, the condemned man is subjected to adjudication, that is, to the reading of a powerful text operating under the guise of law with the machine operating as the mediating judge. But the modern science of law cannot recognise this powerful text as law because the only reason for complying with its dictates is the illegitimate power of terror that combines a tyrannical command with an inhumane execution. The creation of the template, the original law-giving of the old Commandant, is an arche-writing that produces incomprehensible cryptograms, but because these divine laws are illegible, an interpreting mediator or a judge is needed. The machine, however, blurs all attempts to distinguish between writing and reading, between legislative creation and adjudicative interpretation, as the sentence is at once an interpretative reading of a prescribed law and an originary inscription—because the template is illegible, it cannot strictly speaking be "interpreted".[24]

Apparently the old Commandant's commandments have had no power before their engraving on the bodies of the condemned. Law can subject, so it seems, only by taking force (*Gewalt*) for power (*Macht*). In the penal colony, the template law has no power in itself and remains meaningless to the condemned until the sixth hour of their execution. Only by producing a *con*-templation, an understanding, can the template law claim to have any power, but by then force has already corrupted the process. Only then:

> "Understanding [*Verstand*] reaches the most feeble-minded! It begins around the eyes. From there it spreads. A sight that might seduce one to get under the harrow with him".[25]

The execution of the punishment seems to be an embodiment of violent and unlawful force, and this is what is often identified as the Kafkaesque in law. The only true laws in the text seem to be the explorer's sense of justice and the condemned man's contemplation of his own fate midway through the execution, in the understanding he reaches on the threshold of his death. But what is the understanding that the condemned man contemplates? Is it the unjust nature of his fate? Is it the meaning of the individual command he has violated against? Or is it, perhaps, a Kafkaesque science of law, a "juridical wisdom" of modernity?

[23] Koelb, *Kafka's Rhetoric*, pp. 74–75.

[24] On "prescription" and Kafka, see Lyotard, "Prescriptions", in Lyotard, *Lectures d'enfance*, pp. 35–56.

[25] Kafka, "In der Strafkolonie", n. 12 above, p. 108.

At least the reader is led to understand that the relatively autonomous and pseudo-legal display of violent force created by the old Commandant is Kafkaesque in its mechanical cruelty. Although it is conceived of in the domain of literature, the Kafkaesque execution corresponds accurately with the experience of modernity, with the unutterable truth that escapes the attempts of Enlightened reason to conceptualise the world. But what is wrong with law in the penal colony aside from the presumed "clearly unjust nature" of the torture machine? We may, once again, turn to the hierarchic structure of law.

In Kafka's text, the law of the old Commandant is a non-hierarchic system of subjugation based on evidently illegitimate commands whereas the explorer's sense of justice would seem to represent the traditional mode of juridical thinking in which all individual laws are subjected to a prior and higher order, to a substantial understanding of justice.[26] Towards the end of the text, we are offered an objective verification, so it seems, of the existence of such a hierarchy as the officer, having heard the disapproval of the explorer, condemns himself with the ultimate command: "be just [*sei gerecht*]". This ultimate command obliges the officer to respect a requirement of justice that is superior to all individual commands and is the source of their validity and justification.

IV

Such a claim obviously refers to a political Kafka quite apart from the man of letters of mainstream literary criticism. Within the musty traditions of the problematic father relationships and unfortunate love affairs of established Kafka scholarship, Gilles Deleuze and Félix Guattari have attempted to re-evaluate the author's politico-cultural legacy. Their claim is that Kafka should not be read as a self-evident proponent of a "negative theology" of modernity, but as an opening to a politics of desire. Kafka's truth is, then, not in the assertion of the painful destiny of modern man, but in the possibility of a new politics, and this applies to law, as well. Deleuze and Guattari motivate their understanding of Kafka by way of what they call "minor literature": being outside the realms of all major literary traditions, Kafka cannot be read merely as an author trying to describe a particular life and its circumstances, but rather as the initiator of a political programme.[27]

As an artist in the world of law—or perhaps vice versa—Kafka also writes what one could call "minor juridical literature" or "minor jurisprudence".[28] With the gift of insight that is commonly associated with the yearning for truth

[26] For a stunning etymological survey into the origins of *ius*, see Dumézil, "Ius", in Dumézil, *Idées romaines*, pp. 31–45.

[27] Deleuze and Guattari, *Kafka*.

[28] According to Goodrich, a "minor jurisprudence" escapes the phantom of a sovereign law by challenging "the law of masters" and the science that embraces it. I find this formulation, once again, too much of a "critical *œuvre*" of its author: Goodrich, *Law in the Courts of Love*, pp. 1–3.

of an artist, Kafka is granted access to the phenomenological *Wesenschau* that would enable him to unravel the essence of law and see the juridical phenomenon as it truly is. The *Wesen* of law that Kafka reaches but that is presumably unattainable to the professional lawyer is, despite its singular characterisation in Kafka's literature, necessarily also a generalisation of the world of law, a political statement about law. By marginalising his politics in "In der Strafkolonie" and its law, Kafka makes this characterisation into the foundation of a new law that would find its expression by way of negation in relation to the narrative, in an other law.

The danger lies in the interpretative naivete affecting most political readings of Kafka's minor jurisprudence. "In der Strafkolonie" is read as if the text represented a form of literary justice that *e contrario* condemns the forceful functioning of law in modernity. By unveiling the violent nature of juridical power in modern society and the inability of the modern science of law to assume responsibility for it, it is claimed that, in his literature, Kafka sets a normative standard for moral and ethical reform within the traditional notions of social justice.[29] Kafka is read as if he were a spokesman for a non-positivistic "ethics of justice" regardless of the fact that nothing in his texts conclusively justifies such a position.

Such interpretative naivete is reinforced by identifying the reader of the text with the explorer, both sharing cultured learning and enlightened values. During the course of the narrative, the explorer, unlike a reader unaffected by the law of the Kafkaesque, is never in a situation where he cannot believe his eyes or ears. Something like this was to be expected: the officer's presentation of the machine "displeases" the explorer although it is, of course, a penal colony "where extraordinary measures were needed and . . . military discipline must be enforced to the last".[30] He can merely verify meanings and values that precede the text.

An interpretation of such simplicity is, however, blind to the more awesome elements of Kafka's text. It ignores altogether, for example, the conclusion to the narrative and the prophecy inscribed on the gravestone of the old Commandant. If one wishes to deliver the reader from the pre-structuring expectations created by the proper name and the law of the Kafkaesque, the reader should be identified with the condemned man rather than the explorer. In the beginning of the text, the condemned man is portrayed as a common man unable to comprehend the French language spoken by the officer and the explorer. The text describes him as a "stupid-looking wide-mouthed creature with bewildered hair and face" who, like a "submissive dog",[31] "imitated the explorer"[32] in trying to understand the officer's presentation but "could not make head or tail out of it".[33] He is, therefore, unable to follow the presentation

[29] Cf. Emrich, *Franz Kafka*, pp. 220–226.
[30] Kafka, "In der Strafkolonie", n. 12 above, p. 105.
[31] *Ibid.*, p. 100.
[32] *Ibid.*, p. 103.

of the machine. In a similar way, a reader unaffected by the law of the Kafkaesque is very much like the condemned man desperately seeking to understand the author's account of the colony and its law but, being unable to master the meanings that literary language generates, can at first merely imitate comprehension.

But all of a sudden the aim of the execution is fulfilled: "enlightenment comes to the most dull-witted",[34] that is, to the condemned man. There is a considerable change in his understanding of what is happening, and a similar turn occurs in the text and its conception of the validity and justification of the law that regulates the execution. As the officer sets himself between the bed and the harrow, the condemned man realises that the explorer has undoubtedly given a command that somehow rectifies a wrong he has suffered.[35] How does the condemned man, at last displaying the transfiguration of the "radiance of justice", understand and evaluate the law of the colony? On the other hand, how does the reader, so far only able to imitate the explorer's understanding of the execution, perceive Kafka's minor jurisprudence? One answer can be formulated with the help of Nietzsche.[36]

For Nietzsche, the social bond that constitutes a society is based on promise. A promise is a commitment to act in a prescribed way in exchange for which the individual receives the advantages of living in a community. But even if man makes his actions predictable by promising to act in a certain way, he frequently forgets what he has committed himself to. Therefore, a reminder is needed, and this is how Nietzsche conceptualises punishment. Physical punishment is a "mnemonics of pain", a painful way of reminding forgetful man of his commitments and promises, of his social duties and responsibilities to the community. Nietzsche's mnemonic technique is simple: the promise that one has broken is written on the skin of the criminal with fire, because only that which causes ceaseless pain will be remembered. The community partakes in this literary torture but not through identification with the victim and the sensation of just revenge, but by experiencing pure pleasure in inflicting pain to another; punishment is a feast of cruelty.[37]

The festive and mnemonic character of the execution in the penal colony is clear enough. The officer enthusiastically describes the executions in "earlier times" when the valley was full of people who had come down to enjoy the ceremonial killing.[38] The futile intention of the officer seems to be to revive an old

[33] *Ibid.*, p. 104.
[34] *Ibid.*, p. 108.
[35] *Ibid.*, p. 119.
[36] Kafka's philosophical affinities to Kierkegaard and Schopenhauer have been studied to a larger extent. Patrick Bridgwater accounts for the more modest interest in Nietzsche to Max Brod's personal antipathies: Bridgwater, *Kafka and Nietzsche*, pp. 13–14. Brod's "interpretative failure" to see the affinities between Kafka and Nietzsche is also noted in Udoff, "Before the Question of the Laws", in Udoff (ed.), *Kafka and the Contemporary Critical Performance*, pp. 178–213. Kafka's Nietzschean features are amplified in his texts on law.
[37] Nietzsche, *Zur Genealogie der Moral*, pp. 802–804 and 806–808 (Part II, §§ 3 and 6).
[38] Kafka, "In der Strafkolonie", n. 12 above, p. 111.

tradition that is quickly degenerating, and he cannot understand why the explorer does not realise the glory in this tradition. Like Nietzsche's text, the short story also clearly involves three different levels of history: the Dionysian culture of the old Commandant so vividly described by the emotionally moved officer, the degradation of this tragic past into the empty ritual threatened by the Apollonian ideals of the new Commandant and, finally, the Messianic future prophesied by Nietzsche and written into the old Commandant's gravestone.[39]

Such a conception of punishment as ceremonial execution operates in relation to a specific understanding of law and justice. For Nietzsche, law as *Gesetz* is law that is posited and, hence, "positive" law. Law exists only in as much as it is valid, and law is valid if the will that has posited it has the power to do so. In other words, law exists for Nietzsche if it is valid, that is, if it is powerful and effective. According to Philippe Nonet, the identification of validity and existence in Nietzsche is a reference to medieval Christian ontology according to which something exists only in as much as Being is understood as the actuality (*actualitas*) of the power that has created it (*actus purus*). As a command given by a particular will, law would accordingly be the actuality (*Wirklichkeit*) and the efficacy (*Wirksamkeit*) of the power to command. Law would, then, be an effective command in which the command given and the corresponding obedience are indistinguishable.[40]

But in the traditions of juridical thinking, the authority to posit laws is usually subjected to a prior and higher law that does not, in itself, command, but merely founds the authority to command while simultaneously setting conditions for the legitimate use of that authority. In the modern science of law, there is, strictly speaking, no sovereign power. But with Nietzsche, the relationship between a command and its legitimate and just nature or between law and justice has been turned upside down. Justice is a creation of the law-giver, a creature of law. The commanding activity of the sovereign power is executed by positing laws, by law-giving, in the powerful manifestation of what is right (*Recht*) and what is wrong (*Unrecht*). According to Nietzsche, the right and the wrong can only exist through law-giving as posited laws, and to talk of them as such would be senseless.

As an expression of a commanding will, law is, for Nietzsche, the decision of correctness that either justifies or condemns, and the just or unjust nature of any procedure is ultimately based on the positing of laws. The power to command and to posit laws is, accordingly, the foundation of correctness, of all conceptions of right and wrong. But this power must first found its own authority. Coinciding with each individual command, each legislative act deeming what is right and what is wrong, this will must first establish its own power to command prior to the object of the command. The decision of correctness is, in the end, an expression of the will to power (*Wille zur Macht*). The juridical is always an

[39] Cf. Bridgwater, *Kafka and Nietzsche*, pp. 104–111.
[40] Nonet, "What is Positive Law?".

instrumental exception to the infinity of the will to power; universal justice is a principle hostile to life itself.[41]

V

In Kafka's text, an evident source of absolute power in the colony is, of course, the reign of the old Commandant. And as I have tried to indicate before, the old Commandant seems to act in the narrative as a divinity who, with his supreme authority, validates and justifies law in the colony. In other words, the old Commandant functions as a hierarchically sovereign power that guarantees the validity and the justification of law in much the same way as justice would in a conventional understanding of law. But the old Commandant's divine character does not fit well into a Nietzschean conception of law and justice. In addition, there are individual instances of law-giving in the text that constitute law in the Nietzschean sense: the order to guard the Captain's door, the officer's condemnation of its breach, and, most notably, the explorer's participation in the execution of the officer.

After the officer asks the explorer for help in convincing the new Commandant about the merits of the machine, the explorer responds by admitting that he had wondered whether he "had the right [*ob ich berechtigt wäre*]"[42] to intervene and pronounce his own judgement in relation to the execution. This is what he finally does. But at the same time he agrees to participate in the execution of the officer, to take part in the administering of a punishment he has just declared wrong. Were he to be consistent, the explorer would be obliged to condemn the execution as unjust and inhumane even when the officer places himself between the bed and the harrow. The explorer "knew very well what was going to happen, but he had no right [*er hatte kein Recht*] to obstruct the officer in anything".[43] The explorer chooses to remain silent in a situation where he would seem to be obliged to protest, and by remaining silent he gives the command and, at the same time, overrules any superior requirement of justice, subjects justice to his own decision of correctness.

But there is no contradiction. The explorer's two judgements are not regulated by a transcendental requirement of justice; both decisions, the condemning of the execution and participating in the execution of the officer, are also expressions of the explorer's will to power. In Nietzschean terms, the participation of the explorer in the execution of the officer is possible only because the requirement of justice inscribed into the second sheet, "be just [*sei gerecht*]", cannot, in itself, command to do anything. Jean-François Lyotard has attempted to clarify the nature of the requirement of justice as a law of laws from another angle. In Judaic law, "be just" is a meta-law that prescribes

41 Nietzsche, *Zur Genealogie der Moral*, pp. 814–817 (Part II, § 11).
42 Kafka, "In der Strafkolonie", n. 12 above, p. 116.
43 *Ibid.*, p. 119.

justice, but one can never know what it is to be just. In other words, one must be just case by case. Each time one must first decide, commit oneself, and judge, and only then can one meditate on whether what has been done was just or not.[44]

The officer, on the other hand, is "at least partly satisfied" and pronounces that "the time has come". The time has come because something has been prophesied; the prophecy written on the old Commandant's gravestone is, at last, being fulfilled. He then goes on to look at the explorer "with bright eyes that held some challenge, some appeal for cooperation".[45] With the silent command of the missing protest and wilful participation in the execution of the officer, the explorer has subjected the requirement of justice to his own will to power and, having done so, he assumes the position of the saviour foreseen in the prophecy, the Messiah "risen again" that the nameless adherents of the old Commandant, that is, the soldier and the condemned man, follow like faithful disciples.

Who is this Messiah? In his "prelude to a philosophy of the future", Nietzsche prophesies the coming of the new philosophers, "the philosophers of the dangerous 'Perhaps' " who are:

> "*commanders and law-givers* [*Befehlende und Gesetzgeber*]: they say: 'Thus *shall* it be!' They first determine the 'Where' and the 'Why' of mankind, and thereby set aside the previous labour of all philosophical workers and subjugators of the past. . . . Their 'knowing' is *creating*, their creating is a law-giving, their will to truth is—*Will to Power*".[46]

The soldier and the condemned man run from the tea-house after their law-giving Messiah to the harbour and "probably they wanted to force him at the last minute to take them with him".[47] But the explorer gets into the boat and lifts a heavy rope from the floor of the boat preventing his disciples from getting aboard. He denounces the position of the Messiah offered to him, thus escaping the cloak of the master that the prophecy has ordered him to carry. But his escape can only be as successful as his who flees his destiny:

> "A philosopher: alas, a being who often runs away from himself, is often afraid of himself—but whose curiosity always makes him 'come to himself' again".[48]

[44] Lyotard and Thébaud, *Au juste*, pp. 101–102.
[45] Kafka, "In der Strafkolonie", n. 12 above, pp. 117–118.
[46] Nietzsche, *Jenseits von Gut und Böse*, pp. 676–677 (§ 211).
[47] Kafka, "In der Strafkolonie", n. 12 above, p. 123.
[48] Nietzsche, *Jenseits von Gut und Böse*, p. 752 (§ 292).

10

Justice, Finally?

"But to understand God that is not contaminated by Being is as important and as uncertain a human possibility as delivering Being to unconcealement from the forgetfulness into which it has descended in metaphysics and in onto-theology".

Emmanuel Levinas

I

In the first part of this book, I wanted to develop an understanding of the philosophy of law. My claim was that even a philosophy of law is necessarily metaphysics or, in other words, what Aristotle called the *prōtē filosofia*, the "first philosophy". Metaphysical contemplation as theory entailed a promise of fulfilment that, however, I deemed impossible. I attributed this impossibility to the desire (*orexis*) that is involved in thinking. The unappeasable desire of metaphysics, however, induces an evaluation of "correctness", an assessment on the "rightful" and "true" constitution of things even if their divine origin, that is, the primary causes and principles, must necessarily remain unappropriable. The divine origin of things, I further maintained, is what the Greeks understood as "justice". But even if justice cannot be realised, it is, as the sense and direction of metaphysical desire, foundational in correct judgements. This is not, however, a metaphysics that speaks *about* law, it is a philosophy that speaks juridically, in the mode of law.

Later I claimed that if the philosophy of law addresses justice and correctness in the metaphysical senses outlined above, they seem to have very little to do with the way in which contemporary critical legal scholarship understands these notions. The foregoing chapters of the second part of this book have tried to map some confusions that are involved, but there are, surely, many more. It is, I feel, important to emphasise that before the ambitious projects of critical legal scholarship can be realised, the issue of social justice—or rather, the separate issues of the social and the just—must be worked out *as a philosophical question* independently of the political struggles that it is committed to. Such an enterprise does not, of course, inhibit the scholar from participating in political activity, but the transformation of theory into political agency as, for instance, an "applied metaphysics" of sorts seems to involve a misunderstanding of both philosophy and politics.

One such theoretical enterprise is Philippe Lacoue-Labarthe's and Jean-Luc Nancy's philosophical investigation of the "political" (*le politique*). The crisis of modernity, the authors claim, involves the "retreat" or withdrawal of civil society from the modern *polis*, and man is thereafter defined merely by way of work and production. The public sphere only covers the essential conditions of life, and the authoritarian foundation of power has been destroyed. In such conditions, true liberty has become impossible. This new form of totalitarianism cannot be confronted with the traditional devices of political criticism. Classic totalitarianism always included a transcendental point of reference—Lacoue-Labarthe's and Nancy's example is the "historical necessity" of Stalinist communism—but the new totalitarianism is radically immanent in that it entails the disappearance of all otherness. But the disappearance of otherness must not—this also captures well my own reservations about references to a "new ethics"—lead to nostalgia, for classic totalitarian thinking is born from a transcendence that reconstructs itself into the immanent closure of communal life. Lacoue-Labarthe and Nancy claim that the otherness that has withdrawn takes on the form of what Bataille understands as sovereignty, and one postulate must necessarily be that such sovereignty has never "existed", that it has always been in the futural mode of "to come", *à venir*.[1] This is something that Jacques Derrida has also touched upon in relation to democracy:

> "For democracy remains to come, that is its essence to the extent that it lingers: it will not only remain indefinitely perfectible and, therefore, always insufficient and futural, but, belonging to the time of the promise, it always remains to come in each of its future times. Even when there is democracy, it never exists, it is never present, it remains the theme of a non-presentable concept".[2]

The initial question of justice would, then, seem to be the recovering of a transcendence as otherness. As I have previously mentioned, a major vein in the rediscovery of transcendence is distinctly inspired by the philosophy of Emmanuel Levinas. Not only is his ethics often seen as a response to the moral dilemmas of a critical epoch—the prime example here is, of course, the social theory of Zygmund Bauman—but Levinas has also been designated as a significant turning point in, for instance, the political developments in the philosophy of deconstruction. Deconstruction, with its alleged emphases on literary wit and cultivation, has been criticised for its inability to address political issues, but Levinas's understanding of otherness is claimed to not only enable an escape from the impasses of deconstruction, but to also mark some kind of "ethical turn" in Derrida's philosophy. Without wanting to plunge into the details of this very controversial debate, I would only like to point out, once again, that such interpretations and emphases are markedly Anglo-American. They stem from a tradition that understands philosophy essentially as an intervention into the world. Intervention is not the *consequence* of philosophy, it is its *finalistic aim*. Philosophy is preceded by a moral obligation to take part in the politics of the

[1] Lacoue-Labarthe and Nancy, "Le 'retrait' du politique", in Kambouchner et al, *Le retrait du politique*, pp. 191–194.

[2] Derrida, *Politiques de l'amitié*, p. 339.

world, and like all other modes of human action, thinking must also do its share.

It is, therefore, quite easy to understand why the *œuvre* of Levinas with its emphases on otherness and justice has enjoyed such a success in critical legal scholarship. However, I fear that its impact is due to exactly the sort of retreat that Lacoue-Labarthe and Nancy termed "nostalgic". It is the revocation of a transcendence that typified the political overtones of traditional social criticism. It is a retreat—perhaps even an evasive move—from the most fundamental questions concerning law emphasising, once again, the victory of science over philosophy, of "Kant over Heidegger".

What would, then, transcendence and justice involve philosophically if our retreat was *not* nostalgic? And what would its "political" and "social" implications be? I will try to shed light on some essential issues by, first, returning to Erik Wolf. In his "fundamental ontology of law", Wolf formulated an understanding of *dikē* as *Zukommende*, as the advent of truth and justice "to come". Later in his life, he elaborated on the social implications of his theory in a theological project that he called the "law of the neighbour". Despite the distinctly humanistic overtones of Wolf's appeals for neighbourly love, some themes in his theology of law are also audible in Levinas's notion of justice. I will, therefore, also take a brief look at the first section of Levinas's earlier masterpiece, *Totalité et infini*.

We are, then, dealing with nothing less than transcendence. When one thinks transcendence, the question of God is likely to come up sooner or later.[3] In the philosophy of law, God is one name among others for the ultimate source of law's obliging nature. This is *not* a confessional statement, and I am not advocating a religious theory. But to be able to philosophically assess the (possible) relationship between law and justice, one must also be able to address the foundations of responsibility. God is not the source or the origin of responsibility, but the horrified exclamation with which man recognises her own ability to respond.

II

Wolf's theology of law seems to be more or less motivated by a similar juxtaposing of ontology and ethics that has been popular in contemporary critical legal scholarship inspired by the philosophy of Levinas. But despite some common themes and formulations, Wolf's thinking is, nevertheless, quite different and even singular.

For Wolf, the theology of law transcends ontology and ethics, rendering both possible. It is, then, the foundation of all juridical thinking. The science of law usually infers the obliging nature of law from its formal normativity (*Geltung*),

[3] On philosophy and God, see, e.g., Kovacs, *The Question of God in Heidegger's Phenomenology*, pp. 123–132.

but Wolf claims that the ultimate foundation of the obliging essence of law can only be determined from man's unconditional responsibility for his neighbour before God:

> "what *is* law (right) before God, that *ought* to be law (right) for man".[4]

The culmination of Wolf's theology of law is a short essay that investigates the foundational normativity of law through the concept of "neighbour" (*Nächste*). The study is dedicated to Karl Barth whose dialectic theology is a central component of Wolf's thinking. In particular Barth's notion of God as an "absolutely other" gives Wolf's theology of law a philosophical quality that sets it apart from the conventions of natural law doctrine.[5] Man is isolated from God by an unsurmountable qualitative distance. As far as my interpretation is concerned, Barth's critique of anthropomorphic representations suggests that the rapport between God and man is asymmetric. Even though all (human) ethics is subject to the judgement of God, man has no privileged access to God. The word of God cannot be merely "found" at will; it reveals itself as an exterior evaluation to judge man and to determine his responsibility. Only after man has unconditionally accepted his responsibility, God may appear.[6]

The point of departure is the traditional view that excludes love from the domain of law. If the juridical is transformed into love, an abstract other, as it is conceptualised by law, is redefined as a neighbour. A juridical subject is by necessity an abstract other that can enjoy the benefits offered by law under certain specified circumstances. But within the order of love, the other is always a neighbour, and in such a neighbourly relationship, the subject's rapport *vis-à-vis* the other is defined rather by the former's responsibility than the latter's formal rights as they are defined in the law. Wolf cannot accept the notion of a formal and loveless law that would merely recognise an abstract other and its rights without assigning a responsibility to respect them. On the contrary, the love of the neighbour is the foundation on which all law rests.[7]

But love that transcends formal and positive law raises a consequential question concerning the normativity of law. According to traditional juridical thinking, love that is not bound to the form of law also introduces the spectre of relativism. If true normativity only pertains to law that is founded on neighbourly love, can such love *in itself* be regarded as binding? Wolf deems all former attempts to solve the problem of relativism insufficient.[8] The answer cannot be sought in abstract notions of man as the tradition of juridical thinking seems to do, but only from the concreteness of a situation in which the other arrives at man's side as his neighbour. This is Wolf's radical turn, his *metanoia*, and he calls it, following Søren Kierkegaard, a "new order of things":

[4] Wolf, "Rechtsphilosophie", in Wolf, *Rechtsphilosophische Studien*, p. 81.
[5] Wolf, *Recht des Nächsten*, pp. 32–34. See also Wolf, *Das Problem der Naturrechtslehre*.
[6] On human and divine justice, see Barth, *Der Römerbrief*, chs 3 and 4.
[7] Wolf, *Recht des Nächsten*, pp. 11–12.
[8] *Ibid*., pp. 12–15.

"The experience of faith enables one to realise that love is not the limit of law, but one can see it now as the ground of a new order of Dasein [*Daseins-Neuordnung*] within which *God* judges to each her own: he delivers us to our fellow man (and fellow being) 'in order' ".[9]

"Neighbour" suggests a concrete encounter, a proximity in relation to an other Dasein. The essence of this proximity is, however, theological: even if the neighbour can be anybody—or anything—proximity is a concrete situation that is founded on Dasein's responsibility before God. It is not a general abstraction that is inferred from the ideals of classic humanistic thinking.[10]

For Wolf, Dasein's primordial mode of Being is communal, but it does not concern the unauthentic character of Heidegger's *Mitsein*. The theological purport of a communal Dasein unfolds as personality and as solidarity. Man as Dasein is a person in so far as he accepts his responsibility by responding to the call of God. First, personality must be understood as man's existence as the image of God. This image includes a juridical moment, for God has realised his law in his covenant with man. But personality also refers to man's existence as a face. The face is evidence of God's will to see his law respected in the human world; the face of the other is the image of God. Personality as man's communal existence (the image of God, the face) is, then, a vertical relationship that serves as the foundational law (*Urrecht*) that prescribes all basic rights enjoyed by man.

In solidarity, on the other hand, man recognises that his rapport *vis-à-vis* the other is ordered by God. The communal aspect of Dasein is founded on man's response to the call of God, and this transforms the other into a neighbour. For Wolf, the call of God reaches man through Christ, and in the person of Christ, even God can be regarded as man's neighbour. Solidarity is, then, the interconnection of a vertical and a horizontal relationship where the fraternity of men meets communality before God. The two notions of personality and of solidarity make up what is called the law of the neighbour, a theological understanding of law that precedes all other rights and duties.[11]

In other words, a theology of law unfolds as the sovereign law of God and as a law commanding man to care for his neighbour. God's law—Wolf also calls this the Christocratic order—is, however, not the expression of a sovereign will. God is infinitely just, and his will is merely to conciliate divine justice to the order of Dasein. The divine justice of God announces itself in the covenant. In the Old Testament, God's justice takes place as the divine intervention that judges and corrects the injustices of the human world. But the justice that is announced in the New Testament is the mercy that man can recognise in the sacrificial death of Christ. Because the covenant is essentially unilateral, the justice of God always precedes that of man. God's law is absolute; before God, every man is as far from the right as the other.[12]

[9] *Ibid.*, pp. 15–16.
[10] *Ibid.*, pp. 28–31.
[11] *Ibid.*, pp. 16–17.
[12] *Ibid.*, pp. 17–18.

The law that commands man to care for his neighbour—Wolf calls this the fraternal order—is manifest in inter-human relations as the commands of solidarity (*Lex Charitatis*) as well as the absolute obligation to enter the order in which the abstract other is transformed into a neighbour.[13]

The law of the neighbour transcends, then, the difference between an ontology of law and an ethics of law because ontology is defined as man's responsibility for his neighbour before God. As a communal set of obligations, the law of the neighbour does not, however, annul the founding difference of Dasein as singularity (*Selbstsein*) and as social existence (*Alssein*). Quite the contrary, it inscribes itself between the two aspects and maintains the difference. As personality, the law of the neighbour is responsibility before God regardless of Dasein's social existence, and as solidarity, it is fraternity amongst neighbours unaffected by the singularity of each.[14]

Wolf expresses his law of the neighbour with three concrete prescriptions that he deems normatively valid ("*es gilt*"). The neighbour must, first, be given access to law both as a likeness that exists at Dasein's side (*Nebenmensch*) and as something distinct and different existing "with" Dasein (*Mitmensch*). Law must be founded on a notion of the other as a concrete neighbour that enters the domain of rights without the coercive force of a formal mechanism. A law that coerces Dasein to care for an abstract other does not comply with the requirements of the law of the neighbour. Secondly, law must be conferred reciprocally one to an other. It must be founded on rights that are "always already" donated to the other and not on a formal mechanism with which an abstract other may, at will, demand such rights. A law that is founded on the need to demand rights does not comply with the requirements of the law of the neighbour. Finally, a right that is "to come", a right that is "due", so to speak, cannot be demanded even if it is to be expected. The concentration of conferred rights to those who are already privileged is against the main principles of the law of the neighbour, but the unequal distribution of rights cannot be criticised by referring to formal justice, a concept that is in sharp contrast with the concreteness of the notion of the neighbour.[15]

If we understand—or read—the God that Wolf founds his theology of law on as an "absolutely other" in the sense of Barth, Wolf's attempts to deify the neighbour reveal certain affinities with Levinas. Access to law as "being (in the) right" is understood as futural, it is the advent "to come" (*Zukommende*). A futural right is not a political or a social ideal that is projected into the future as a possible realisation; it is not a project of social justice. It is something that must remain futural, a temporal structure that resists totalisation. In addition, the normative essence of law and the corresponding responsibility to care for the other as a neighbour are not consequences that are derived from a socio-

[13] Wolf, *Recht des Nächsten*, pp. 18–19.

[14] *Ibid*., p. 20. Cf. Maihofer, "Anthropologie der Koexistenz", in Hollerbach et al (eds), *Mensch und Recht*, pp. 162–211.

[15] Wolf, *Recht des Nächsten*, pp. 24–27.

political institution of power. Responsibility, and especially juridical responsibility, is realised as Dasein encounters the other in its divine transcendence and absolute alterity. The responsibility of neighbourly love precedes all social forms of law simultaneously making them possible and determining their (possible) normative authority. Law without love cannot be justice; it is merely factual efficacy.

But despite these similarities, Wolf's law of the neighbour is closer to an onto-theology in the sense that Heidegger understands the tradition of philosophy than an ethics as "metaphysics" in the Levinasian sense. Being (in the) right—an ontological question for Wolf—is defined before the absolutely other, but this absolutely other is by necessity the God who calls on man to respond in the name of faith. On the other hand, ethics is understood as the consequence of this overwhelming encounter with divinity, as a fundamentally humanistic morality that also accounts for the normative essence of law.

How does, then, Levinas understand ethics as metaphysics? And how does it concern justice?

III

Franz Rosenzweig begins his monumental work *Der Stern der Erlösung* with an observation on the relationship between metaphysics and the finitude of human existence:

> "From death, from the fear of death, all knowledge of the all arises. Philosophy aspires to overcome the anxiety of the worldly, to defeat the death of its poisonous thorn and the Hades of its pestilent whisper. Everything mortal lives in this fear of death".[16]

In order to respect fully the philosophical nature of Levinas's work, I believe that one must understand his profound affinity to Rosenzweig. The "fear of death" cited above represents man's motivation to transcend the limits of his mundane existence, the desire to overcome the finite Being of Dasein and to join the gods. I have tried to indicate how this aspiration is already present in the Aristotelian *orexis tou eidenai* and how it relates to Dasein's unauthentic existence in the world. But Rosenzweig's unique contribution to this discussion is the "all", the totality towards which metaphysics aspires as it is driven by the fear of death, and the alternative possibility of true redemption. Rosenzweig's "all" is, of course, the totality that Levinas's *Totalité et infini* is so firmly opposed to.[17] But some key elements of Levinas's thinking are already present in his earliest texts. In *De l'évasion*, originally an article from as early as 1935, the central issue is the nauseating shame with which man encounters Being in its simplicity and purity. Such an encounter, compelling man to compare his

[16] Rosenzweig, *Der Stern der Erlösung*, p. 3.

[17] See Levinas, *Totalité et infini*, p. 14. On Rosenzweig and Levinas, see, e.g., Gibbs, *Correlations in Rosenzweig and Levinas*, pp. 23–30.

adequateness—for the Levinas of the period, "adequateness" was the creed of petty bourgeois materialism: "I am enough"—in relation to the simple Being of things, leaves man in shame inducing a demand to escape. But the subject cannot flee its limits to an allegedly infinite existence and a consequent inner harmony. Quite the contrary, it can only escape "itself", the fact that it "is".[18]

Although this early text is not outspoken about it, escape as "evading" clearly implies an avoiding of sorts, a flight from something essential with clear ethical overtones. The escape from being is, then, the central theme of what has later come to be known as a Levinasian ethics. In trying to formulate a "pre-ontological ethics", Levinas's main concern has been the recovering of transcendence as something other than Being, as something "*autrement qu'être*".[19] And it is in this enterprise that the notion of justice plays an essential role. My aim here is to touch upon certain aspects of Levinas's philosophy in the first section of *Totalité et infini* and to designate the element of "rectitude" or "correctness" as *droiture*. Here is one of his (many) formulations of justice:

> "The other as other is the Other [*Autrui*]. Only a discursive relation can 'let it be'; a pure 'unveiling' in which it comes up as a theme does not respect it adequately for this to happen. We call justice this facial encounter in discourse. If truth arises in the absolute experience in which a being sheds its proper light, then only true discourse or justice can produce the truth".[20]

But it is, I feel, important to emphasise that Levinas is not writing an ethics for an era of crises as many contemporary interpreters seem to presume, but, indeed, to address the question of the *prōtē filosofia*: what is the "first philosophy"? "Ethics", "other" and "justice" are, then, all notions that belong to Levinas's understanding of *ethics as metaphysics*, and not to ethics as a "practical science" in the sense of Aristotle. *Totalité et infini* begins with an elaboration of what "metaphysical desire" might be. Because truth is what is absent, metaphysical desire reaches out towards otherness, towards an other being as *kath'auto* or as "in accordance with itself". In accordance with itself, the other must necessarily be "absolutely other" in relation to the Self. Otherness is nothing that can be recovered which would imply that it has once been part of the Self. But neither is it appropriable in the sense that metaphysical desire could somehow be appeased. Indeed, the otherness that desire understands or "hears" (*entendre*) is also its "sense" and "direction" (*sens*). Metaphysical desire, then, reaches out towards something in which it can only hear a divinity:

> "[Otherness] is understood as the alterity of the Other and of the Very-High [*Très-Haut*]. Metaphysical desire opens up the very dimension of highness [*hauteur*]".[21]

Highness is true sovereignty, and the overtones that Levinas gives to it clearly suggest a divine consideration. It is, however, specifically noted that metaphys-

[18] Levinas, *De l'évasion*, pp. 73–74.
[19] See, e.g., Levinas, *Autrement qu'être*, pp. 13–15.
[20] Levinas, *Totalité et infini*, p. 67 (emphases deleted).
[21] *Ibid.*, p. 23.

ical desire is not a consequence of man's finitude. Although the highness of the other, that is, its majesty as the union of the teacher and what is taught,[22] clearly touches upon infinity and the divine, the object of metaphysical desire is not immortality in the form of divinity. The Other reveals itself in its highness and sanctity, but its infinite character does not "burn the eyes of the onlooker," as Levinas puts it. There is no sacred violence involved, and this means that the metaphysical encounter with the Other must be fundamentally atheistic. Metaphysics can, however, also account for God that is *kath'auto*. To hear divine speech does not involve the comprehension of an object. It is entering into a relation with a substance that exceeds beyond its idea as objective existence:

> "The discourse in which [the divine] is simultaneously alien and present defers participation, and instead of the recognition of an object, it establishes the pure experience of a social relation in which a being does not infer its existence from its contact with the other".[23]

The divine dimension is revealed as the Other appears as a *human* face. The relationship with the transcendent being—God, if you will—is, then, by nature atheistic and social. God arises to his supreme and ultimate presence as the correlative of justice rendered to man. One cannot have direct knowledge of God by turning one's attention to him, not because man's noetic abilities are limited, but because metaphysics as the relation to infinity already respects the unconditional transcendence of the Other. If the Other is the domain of metaphysical truth, it is also fundamental in defining man's relationship to God; the absolute highness in which God reveals himself is already manifest in the face of the Other. Nothing is more direct than such a face-to-face encounter of the Self and the Other in all its uncanny otherness, and Levinas also characterises this encounter with the term "rectitude" (*droiture*):

> "An act of justice—the rectitude of the face-to-face—is required so that the opening will prepare the appearance of God, and here 'vision' concurs with the act of justice".[24]

The Other reveals itself in discourse, but Levinas understands discourse in a rather specific way. As the medium bridging one to an other, language makes universality possible and, accordingly, presupposes a plurality of interlocutors. But it also presupposes the radical strangeness of these interlocutors in relation to each other, a transcendence:

> "language speaks where common relational terms are missing, where the common ground is missing or should only constitute itself. It installs itself in this transcendence. Discourse is, then, the experience of something absolutely strange, a *pure* 'knowledge' or 'experience', the *trauma of wonder*".[25]

[22] "Justice consists of recognising my master in the Other": *ibid.*, p. 68.

[23] *Ibid.*, p. 76.

[24] *Ibid.*, p. 77. On the "facial" character of Rosenzweig's notion of dialogue, see Rosenzweig, *Der Stern der Erlösung*, p. 80.

[25] Levinas, *Totalité et infini*, pp. 70–71.

But the Other will reveal itself in its full majesty only in certain kinds of discourse. Rhetorics, for instance, is not a mode of discourse that could enable the revelation, to "let the Other be" in all its divine glory. The Same must, then, take upon itself to "receive" (*accueillir*) the Other in a rather specific way. It must commit itself to "respect" the Other *before* any ethics as metaphysics is possible. This commitment to "rectitude", the respectful and "right" reception of the Other, is intimately bound to the way in which Levinas understands subjectivity. The absolute otherness on which an ethics as metaphysics is founded arises from Being, and only then is any thinking or subjectivity possible. Subjectivity is, accordingly, possible only to the extent that the gap between Being and transcendence is realised. The gap can, however, only be realised by *according a right*, that is, by taking the "correct" decision and letting the Other affirm itself as subject in discourse:

> "the very fact of being engaged in a discourse consists of granting the Other *a right* to this egoism and, consequently, to justify itself. It is in the essence of discourse that, in this apology, the ego [*le moi*] simultaneously affirms itself and yields before the transcendant".[26]

Justice is the taking place of transcendence through the face-to-face encounter in which the Other reveals itself in all its alterity and highness. In other words, justice, for Levinas, is the event of metaphysical truth as ethics. But it would seem that the event is concurrent with a judgement of "rectitude", a commitment made by a pre-subjective consciousness of sorts. As the ethical truth of metaphysics, justice must by necessity precede all human laws, but paradoxically there seems to be a law of "rectitude" that precedes the taking place of justice, that is, the reception of the Other in discourse.

As an ethics before ontology, metaphysics involves the face-to-face encounter with the Other. Such a foundational notion of justice must precede all socio-political statutes that, for example, codify the reciprocal responsibilities and obligations of the citizens of the *polis*. But a pre-ontological ethics and the corresponding notion of justice would not be possible without another kind of law. This other law orders the way in which the Other should be received in discourse. It is a critical law in the sense that it compels one to engage in true discourse and to avoid corrupt variants such as rhetorics. But the obligation to receive the Other in true discourse is coupled with a responsibility that precedes the formation of any subject, for subjectivity is conceivable only after the Other has revealed itself. There are, then, two laws. The first law—the very first one—and the responsibility it entails require a commitment of "rectitude", a decision to respond to an original call, and this first law is undoubtedly of divine origin. The first law is the call of God that establishes man's ability to respond, his original responsibility. And only after one has committed oneself to true discourse is the event of a justice "to come" conceivable and the correct laws of society

[26] Levinas, *Totalité et infini*, p. 29.

possible. This odd paradox—"law before justice before law"—is what I understand by the aporetic nature of law.

IV

Marguerite Duras, an author, gives me the pretext to develop some concluding remarks on the aporetic nature of law. Another French author, Maurice Blanchot, touches upon the subject in a short book, *La communauté inavouable*, which has during the past few years become one of the best known social and political texts within contemporary French philosophy. The latter of the book's two essays, "La communauté des amants", is Blanchot's reading of Duras's short prose text *La maladie de la mort*. When literature encounters the political, one should, perhaps, examine the degree to which Duras is a pretext for Blanchot as well to continue a discourse on love, friendship, and community, themes which have previously been dealt with especially in the collection *L'amitié*. At the closing pages of the collection, we find Blanchot's often cited characterisation of friendship:

> "Friendship, this relation without dependence, without episode and into which all the simplicity of life nevertheless enters, passes by way of the recognition of the common strangeness that does not permit us to speak of our friends, but only to speak to them, not to make them a theme of conversations (or articles), but the movement of listening in which, speaking to us, they reserve, even in the greatest familiarity, the infinite distance, the fundamental separation from which that which separates becomes relation".[27]

Strangeness, distance, separation; Blanchot's friendship is incommensurability, friendship that exists only in separation.

In his book, Blanchot also speaks of his relation to Duras's text with expressions that resonate with friendship. He notes that his essay consists of observations that "accompany" the reading of Duras's text. Blanchot's company is, however, not without ambiguity. Duras's text, the *récit* or the account that Blanchot wishes to accompany, is characterised by a certain completeness: it is "in itself sufficient", "perfect", "without a way out".[28] But later Blanchot refers to Duras's "declarative text" as being merely apparently a *récit*.[29] Blanchot says that he is trying to extract the secret of the account by turning the text around30 but, in doing so, he must also "betray" the text.[31] What is Duras's mystery, the secret of the account that requires Blanchot's betrayal?

This is the social question that Blanchot is asking: what are the conditions of community? The answer is sought from the relation between a woman and a

[27] Blanchot, *L'amitié*, p. 328.
[28] Blanchot, *La communauté inavouable*, p. 51.
[29] *Ibid.*, p. 59.
[30] *Ibid.*, p. 81.
[31] *Ibid.*, p. 83.

man in Duras's text. The lethal disease that the name of the novel indicates is the man's inability to love. According to Blanchot, the moral or physical evil of the disease cannot, however, be appointed to a subject. It concerns the other's suffering, a suffering which is incomprehensible and, yet, demands a response.[32]

At first, the symptoms of the disease seem to be fairly easy to decipher. In the story, a man who knows only those like himself enters into a contractual relationship with an unknown woman. Addressing the man, the narrator of the *récit* gives us a motive:

> "You tell her that you would like to try, try for several days perhaps. Perhaps for several weeks. Perhaps even for your whole life. She asks: Try what? You say: To love".[33]

The diagnosis or the verdict seems clear enough. Being unable to love, the man can approach the woman only by stipulating the terms of their relationship with a contract that is binding to both parties. On the other hand, the woman commits herself to a relationship in which she appears to be surrendering herself completely to the sexual desires of the man but, in reality, retains a certain liberty that is beyond the terms of the agreement—only spurious love, then, based on commerce, a relationship that could hardly furnish the foundation for friendship any more than community. The sick man's inability to love is not, however, sexual. He even satisfies the woman but cannot recognise the signs of a life alien to him and, therefore, annuls the pleasure. This is his "malady of death".[34]

Blanchot asserts, however, that we cannot reduce the account to our preliminary diagnosis.[35] The mystery that escapes a facile reading of the text has to be searched for in the woman whose existence transcends the reality of the story: she is more than Dasein.[36] In a certain sense, only the woman is in the story, the narrator gives us only her:

> "She is very thin, almost slender, the beauty of her legs is of a different kind than that of the body. They are not properly implanted into the rest of the body".[37]

The man attempts to see the beauty but, being unable to recognise anything but his own kind, he cannot. The woman is also the man's first and, according to Blanchot, the first woman for everyone:

> "The body would have been long, made in a single casting, with a single stroke, as if by God himself, with the indelible perfection of individual coincidence".[38]

The narrator does not name the woman that no name could possibly describe. She is God's creation but without nominal existence. She is also fragile, and such weakness arouses deadly desires in the man:

[32] Blanchot, *La communauté inavouable*, p. 59.
[33] Duras, *La maladie de la mort*, pp. 8–9.
[34] Blanchot, *La communauté inavouable*, pp. 35–36.
[35] *Ibid.*, pp. 62–65.
[36] Cf. Levinas, *Totalité et infini*, pp. 164–167.
[37] Duras, *La maladie de la mort*, p. 21.
[38] *Ibid.*, p. 20.

> "The body has no defenses at all, it is smooth from the face to the feet. It entices strangulation, rape, maltreatments, insults, cries of hatred, the rage of austere, lethal passions".[39]

But the man perceives the fragility of the woman as an unforeseen power:

> "You look at this figure, at the same time you discover its infernal power, its abominable fragility, its weakness, the invincible force of its unparalleled weakness".[40]

The woman also sleeps practically all the time. Because of her continuous sleep, her Being sways in a familiar game: there, not-there:

> "She sleeps. You do not wake her. The anxiety grows in the room at the same time as her sleep expands".[41]

According to Blanchot, the woman acquires her enigmatic character from the peculiar closeness with which she offers herself to the man. The man must confront the difference of another species, of the absolutely other. The malady of death is, then, not only the man's inability to recognise the other, but the illness itself germinates in the absolute alterity of the woman:[42]

> "You only know the grace of the bodies of the dead, the grace of those like you. All of a sudden you realise the difference between this grace of the bodies of the dead and the grace found here made of the utmost weakness that a mere gesture could crush, this royalty. You discover that it is here, in her, that the malady of death is fomenting, that it is this displayed figure before you that decrees the malady of death".[43]

The man tormented by his disease attempts continuously to love, to detect in the woman a recognisable and common similarity that he seems to regard as the precondition of love. But his attempts are all in vain and, therefore, he cries. The woman sees only self-pity in the tears that he sheds, but the narrator reads from them the first and original commandment of ethics: "Do not kill":

> "You think you cry because you cannot love. You cry because you cannot impose death".[44]

Blanchot indicates that the asymmetric difference between the unable man and the woman acting as love's chosen emissary indicates an ethical relation. Blanchot's ethics is—following Levinas—a relation in which the other is always granted a place closer to God.[45] Blanchot extracts an ethics from the following passage in Duras's text:

39 *Ibid.*, p. 21.
40 *Ibid.*, p. 31.
41 *Ibid.*, p. 17.
42 Blanchot, *La communauté inavouable*, p. 65.
43 Duras, *La maladie de la mort*, pp. 37–38.
44 *Ibid.*, p. 48.
45 Cf. Levinas, *Totalité et infini*, pp. 236–238.

> "You ask how the emotion of loving could come about. She answers you: Perhaps from a sudden flaw in the logic of the universe. She says: For example from an error. She says: never from a will".[46]

From homogeneity required by understanding arises heterogeneity, the absolutely other that cannot be wanted or desired. Love is the incommensurability between the subject and the absolutely other. That is why the man's efforts at love, his attempts to detect in the woman a recognisable semblance, are doomed to fail. The woman's answer on the possibility of love continues:

> "She says: From everything, from the flight of a night bird, from a sleep, from a sleeping dream, from the approach of death".[47]

The ambiguity of death: as a disease, the inability to love, the inability to recognise the other, but, at the same time, also the movement of love itself in which the unrecognisable other arises in its absolute alterity.[48] Therefore, true love can take place only in the mode of loss. One day, after the contract has expired, the woman has disappeared. At first, the man searches for her everywhere but:

> "Very soon you give up, you do not look for her any more, not in the town, not in the night, nor in the day. Even so this way you have managed to live this love in the only way you could, by losing it before it came to be".[49]

The man does not live in the same time as the woman. He has not lost a woman that he has once had as his own. The disappearance of the woman is the perfection of love itself that has not yet begun and has, by the same token, already ceased to exist. According to Blanchot, the first words of ethics are spoken in this impossible love. The suffering of the other places her above all that is existent. Confronting the absolute alterity of the woman, the man is put into question, and the only possible response to the question of alterity is the limitless responsibility that exceeds its own existence without, however, exhausting itself. Such a responsibility cannot be reduced to law but, quite the contrary, it must precede all law. Nevertheless, it is precisely law that obliges a response. The limitless responsibility towards the other is the singular exception to the universally binding law, an exception that cannot be articulated in the formal language of the juridical.[50]

Is this the aporia of law?

Blanchot's short book continues his social and political thinking that is deeply inspired by Bataille. Through Bataille, the book takes part in the so-called "community" discourse. The first essay of the book, "La communauté négative", is Blanchot's reply to Nancy's text "La communauté désœuvrée", an

[46] Duras, *La maladie de la mort*, p. 52.
[47] *Ibid.*, p. 52.
[48] Blanchot, *La communauté inavouable*, pp. 67–70.
[49] Duras, *La maladie de la mort*, p. 57.
[50] Blanchot, *La communauté inavouable*, pp. 71–73.

essay which was later published as the opening text of the book of the same name.[51]

A third important contribution to this discussion is Derrida's *Politiques de l'amitié*. Derrida indicates that both Nancy and Blanchot have been notable sources of inspiration for the book, but the themes through which Derrida takes his analysis of friendship—ethics, the other, responsibility—seem to be closer to Blanchot and Levinas than to Nancy.[52] In a slightly different tone, Derrida repeats the question that we have already encountered in Blanchot: Who is the friend? What is friendship? Derrida finds that the philosophies of friendship have traditionally been articulated with the help of a distinction between true and apparent friendship. Common friendship, friendship here and now, does not measure up to the requirements of true friendship. Therefore, friendship is never what it seems, true friendship is never present. Blanchot's notion of community seems to reiterate the distinction:

> "Which is, indeed, one of the traits of community, when that community dissolves itself, giving the impression that it could never have been, even when it had been".[53]

As friendship here and now cannot fulfil the requirements of true friendship, the latter is postponed or delayed into the future with a promise. The promise of a true friendship to come also entails the obligation to participate in its realisation. One can prepare the way for the Messiah by studying the Torah; according to Derrida, the discourse of friendship also takes place in the mode of prayer. It is a request, a plea, or an appeal (*appel*) that is not addressed to the present but, rather, to a responsibility opening into the future. But in the prayer, one must also address the past: for the appeal to be heard, it must carry within itself the signs of a minimum friendship, a recollection (*rappel*) of a friendship preceding all other friendships, a being-together that is anterior to all speech—be it an acknowledgment of friendship or a declaration of war.[54]

Blanchot also formulates the obliging appeal of the "unavowable community" as a responsibility:

> "it does not permit us to lose interest in the present time which, by opening up unknown spaces of freedom, makes us responsible for new relations, always threatened, always hoped for".[55]

According to Derrida, the movement and the time of friendship is the *futur antérieur* in which the making present of the future and past traces of friendship implies their concurrent repudiation.[56] If friendship does not exist in the

[51] Cf. Nancy, *La communauté désœuvrée*, pp. 103–105. For a comparison of Nancy and Blanchot, see Bernasconi, "On Deconstructing Nostalgia for Community within the West". A further, so far only little analysed, addition to this debate would be Agamben, *La communità che viene*.

[52] Derrida, *Politiques de l'amitié*, n. 2 above, p. 56, n. 1.

[53] Blanchot, *La communauté inavouable*, p. 88 (emphasis deleted).

[54] Derrida, *Politiques de l'amitié*, pp. 260–264.

[55] Blanchot, *La communauté inavouable*, p. 93.

[56] Derrida, *Politiques de l'amitié*, pp. 279–280.

present, if it cannot be made present but must always be delayed into the future, how is one to understand the responsibility that is necessarily associated with friendship? How is one to understand ethics in a friendship that will never be present?

For both Blanchot and Derrida, responsibility correlates with understanding or "hearing" (*entendre*) and with answering or responding (*répondre*). Derrida maintains that answering is, first, answering *for* oneself in as much as a thing or a happening bears a proper name, when one answers "in one's name". But a response is also forwarded *to* an other. Of these two modes of responding, answering to an other is more original because, when answering for oneself, the response is necessarily addressed to an other. Lastly, answering takes place *before* an other, but in this case it is a universal and institutional representative (law, the tribunal, and so on) of a singular other. According to Derrida, the ability to answer for oneself is understood as responsibility which is associated with time, voice, and hearing. Answering to and before the other is, on the other hand, identified with space, regard, and distance, a respect which is, in the Occidental philosophies of friendship, usually understood as the distinctive character separating friendship from love.[57]

Derrida claims that the ethics of friendship pertaining to the ideals of the Enlightenment can be located at the intersection of responsibility and respect. It is a brotherly responsibility before reason in which the latter furnishes equality with a compelling character. In this scheme built around familial relations, friendship is absolute respect and responsibility amongst brethren before the father that represents reason. The relation between father and sons is, rather, characterised by a reciprocal but unequal love.

In an ethics of friendship thus formulated, the other maintains its absolute singularity in principle, but the relation to the other is determined through the universality of law. According to Derrida, the discourse of universality refers to a third that oversees the face-to-face encounter of two absolutely singular beings. It seems, then, that we have two models of friendship. The first pertains to narcissism, the second to desire.

In narcissistic friendship, the subject recognises in the friend a semblance, an other ego. In the dual relation, law operating as the third obliges the retention of a respectable distance required by friendship and, thus, prevents the two absolutely singular beings from plunging into the destructive abyss of narcissism. In friendship as desire—for Derrida, Blanchot seems to represent this model—the other intervenes in the relation between the subject and the ego. But Derrida argues that even in the model of desire, a third—that is, law—that originates in the singularity of the other commands the recognition of the transcendental alterity of the other. Even the transcendental alterity of the other requires a law the command of which furnishes the foundation for the recognition of alterity.[58]

The aporia of law?

[57] Derrida, *Politiques de l'amitié*, pp. 280–283.
[58] *Ibid.*, pp. 306–308.

V

I would, finally, like to touch upon the structuring of the rapport between the subject, the ego, and the other in relation to law from the position of the narrator in *La maladie de la mort*. In an earlier text, Blanchot states that the neuter narrator "*il*" is the third person that, nonetheless, does not have the position of a subject. In the neuter space of the *récit*, the narrative voice destroys the possibility of relations determined through a subject/object scheme; the acting subjects of the *récit* lose their ability to say "I" (*je*). In the narrative voice, the other understood as the neuter imposes itself into the account in its irreducible strangeness and deceitful perversity: "The other speaks".[59]

The narrator of *La maladie de la mort* may not, however, be a voice in which only the other speaks. Its tone of voice, addressing the man in the second person present, is rather imperative than majestic:

> "You would not know anything either, never, neither you nor anybody, about how she thinks of the world or you, about your body or your soul, or about the disease that she says you have caught".[60]

Perhaps the specific nature of the narrator is the reason why Blanchot regards Duras's "declarative text" as only apparently an account. Blanchot hears something godly in the imperative voice:

> "Everything is decided by an initial 'You' that is more than authoritative, that demands and determines what will happen or what could happen to one who has fallen into the snare of an inexorable fate. For the sake of ease, we will say that it is the 'you' of the stage director giving indications to the actor who must make the passing figure he is to incarnate appear from nothing. So be it, but it must be, then, understood as the supreme Director: the biblical 'You' that comes from high above and prophetically fixes the major traits of the plot in which we proceed ignorant of what has been prescribed for us".[61]

The authoritative voice directing the encounter of the woman and the man structures the confrontation like a law. First, it localises the account in a room by the sea where the contract is put into effect. In addition, the narrator also orders the relationship between the woman and the man into a hierarchy by empowering the woman to make the original diagnosis and, later on, a distressing prognosis of the man's illness:

> "You ask her if she thinks you can be loved. She says that you cannot under any circumstances".[62]

[59] Blanchot, "La voix narrative", in Blanchot, *L'entretien infini*, pp. 563–565.

[60] Duras, *La maladie de la mort*, p. 19. On the present tense and commandment, see Rosenzweig, *Der Stern der Erlösung*, pp. 197–198. On law, see also Rosenzweig, "Die Bauleute. Über das Gesetz," in Rosenzweig, *Zweistromland*, pp. 699–712.

[61] Blanchot, *La communauté inavouable*, p. 59.

[62] Duras, *La maladie de la mort*, p. 46.

Blanchot hears the voice of the woman from the same distant position as the narrator's:

> "A response so categorical that it cannot come from an ordinary mouth, but from very high above and very far away, a higher instance that also expresses itself in him with partial and trivial truths".[63]

The narrator—law—empowers the other to address the subject "from very high above and very far away", from the highness of the supreme authority from which the "biblical 'You' " also animates the intrigue. At the end of the book, Duras—a director perhaps even higher than the supreme—has included her own indications on how the text should be set on stage. In these notes, Duras, however, impairs the supposed force of law. On stage, there would only be the woman and a male narrator, only the other in its absolute strangeness and law. With speech—a jurisdiction—the narrator localises and orders the encounter between the woman and the man, but:

> "The man reading the story would be struck by an essential and mortal weakness that would be the weakness of the other man—the one not represented".[64]

A pretext: something that precedes the text, but also a preceding text. Not only the relation to the absolutely other that precedes responsibility prescribed by law, but also law itself, a prescription that becomes the covenant of a lovers' discourse founded on pretext.

Justice, finally? Or only the aporia of law?

[63] Blanchot, *La communauté inavouable*, p. 90.
[64] Duras, *La maladie de la mort*, p. 60.

Appendix

"Thinking Without Desire"

In 1894, the celebrated Austrian artist Gustav Klimt was commissioned to produce three large paintings for the foyer of a new university building in Vienna. The images were to represent three of the four classical faculties, that is, philosophy, medicine, and law.[1] The three completed "faculty paintings", "Medizin", "Philosophie", and "Jurisprudenz", were all burned in 1945 in the castle of Immendorf that the SS troops, retreating from Austria, had set on fire. Today only photographs remain of these paintings.

"Jurisprudenz" was a scandal when it was presented to the public in 1907. The common reaction of the legal community was to accuse Klimt of reducing the function of law in society to the execution of punishment and, consequently, of deliberately understating the constructive possibilities of the juridical system. In contrast, many of Klimt's defenders at the time understood the painting as a painfully acute portrayal of the fundamentally violent essence of law, as a critique of what we would today perhaps understand as the dilemma of modern law. A single interpretation, then, but two opposing evaluations.

Such an interpretation can, of course, be supported by emphasising, in a particular way, the role of the human figure that Klimt offers for our view at the fore of the image. A sea-monster, a Leviathan, has entangled its octopus-like tentacles around a nude man who stands powerless and stooped with his hands behind his back. He is evidently both physically and psychically humiliated. This violent "taking place of justice" is administered by three furies, the Erinyes of Aeschylus's Oresteian trilogy, who have gathered together to celebrate the cruel feast:

> "a hymn that comes from the Erinyes fettering the brain, sung without the lure, withering to mortals".[2]

But the image, rich in details, refuses to exhaust itself into such a facile and consistent interpretation. Is this a law that Klimt—biased by personal misfortunes, some claim—wishes to criticise? Or are there, perhaps, other dimensions involved, other reserves of sense and meaning that escape our enlightened eyes?

Klimt chose to call this faculty painting "Jurisprudenz". Not "Recht" or "Rechtswissenschaft", but *iurisprudentia*. The painting is not, then, about law as such; it is about a juridical mode of "prudence", of a "foresight" and a "providence" that is related to law. Perhaps law is looked upon in a particular way.

[1] The fourth painting representing theology was commissioned from Franz Matsch.

[2] Aeschylus, *Eu.* 331–333. The translations of the *Oresteia* are by Hugh Lloyd-Jones.

Or, rather, law itself is a "foresight", a way of somehow seeing the world in advance. But what sort of seeing would we be talking about?

The eyes of the human figure—Is he "us", you and me?—they are clearly turned down, so part of his humiliation may be the blindness with which he must endure his own execution. In addition, the other human faces that are visible in the cracks are all looking away. But this grotesque event is witnessed from two other positions. While the furies are enjoying the carnage at the fore, three other female deities traditionally associated with law, *Veritas*, *Iustitia*, and *Lex*, stand in the background. They are placed high at the rear end of the painting where the light still manages to distinguish colours and shades.

Two ways of seeing, then. One exemplified by the goddesses, the other by the furies. One representing the composed and well-reasoned way in which law, guided by truth and tempered with justice, manages the intricacies of the human world, the other emphasising the brute and fierce force with which this task is fulfilled.

Klimt seems to structure the painting by using these two sets of feminine figures. The goddesses have assumed a priority in relation to their savage sisters by occupying a superior position in the luminous upper-levels of the image. But although they are standing erect in the light, they are also at a distance and seem to have little control over the events taking place in the dark foreground. One might even be tempted to assume that they are somehow helpless, wanting to intervene, but are held back, frozen by what they are witnessing.

By way of contrast, the furies standing in the dark foreground are too caught up in the revelries to even notice the probing of their siblings. Their relentless stare implies a bestial appetite that Klimt often identified with feminine sexuality.

Is this, then, the core of Klimt's alleged criticism? Is he inviting the goddesses, that is, truth, justice, and law, to intervene and to illuminate the darkness that we live in? Is this the enlightened interpretation, a reading that would also call upon the philosophy of law to participate and relieve the suffering that is so emblematic of our modern era?

Or is it the other way around? Perhaps it is "jurisprudence" itself that has introduced the furies into the world. Perhaps Klimt is reinstating the ancient chthonic gods to their rightful place after Athene, with the cunning of a master-advocate, persuaded them to trade in their grim powers for the vain glitter of human worship. So is it the task of the philosophy of law to tell the naked truth, to affirm that justice cannot take place without these dark forces, that, in the end, law *is* violence?

The image tells us something about different ways of seeing, of darkness and of light. One of the best known Western accounts of philosophy as the ability to see is Plato's allegory of the cave.[3] In the darkness of the cave, the imprisoned men are only able to see objects that are brought in front of them and the shad-

[3] Plato, *Rep.* 514a–518b.

ows that are cast on the walls due to a fire burning inside. Plato suggests that the inhabitants of the cave must first be freed from their chains, then forced to confront the light of the fire and, eventually, the sunlight coming from the entrance of the cave, and, finally, ushered outside to come to terms with the truth of the ideational world.

But what distinguishes the man who has seen the light from the cave-dweller is *not* the former's more acute ability to see. In fact, the cave-dweller sees perfectly well, and Plato even emphasises that the better he sees, the more his knowledge serves evil.[4] It is, then, not the ability to see that distinguishes the two, but the direction into which they are looking. One is focused on the shadows and trivial objects in the cave, the other on the eternal and divine ideas that shine in the light of the sun.

The Russian philosopher Léon Chestov notes that Plato is talking of two distinct philosophies.[5] On the one hand, there is an *optimal philosophy*. It attempts to force the cave-dweller to turn his eyes towards the sunlight radiating from the opening of the cave. The philosopher cannot give eyesight to the blind, but he can attempt to turn the eyes of someone who already sees towards the truth that lies outside the cave.

But such an edifying philosophy is preceded by something that has originally uncovered the truth. Optimal philosophy is not the search for truth; it is the forcing-upon of a truth that has already revealed itself in a *true philosophy*. Chestov argues that, for Plato, such a true philosophy is exemplified in the way in which Socrates waits for his death sentence to be executed. True philosophy is not a science at all, but neither is it identifiable with a supposedly more acute ability to see. True philosophy is always "the preparation for death".[6]

When he encounters the dilemma between true and optimal philosophy, Plato does not hesitate to choose the latter. He has no use for true philosophy. Indeed, true philosophy is by its very nature "useless", as the allegory of the shipmaster attempts to tell us.[7] But Chestov inquires about the justification of such a choice: By what right do we choose? What is the "legal title" that authorises the making of such a choice? How can Plato—or we, for that matter—justify the choice of a "useful" optimal philosophy? And further, reformulated in a striking juridical image:

> "Whose duty is it to grant [this authorisation] that is called a *justus titulus* by jurists (in other words, by these men that, in accordance with their vocation and their mentality, are called upon to defend the pseudo-reality that they have found in the cave)?".[8]

For Chestov, then, the jurist is the cave-dweller, a man who lives in the dark. But what distinguishes him from the philosopher is his unwillingness to turn his

[4] Plato, *Rep*. 518c–d.
[5] Chestov, "Des sources des vérités métaphysiques".
[6] Plato, *Faid*. 67a–69c.
[7] Plato, *Rep*. 487e–489d.
[8] Chestov, "Des sources des vérités métaphysiques", p. 46 (emphases altered).

eyes towards the world outside. Although there is nothing wrong with his ability to see, he keeps his eyes focused on the umbrage on the walls of his cave. And what Plato seems to fear is that, because this jurist can see just as well as anybody, he can only make things worse in the cave; his insight can only serve evil.

But if the philosopher understands his vocation as forcing the cave-dweller to turn his eyes towards the light, he is no closer to truth than the jurist. This is what the optimal philosopher does; his calling, his "legal title", is education, not truth.

Three figures, then: the jurist who has settled for his dark world, the optimal philosopher who ushers the former towards the light, and the true philosopher who can but fraternise with death. And usually the relationship between philosophy and law is articulated as an alliance between the jurist and the optimal philosopher: philosophy facilitates law by providing it with the required theoretical and conceptual tools with which it can reach out towards the light.

But what about truth?

The slanting perspective of Klimt's painting is very much like a view from the dark pit towards the light of the ideational world shining in the distance. The Erinyes have been banished from Hades into the dim light of the cave where they now portray the jurist who refuses to leave the world of the shadows. On the other hand, the goddesses in the luminous background represent the philosopher who looks back into the cave helplessly. Both see equally well; neither is impaired in sight. But the philosopher seems to have accepted his inability to convince the jurist to turn. For something keeps the jurist focused on his world of shadows, just like the furies who cannot take their eyes off the event that is taking place at the fore. This is why the cave-dwellers are also captives.

If truth uncovers itself in a philosophical way of seeing or, in other words, in thinking, Aristotle continues to say that law is "thinking without desire".[9] So in its purity, law is the most immediate association between thinking and truth. It is a divine relationship that has been purged of the human flaw that tarnishes thinking, namely, desire.

But in Klimt's painting, the eyes of the furies are ablaze with desire. Even Orestes fears his pursuers because: "they drip from their eyes a hateful stream".[10]

And it is with a similar craving that we, as witnesses and as onlookers positioned at eye-level with the furies, recognise some truth in the image. And further, the goddesses in the background are no more unaffected than we; they have also been humanised to the extent that they look upon the events attentively but are simultaneously left powerless.

The only desireless figure in the image can be the man who humbly accepts his execution, just like Socrates who, being the true philosopher he is, "prepares for death." Maybe at first the man has escaped our attention, or maybe we have

[9] Aristotle, *Pol.* 1287a 32.

[10] Aeschylus, *Choe.* 1058.

saturated our gaze with an unfounded pity. But in the end, all eyes are on him: the goddesses', the furies', ours. We all watch him with desire trying desperately to unravel some mysterious truth that his deplorable figure embodies, just as Socrates's disciples follow in awe how their master peacefully awaits his own death.

Truth is the ultimate object of thinking, but because it is also the object of our desire, it must necessarily remain unresolved, an aporia. Thinking without desire and, by the same token, law as such, are authentic paradoxes. Desiring to know, we can only anticipate how truth as justice would take place and, while doing so, decide on what is "right," what is "correct".

This is "jurisprudence", a juridical foresight, an anticipation of truth and of justice that are forever delayed.

Bibliography

Numerous editions of the classics of Antiquity have been consulted. All translations are mine and are based on a variety of sources: Greek, Latin, Finnish, English, German and French. The abbreviations used correspond with those of *A Greek-English Lexicon* compiled by H.G. Liddell and R. Scott (Oxford: Clarendon Press, 1996) and *A Latin Dictionary* compiled by C.T. Lewis and C. Short (Oxford: Claredon Press, 1969).

All other translations in the text are mine, as well, but, once again, they are often a composite from a variety of sources. Whenever available, I used the standard English edition as the basis of my own translation.

AGAMBEN, Giorgio, *La communità che viene (*Torino: Einaudi, 1990).

——, *Homo sacer. Le pouvoir souverain et la vie nue* (Paris: Seuil, 1997).

ALTHUSSER, Louis, *Écrits sur la psychanalyse. Freud et Lacan* (Paris: STOCK/IMEC, 1993).

AMSELEK, Paul, *Méthode phénoménologique et théorie du droit* (Paris: L.G.D.J., 1964).

——, "La phénoménologie et le droit", (1972) XVII *Archives de la philosophie du droit* 195–259.

ARNAUD, André-Jean, *Critique de la raison juridique. 1. Où va la sociologie du droit?* (Paris: L.G.D.J., 1981).

BAAS, Bernard, *Le désir pur. Parcours philosophiques dans les parages de J. Lacan* (Louvain: Éditions Peeters, 1992).

BALIBAR, Etienne et al, *Rejouer le politique* (Paris: Galilée, 1981).

BALKIN, J.M., "Deconstructive Practice and Legal Theory", (1987) 96 *Yale Law Journal* 743–786.

——, "Understanding Legal Understanding: The Legal Subject and the Problem of Legal Coherence", (1993) 103 *Yale Law Journal* 105–176.

BARION, Hans et al (eds), *Epirrhosis. Festgabe für Carl Schmitt* (Berlin: Duncker & Humblot, 1968).

BARTH, Karl, *Der Römerbrief. Gesamtausgabe. Band 16* (Zürich: Theologischer Verlag, 1985).

BAUDRILLARD, Jean, *Le transparence du Mal. Essai sur les phénomènes extrêmes* (Paris: Galilée, 1989).

BEARDSWORTH, Richard, *Derrida & the Political* (London/New York: Routledge, 1996).

BENNINGTON, Geoffrey, *Dudding. Des noms de Rousseau* (Paris: Galilée, 1991).

——, and DERRIDA, Jacques, *Jacques Derrida* (Paris: Seuil, 1991).

BERNASCONI, Robert, *Heidegger in Question. The Art of Existing* (New Jersey: Humanities Press, 1993).

——, "On Deconstructing Nostalgia for Community within the West: The Debate between Nancy and Blanchot", (1993) XXIII *Research in Phenomenology* 3–21.

BEUTNER, Barbara, *Die Bildsprache Franz Kafkas* (München: Wilhelm Fink, 1973).

BINDER, Hartmut (ed.), *Kafka. Handbuch in zwei Bänden* (Stuttgart: Alfred Kröner, 1979).

BLANCHOT, Maurice, *L'entretien infini* (Paris: Gallimard, 1969).
——, *L'amitié* (Paris: Gallimard, 1971).
——, *La communauté inavouable* (Paris: Minuit, 1983).
——, *Michel Foucault tel que je l'imagine* (Paris: Fata Morgana, 1986).
BOBBIO, Norberto, "Hans Kelsen", (1973) *Rivista internazionale di Filosofia del Diritto*, Vol. L, 425–449.
BOULOUMIÉ, Arlette, "*Vendredi ou les limbes du Pacifique*" *de Michel Tournier* (Paris: Gallimard, 1991).
BRIDGWATER, Patrick, *Kafka and Nietzsche* (Bonn: Bouvier & Herbert Grundmann, 1974).
CACCIARI, Massimo, *Icone della Legge* (Milano: Adelphi, 1985).
CAPUTO, John D., *Radical Hermeneutics. Repetition, Deconstruction, and the Hermeneutic Project* (Bloomington/Indianapolis: Indiana University Press, 1987).
CARBONNIER, Jean, *Flexible droit. Pour une sociologie du droit sans rigueur* (Paris: L.G.D.J., 1988).
CERRONI, Umberto, "Per la critica della dommatica giuridica", (1960) *Rivista internazionale di Filosofia del Diritto*, Vol. XLI, 62–70.
CHESTOV, Léon, "Des sources des vérités métaphysiques (*Παρμενίδης δεσμώτες*)", (1930) *Revue Philosophique de la France et de l'Étranger*, Vol. CX, 13–85.
CIXOUS, Hélène, *Readings. The Poetics of Blanchot, Joyce, Kafka, Kleist, Lispector, and Tsvetayeva* (Minneapolis: University of Minnesota Press, 1991).
COING, Helmut, *Grundzüge der Rechtsphilosophie* (Berlin: Walter de Gruyter & Co, 1950).
CORNELL, Drucilla et al (eds), *Deconstruction and the Possibility of Justice* (New York/London: Routledge, 1992).
DALLMAYR, Fred, "Self and Other: Gadamer and the Hermeneutics of Difference", (1993) 5 *Yale Journal of Law & the Humanities* 507–529.
DEFOE, Daniel, *The Life and Strange Surprizing Adventures of Robinson Crusoe, of York, Mariner* . . . (Oxford/New York: Oxford University Press, 1972).
DELEUZE, Gilles, *Logique du sens* (Paris: Minuit, 1969).
——, *Foucault* (Paris: Minuit, 1986).
——, "Désir et plaisir", (1994) *Magazine littéraire*, No 325, 57–65.
——, and Félix Guattari, *Capitalisme et schizophrénie. L'anti-Œdipe* (Paris: Minuit, 1972).
—— and ——, *Kafka: Pour une littérature mineure* (Paris: Minuit, 1975).
DEL VECCHIO, Giorgio, *Lezioni di filosofia del diritto. Ottava edizione riveduta e accresciuta* (Milano: A. Giuffrè, 1952).
DE MAN, Paul, *Blindness and Insight. Essays in the Rhetoric of Contemporary Criticism* (Minneapolis: University of Minnesota Press, 1971).
DERRIDA, Jacques, *L'écriture et la différence* (Paris: Seuil, 1967).
——, *Marges—de la philosophie* (Paris: Minuit, 1972).
——, *D'un ton apocalyptique adopté naguère en philosophie* (Paris: Galilée, 1983).
——, *Psyché. Inventions de l'autre* (Paris: Galilée, 1987).
——, *Mémoires pour Paul de Man* (Paris: Galilée, 1988).
——, *Du droit à la philosophie* (Paris: Galilée, 1990).
——, *Spectres de Marx. L'État de la dette, le travail du deuil et la nouvelle Internationale* (Paris: Galilée, 1993).
——, *Force de loi. Le "fondement mystique de l'autorité"* (Paris: Galilée, 1994).

——, *Politiques de l'amitié* (Paris: Galilée, 1994).
——, et al, *La faculté de juger* (Paris: Minuit, 1985).
DETHIER, Luc, "Le droit par la bande. Sur la logique du dispositif discursif juridique", (1990) *Revue interdisciplinaire d'études juridiques*, No. 25, 1–68.
DONIUS, Charles, "Existentialisme, phénoménologie et philosophie du droit", (1957) *Archives de la philosophie du droit*, No. IV, 221–231.
DONZELOT, Jacques, *La police des familles* (Paris: Minuit, 1977).
DOR, Joël, *Introduction à la lecture de Lacan. 1. L'inconscient structuré comme un langage* (Paris: Denoël, 1985).
——, "Approche épistémologique des paradigmes mathématiques lacaniens", (1991) *Esquisses psychanalytiques*, No. 15, 87–97.
——, *Introduction à la lecture de Lacan. 2. La structure du sujet* (Paris: Denoël, 1992).
DREYFUS, Hubert L. and RABINOW, Paul, *Michel Foucault. Beyond Structuralism and Hermeneutics* (Chicago: University of Chicago Press, 1982).
DUMÉZIL, Georges, *Idées romaines* (Paris: Gallimard, 1969).
DURAS, Marguerite, *La maladie de la mort* (Paris: Minuit, 1982).
DWORKIN, Ronald, *Taking Rights Seriously. New Impression with a Reply to Critics* (London: Duckworth, 1978).
——, *A Matter of Principle* (Cambridge/London: Harvard University Press, 1985).
——, *Law's Empire* (London: Fontana Press, 1986).
EHRENZWEIG, Albert A., "Pysychoanalytical Jurisprudence: A Common Language for Babylon", (1965) 65 *Columbia Law Review* 1131–1360.
——, *Psychoanalytic Jurisprudence. On Ethics, Aesthetics, and "Law"—On Crime, Tort, and Procedure* (Leiden/Dobbs Ferry: A.W. Sijthoff/Oceana, 1971).
EMRICH, Wilhelm, *Franz Kafka* (Bonn: Athenäum, 1958).
EWALD, François, *L'État providence* (Paris: Grasset, 1986).
——, *Histoire de l'État providence. Les origines de la solidarité* (Paris: Grasset, 1996).
FARGE, Arlette and FOUCAULT, Michel, *Le désordre des familles. Lettres de cachet des Archives de la Bastille* (Paris: Gallimard/Julliard, 1982).
FECHNER, Erich, *Rechtsphilosophie. Soziologie und Metaphysik des Rechts* (Tübingen: J.C.B. Mohr, 1956).
FINK, Bruce, *The Lacanian Subject. Between Language and Jouissance* (Princeton: Princeton University Press, 1995).
FINNIS, John, *Natural Law and Natural Rights* (Oxford: Clarendon Press, 1980).
FISH, Stanley, *Doing What Comes Naturally. Change, Rhetoric, and the Practice of Theory in Literary and Legal Studies* (Oxford: Clarendon Press, 1989).
FITZPATRICH, Peter and HUNT, Alan (eds.), *Critical Legal Studies* (Oxford/New York: Basil Blackwell, 1987).
FOUCAULT, Michel, *Les mots et les choses. Une archéologie des sciences humaines* (Paris: Gallimard, 1966).
——, *L'archéologie du savoir* (Paris: Gallimard, 1969).
——, *Surveiller et punir. Naissance de la prison* (Paris: Gallimard, 1975).
——, *La volonté de savoir. Histoire de la sexualité 1* (Paris: Gallimard, 1976).
——, *La verdad y las formas jurídicas* (Mexico: Gedisa, 1983).
——, *Résumé des cours 1970–1982* (Paris: Julliard, 1989).
——, *Dits et écrits II. 1970–1975* (Paris: Gallimard, 1994).
——, *Dits et écrits III. 1976–1979* (Paris: Gallimard, 1994).
FRANKENBERG, Günter, "Die Ernst im Recht", (1987) 20 *Kritische Justiz* 281–307.

FREUD, Sigmund, *Totem und Tabu. Gesammelte Werke. Neunter Band* (London: Imago, 1940).
——, *Werke aus den Jahren 1925–1931. Gesammelte Werke. Vierzehnter Band* (London: Imago, 1940).
——, *Werke aus den Jahren 1909–1913. Gesammelte Werke. Achter Band* (London: Imago, 1943).
——, *Neue Folge der Vorlesungen zur Einführung in die Psychoanalyse. Gesammelte Werke. Fünfzehnter Band* (London: Imago, 1948).
——, *Werke aus den Jahren 1932–1939. Gesammelte Werke. Sechzehnter Band* (London: Imago, 1950).
GADAMER, Hans-Georg, *Hermeneutik I. Wahrheit und Methode. Grundzüge einer philosophischen Hermenutik. Gesammelte Werke. Band 1* (Tübingen: J.C.B. Mohr, 1986).
——, *Hermeneutik II. Wahrheit und Methode. Ergränzungen, Register. Gesammelte Werke. Band 2* (Tübingen: J.C.B. Mohr, 1986).
——, *Neuere Philosophie I. Hegel—Husserl—Heidegger. Gesammelte Werke. Band 3* (Tübingen: J.C.B. Mohr, 1987).
GARAPON, Antoine, "Kafka ou le non-lieu de la loi", (1992) *Revue interdisciplinaire des études juridiques*, No. 28, 1–19.
GARLAND, David, *Punishment and Welfare. A Study in Social Theory* (Oxford: Clarendon Press, 1990).
GASCHÉ, Rodolphe, *The Tain of the Mirror. Derrida and the Philosophy of Reflection* (Cambridge/London: Harvard University Press, 1986).
——, "On Critique, Hypercriticism, and Deconstruction: The Case of Benjamin", (1991) 13 *Cardozo Law Review* 1115–1132.
——, *Inventions of Difference. On Jacques Derrida* (Cambridge/London: Harvard University Press, 1994).
GIBBS, Robert, *Correlations in Rosenzweig and Levinas* (Princeton: Princeton University Press, 1992).
GIRARDOT, Rafael Gutiérrez, "Ist Rechtsphilosophie überhaupt möglich?", (1965) *Archiv für Rechts- und Sozialphilosophie*, Beiheft Nr. 41—Neue Folge Nr. 4, 155–162.
GOODRICH, Peter, *Languages of Law. From Logics of Memory to Nomadic Masks* (London: Weidenfeld and Nicholson, 1991).
——, *Oedipus Lex. Psychoanalysis, History, Law* (Berkeley/Los Angeles/London: University of California Press, 1995).
——, *Law in the Courts of Love. Literature and other Minor Jurisprudences* (London/New York: Routledge, 1996).
GUIBERT, Hervé, *À l'ami qui ne m'a pas sauvé la vie* (Paris: Gallimard, 1990).
HABERMAS, Jürgen, *Der philosophische Diskurs der Moderne. Zwölf Vorlesungen* (Frankfurt am Main: Suhrkamp, 1988).
HAFT, Fritjof et al (eds), *Strafgerechtigkeit. Festschrift für Arthur Kaufmann zum 70. Geburtstag* (Heidelberg: C.F. Müller, 1993).
HEGEL, G.W.F., *Vorlesungen über Rechtsphilosophie 1818–1831. Vierter Band* (Stuttgart/Bad Constatt: Frommann—Holzboog, 1974).
HEIDEGGER, Martin, *Vorträge und Aufsätze* (Pfullingen: Neske, 1954).
——, *Die Grundprobleme der Phänomenologie. Gesamtausgabe. Band 24* (Frankfurt am Main: Vittorio Klostermann, 1975).
——, *Wegmarken. Gesamtausgabe. Band 9* (Frankfurt am Main: Vittorio Klostermann, 1976).

——, *Holzwege. Gesamtausgabe. Band 5* (Frankfurt am Main: Vittorio Klostermann, 1977).

——, *Sein und Zeit. Gesamtausgabe. Band 2* (Frankfurt am Main: Vittorio Klostermann, 1977).

——, *Hölderlins Hymnen "Germanien" und "Der Rhein". Gesamtausgabe. Band 39* (Frankfurt am Main: Vittorio Klostermann, 1980).

——, *Parmenides. Gesamtausgabe. Band 54* (Frankfurt am Main: Vittorio Klostermann, 1982).

——, *Einführung in die Metaphysik. Gesamtausgabe. Band 40* (Frankfurt am Main: Vittorio Klostermann, 1983).

——, *Zollikoner Seminare. Protokolle—Gespräche—Briefe* (Frankfurt am Main: Vittorio Klostermann, 1987).

HENKEL, Heinrich, *Einführung in die Rechtsphilosophie. Grundlagen des Rechts* (München: C.H. Beck, 1964).

HERNMARCK, Gustaf C. (ed.), *Festschrift zu Ehren von Rudolf Laun anlässlich der Vollendung seines 65. Lebensjahres am 1. Januar 1947* (Hamburg: J.P. Toth, 1948).

HOFMANN, Hasso, *Legitimität gegen Legalität. Der Weg der politischen Philosophie Carl Schmitts* (Neuwied/Berlin: Luchterhand, 1964).

HOLLERBACH, Alexander et al (eds), *Mensch und Recht. Festschrift für Erik Wolf zum 70. Geburtstag* (Frankfurt am Main: Vittorio Klostermann, 1972).

HOY, David Couzens, "Dworkin's Constructive Optimism v. Deconstructive Legal Nihilism", (1987) 6 *Law and Philosophy* 321–356.

HUNT, Alan and WICKHAM, Gary, *Foucault and Law: Towards a Sociology of Law as Governance* (London: Pluto Press, 1994).

HUSSERL, Edmund, *Ideen zu einer reinen Phänomenologie und phänomenologischen Philosophie. Drittes Buch. Die Phänomenologie und die Fundamente der Wissenschaften. Husserliana: gesammelte Werke. Band V* (Haag: Martinus Nijhoff, 1952).

——, *Ideen zu einer reinen Phänomenologie und phänomenologischen Philosophie. Erstes Buch. Allgemeine Einführung in die reine Phänomenologie. Husserliana: gesammelte Werke. Band III* (Haag: Martinus Nijhoff, 1976).

——, *Aufsätze und Vorträge (1911–1921). Husserliana: gesammelte Werke. Band XXV* (Dodrecht/Boston/Lancaster: Martinus Nijhoff, 1987).

HUSSERL, Gerhart, *Recht und Zeit. Fünf rechtsphilosopische Essays* (Frankfurt am Main: Vittorio Klostermann, 1955).

——, *Recht und Welt. Rechtsphilosophische Abhandlungen* (Frankfurt am Main: Vittorio Klostermann, 1964).

JASPERS, Karl, *Existenzphilosophie* (Berlin: De Gruyter, 1956).

JÖCKEL, Wilhelm, *Hans Kelsens rechttheoretische Methode. Darstellung und Kritik ihrer Grundlagen und hauptsächlichen Ergebnisse* (Tübingen: J.C.B. Mohr/Paul Siebeck, 1930).

KAFKA, Franz, *Der Prozeß* (Frankfurt am Main/Hamburg: S. Fischer, 1935).

——, *Briefe an Milena* (Frankfurt am Main/Hamburg: S. Fischer, 1952).

——, *Sämtliche Erzählungen. Herausgegeben von Paul Raabe* (Frankfurt am Main/Hamburg: S. Fischer, 1970).

KAMBOUCHNER, Denis et al, *Le retrait du politique* (Paris: Galilée, 1983).

KANT, Immanuel, *Kritik der reinen Vernunft. Elfte Auflage* (Leipzig: Felix Meiner, 1919).

KAUFMANN, Arthur, *Rechtsphilosophie im Wandel. Stationen eines Weges* (Frankfurt am Main: Athenäum, 1972).

KAUFMANN, Erich, *Kritik der neukantischen Rechtsphilosophie. Eine Betrachtung über die Beziehungen zwischen Philosophie und Rechtswissenschaft* (Tübingen: J.C.B. Mohr, 1921).

KELSEN, Hans, *Hauptprobleme der Staatrechtslehre entwickelt aus der Lehre von Rechtssatze* (Tübingen: J.C.B. Mohr, 1911).

——, *Der soziologische und der juristische Staatsbegriff. Kritische Untersuchung des Verhältnisses von Staat und Recht* (Tübingen: J.C.B. Mohr, 1928).

——, *Reine Rechtslehre. Zweite, vollständig neu bearbeitete und erweiterte Auflage* (Wien: Franz Deuticke, 1960).

——, *Allgemeine Theorie der Normen* (Wien: Manz, 1979).

——, *Reine Rechtslehre. Einleitung in die rechtswissenschaftliche Problematik. Erste Auflage* (Aalen: Scientia, 1985).

KENNEDY, Duncan and KLARE, Karl E., "A Bibliography of Critical Legal Studies", (1984) 94 *Yale Law Journal* 461–490.

KOELB, Clayton, *Kafka's Rhetoric. The Passion of Reading* (Ithaca/London: Cornell University Press, 1989).

KOJEVE, Alexandre, *Introduction à la lecture de Hegel. Leçons sur la* Phénoménologie de l'Esprit *professées de 1933 à 1939* (Paris: Gallimard, 1947).

——, *Esquisse d'une phénoménologie du droit* (Paris: Gallimard, 1981).

KOVACS, George, *The Question of God in Heidegger's Phenomenology* (Evanston: Northwestern University Press, 1990).

KROCKOW, Christian Graf von, *Die Entscheidung. Eine Untersuchung über Ernst Jünger, Carl Schmitt, Martin Heidegger* (Stuttgart: Ferdinand Enke, 1958).

LACAN, Jacques, "L'identification" (unpublished manuscript, 1961–1962).

——, "Problèmes cruciaux pour la psychanalyse" (unpublished manuscript, 1964–1965).

——, *Écrits* (Paris: Seuil, 1966).

——, "Radiophonie", (1970) *Scilicet*, No. 2/3, 55–99.

——, *Le séminaire. Livre XI. Les quatre concepts fondamentaux de la psychanalyse* (Paris: Seuil, 1973).

——, *Le séminaire. Livre I. Les écrits techniques de Freud* (Paris: Seuil, 1975).

——, *Le séminaire. Livre XX. Encore* (Paris: Seuil, 1975).

——, *Le séminaire. Livre II. Le moi dans la théorie de Freud et dans la technique de la psychanalyse* (Paris: Seuil, 1978).

——, *Le séminaire. Livre III. Les psychoses* (Paris: Seuil, 1981).

——, *Le séminaire. Livre VII. L'éthique de la psychanalyse* (Paris: Seuil, 1986).

——, *Le séminaire. Livre VIII. Le transfert* (Paris: Seuil, 1991).

——, *Le séminaire. Livre XVII. L'envers de la psychanalyse* (Paris: Seuil, 1991).

——, *Le séminaire. Livre IV. La relation d'objet* (Paris: Seuil, 1994).

LACOUE-LABARTHE, Philippe, *L'imitation des modernes. Typographies II* (Paris: Galilée, 1986).

——, and NANCY, Jean-Luc, *Le titre de la lettre. Une lecture de Lacan* (Paris: Galilée, 1990).

LADEUR, Karl-Heinz, *Postmoderne Rechtstheorie. Selbstreferenz—Selbstorganisation—Prozeduralisierung* (Berlin: Duncker & Humblot, 1995).

LANG, Hermann, *Die Sprache und das Unbewußte. Jacques Lacans Grundlegung der Psychoanalyse* (Frankfurt am Main: Suhrkamp, 1973).

LE GAUFEY, Guy, *L'incomplétude du symbolique. De René Descartes à Jacques Lacan* (Paris: E.P.E.L., 1991).

LEGENDRE, Pierre, *Histoire de l'administration de 1750 à nos jours* (Paris: P.U.F., 1968).
——, *Jouir du pouvoir. Traité de la bureaucratie patriote* (Paris: Minuit, 1976).
——, *Leçons II. L'empire de la vérité. Introduction aux espaces dogmatiques* (Paris: Fayard, 1983).
——, *Leçons VII. Le désir politique de Dieu. Étude sur les montages de l'État et du Droit* (Paris: Fayard, 1988).
LEVINAS, Emmanuel, *Totalité et infini. Essai sur l'extériorité* (Paris: Kluwer, 1971).
——, *Autrement qu'être ou au-delà de l'essence* (Paris: Kluwer, 1974).
——, *De l'évasion* (Paris: Fata Morgana, 1982).
LÉVI-STRAUSS, Claude, *Anthropologie structurale deux* (Paris: Plon, 1973).
LÉVY-BRUHL, Henri, *Aspects sociologiques du droit* (Paris: Marcel Rivière, 1955).
LÖWITH, Karl, *Heidegger—Denker in dürftiger Zeit. Sämtliche Schriften 8* (Stuttgart: Carl Ernst Poeschel, 1984).
LYOTARD, Jean-François, *Lectures d'enfance* (Paris: Galilée, 1991).
——, and THÉBAUD, Jean-Loup, *Au juste. Conversations* (Paris: Christian Bourgois, 1979).
MAIHOFER, Werner, *Recht und Sein. Prolegomena zu einer Rechtsontologie* (Frankfurt am Main: Vittorio Klostermann, 1954).
——, *Vom Sinn menschlicher Ordnung* (Frankfurt am Main: Vittorio Klostermann, 1956).
MARX, Werner, *Heidegger und die Tradition. Eine problemgeschichtliche Einführung in die Grundbestimmungen des Seins* (Stuttgart: W. Kohlhammer, 1961).
MAUSS, Marcel, *Anthropologie et sociologie* (Paris: PUF, 1950).
MEHRING, Reinhard, *Pathetisches Denken. Carl Schmitts Denkweg am Leitfaden Hegels: Katholische Grundstellung und antimarxistische Hegelstrategie* (Duncker & Humblot, 1989).
MERLEAU-PONTY, Maurice, *Phénoménologie de la perception* (Paris: Gallimard, 1945).
MILLER, Jacques-Alain, "La suture (Éléments de la logique du signifiant)", in *Cahiers pour l'analyse. 1 & 2* (Paris: Graphe/Seuil, 1966), pp. 39–51.
MILNER, Jean-Claude, *L'Œuvre claire. Lacan, la science, la philosophie* (Paris: Seuil, 1995).
MOUFFE, Chantal (ed.), *Deconstruction and Pragmatism* (London/New York: Routledge, 1996).
MÜLLER, Max, *Existenzphilosophie im geistigen Leben der Gegenwart* (Heidelberg: F.H. Kerle, 1964).
NANCY, Jean-Luc, *L'impératif catégorique* (Paris: Flammarion, 1983).
——, *L'expérience de la liberté* (Paris: Galilée, 1988).
——, *La communauté désœuvrée* (Paris: Christian Bourgois, 1990).
——, *Le sens du monde* (Paris: Galilée, 1993).
NIETZSCHE, Friedrich, *Jenseits von Gut und Böse. Vorspiel einer Philosophie der Zukunft. Werke in drei Bänden. Band II* (München: Carl Hanser, 1960).
——, *Zur Genealogie der Moral. Eine Streitschrift. Werke in drei Bänden. Band II* (München: Carl Hanser, 1960).
NONET, Philippe, "What is Positive Law?", (1990) 100 *Yale Law Journal* 667–699.
——, "Reply", (1990) 100 *Yale Law Journal* 723–733.
NORRIS, Christopher, *The Contest of Faculties. Philosophy and Theory After Deconstruction* (Cambridge: Methuen, 1985).
——, *Paul de Man. Deconstruction and the Critique of Aesthetic Ideology* (New York/London: Routledge, 1988).

PFISTER, Oscar, "Die Illusion einer Zukunft", (1928) *Imago*, Vol. XIV, 149–184.

PIERRE, Rolland, *Odradek. Loi de Kafka* (Paris: Les Éditeurs Français Réunis, 1976).

POLITZER, Heinz, *Franz Kafka, der Künstler* (Frankfurt am Main/Hamburg: S. Fischer, 1965).

PÖSCHL, Arnold Ernst, *Raum und Raumordnung* (Berlin: Duncker & Humblot, 1965).

POULANTZAS, Nicos, "Notes sur la phénoménologie et l'existentialisme juridiques", (1963) *Archives de philosophie du droit*, No. VIII, 213–235.

——, *Nature des choses. Essai sur la dialectique du fait et de la valeur* (Paris: L.G.D.J., 1965).

QUARITSCH, Helmut (ed.), *Complexio Oppositorum. Über Carl Schmitt* (Berlin: Duncker & Humblot, 1988).

RADBRUCH, Gustav, *Rechtsphilosophie. Vierte Auflage* (Stuttgart: K.F. Koehler, 1950).

——, *Vorschule der Rechtsphilosophie. 2. Auflage* (Göttingen: Vandenhoeck & Ruprecht, 1959).

RAPAPORT, Herman, *Heidegger and Derrida. Reflections on Time and Language* (Lincoln/London: University of Nebraska Press, 1989).

REINACH, Adolf, *Zur Phänomenologie des Rechts. Die apriorischen Grundlagen des bürgerlichen Rechts* (München: Kösel, 1953).

RENAUT, Alain, *Le système du droit. Philosophie et droit dans la pensée de Fichte* (Paris: PUF, 1986).

RICŒUR, Paul, *Le conflit des interprétations. Essais d'herméneutique* (Paris: Seuil, 1969).

——, *Du texte à l'action. Essais d'herméneutique II* (Paris: Seuil, 1986).

RORTY, Richard, *Philosophy and the Mirror of Nature* (Oxford: Basil Blackwell, 1980).

——, *Consequences of Pragmatism (Essays: 1972–1980)* (Brighton: Harvester, 1982).

——, *Essays on Heidegger and Others. Philosophical Papers. Vol. 2* (Cambridge, etc.: Cambridge University Press, 1991).

ROSE, Gillian, *Dialectic of Nihilism. Post-Structuralism and Law* (Oxford/New York: Basil Blackwell, 1984).

ROSENMAYR, Leopold, "Gesellschaftsbild und Kulturkritik Martin Heideggers", (1960) *Archiv für Rechts- und Sozialphilosophie*, Vol. XLVI, 1–38.

ROSENZWEIG, Franz, *Zweistromland. Kleinere Schriften zu Glauben und Denken. Gesammelte Schriften. Band III* (Dordrecht: Martinus Nijhoff, 1984).

——, *Der Stern der Erlösung* (Frankfurt am Main: Suhrkamp, 1988).

ROSS, Alf, *Towards a Realistic Jurisprudence. A Criticism of the Dualism of Law* (Copenhagen: Einar Munksgaard, 1946).

ROUDINESCO, Elisabeth, *Jacques Lacan. Esquisse d'une vie, histoire d'un système de pensée* (Paris: Fayard, 1993).

ROULAND, Norbert, *Anthropologie juridique* (Paris: PUF, 1988).

ROUSSEAU, Jean-Jacques, *Œuvres politiques* (Paris: Bordas, 1989).

ROUSTANG, François, *Lacan, de l'équivoque à l'impasse* (Paris: Minuit, 1986).

SANDER, Fritz and KELSEN, Hans, *Die Rolle des Neukantianismus in der Reinen Rechtlehre. Eine Debatte zwischen Sander und Kelsen* (Aalen: Scientia, 1988).

SANTOS, Boaventura de Sousa, "Three Metaphors for a New Conception of Law: The Frontier, the Baroque, and the South", (1995) 29 *Law & Society Review* 569–584.

SARRAUTE, Nathalie, *Tropismes* (Paris: Minuit, 1950).

SARTRE, Jean-Paul, *L'être et le néant. Essai d'ontologie phénoménologique* (Paris: Gallimard, 1943).

SCHMITT, Carl, *Der Nomos der Erde im Völkerrecht des Jus Publicum Europaeum* (Berlin: Duncker & Humblot, 1950).
——, *Verfassungsrechtliche Aufsätze aus den Jahren 1924–1954. Materialen zu einer Verfassungslehre* (Berlin: Duncker & Humblot, 1958).
——, *Der Begriff des Politischen. Text von 1932 mit einem Vorwort und drei Corollarien* (Berlin: Duncker & Humblot, 1963).
——, *Land und Meer. Eine weltgeschichtliche Betrachtung* (Köln/Lövenich: Hohenheim, 1981).
——, *Legalität und Legitimität* (Berlin: Duncker & Humblot, 1988).
——, *Staat, Großraum, Nomos. Arbeiten aus den Jahren 1916–1969* (Berlin: Duncker & Humblot, 1995).
SCHMÖLTZ, Franz-Martin (ed.), *Das Naturrecht in der politischen Theorie* (Wien: Springer, 1963).
SCHOPENHAUER, Arthur, *Parerga und Paralipomena II. Erster Teilband. Zürcher Ausgabe. Werke in zehn Bänden. Band IX* (Zürich: Diogenes, 1977).
SCHREIER, Fritz, *Grundbegriffe und Grundformen des Rechts. Entwurf einer phänomenologisch begründeten formalen Rechts- und Staatslehre* (Leipzig/Wien: Franz Deuticke, 1924).
SCHÜRMANN, Reiner, *Le principe d'anarchie. Heidegger et la question de l'agir* (Paris: Seuil, 1982).
SOKEL, Walter H., *Franz Kafka—Tragik und Ironie. Zur Struktur seiner Kunst* (München/Wein: Albert Langen & Georg Müller, 1964).
STAMMLER, Rudolf, *Die Lehre von dem richtigen Rechte* (Berlin: J. Guttentag, 1902).
——, *Theorie der Rechtswissenschaft* (Halle an der Saale: Waisenhause, 1911).
——, *Rechtsphilosophische Abhandlungen und Vorträge. Erster Band* (Aalen: Scientia, 1970).
——, *Rechtsphilosophische Abhandlungen und Vorträge. Zweiter Band* (Aalen: Scientia, 1970).
STAROBINSKI, Jean, *Le remède dans le mal. Critique et légitimation de l'artifice à l'âge des Lumières* (Paris: Gallimard, 1989).
STRAUSS, Leo, *Natural Right and History* (Chicago: University of Chicago Press, 1953).
TAURECK, Bernhard H.F. (ed.), *Psychoanalyse und Philosophie. Lacan in der Diskussion* (Frankfurt am Main: Fischer, 1992).
THYSSEN, Johannes, "Zur Rechtsphilosophie des Als-seins", (1957) *Archiv für Rechts- und Sozialphilosophie*, Band XLIII, 87–96.
TODOROV, Tzvetan, *La conquête de l'Amerique. La question de l'autre* (Paris: Seuil, 1982).
——, *Nous et les autres. La réflexion française sur la diversité humaine* (Paris: Seuil, 1989).
TOURNIER, Michel, *Vendredi ou les Limbes du Pacifique* (Paris: Gallimard, 1972).
——, *Vendredi ou la Vie sauvage* (Paris: Gallimard, 1982).
TROLLER, Alois, *Überall gültige Prinzipien der Rechtswissenschaft* (Frankfurt am Main/Berlin: Alfred Metzner, 1965).
TUSHNET, Mark, "Critical Legal Studies: A Political History", (1990) 100 *Yale Law Journal* 1515–1544.
UDOFF, Alan (ed.), *Kafka and the Contemporary Critical Performance. Centenary Readings* (Bloomington/Inidianapolis: Indiana University Press, 1987).

VAIHINGER, Hans, *Die Philosophie des Als Ob. System der theoretischen, praktischen und religiösen Fiktionen der Menschheit auf Grund einer idealistischen Positivismus* (Aalen: Scientia, 1986).

VEYNE, Paul, *Comment on écrit l'histoire* (Paris: Seuil, 1971).

WEBER, Max, *Gesammelte Aufsätze zur Wissenschaftslehre. 2. Auflage* (Tübingen: J.C.B. Mohr, 1951).

WEINSTEIN, Arnold L., *Vision and Response in Modern Fiction* (Ithaca/London: Cornell University Press, 1974).

WOLF, Erik, *Vom Wesen des Rechts in deutscher Dichtung. Hölderlin, Stifter, Hebel, Droste* (Frankfurt am Main: Vittorio Klostermann, 1946).

——, *Griechisches Rechtsdenken I. Vorsokratiker und frühe Dichter* (Frankfurt am Main: Vittorio Klostermann, 1950).

——, *Recht des Nächsten. Ein rechtstheologischer Entwurf* (Frankfurt am Main: Vittorio Klostermann, 1958).

——, *Das Problem der Naturrechtslehre. Versuch einer Orientierung* (Heidelberg: C.F. Müller, 1964).

——, *Rechtsphilosophische Studien. Ausgewählte Schriften I* (Frankfurt am Main: Vittorio Klostermann, 1972).

WÜRTENBERGER, Thomas (ed.), *Quaestiones et responsa. Ein rechtsphilosophisches Gespräch für Erik Wolf zum 65. Geburtstag* (Frankfurt am Main: Vittorio Klostermann, 1968).

ŽIŽEK, Slavoj, *For They Know Not What They Do. Enjoyment as a Political Factor* (London/New York: Verso, 1991).

Index